# DATE DUE

| APR 2 9 1993 JUL 1 6 2003 | | | |
|---|---|---|---|
| | | | |
| | | | |
| | | | |
| | | | |
| | | | |
| | | | |
| | | | |
| | | WITHDRAWN | |
| | | | |
| | | | |
| | | | |
| | | | |

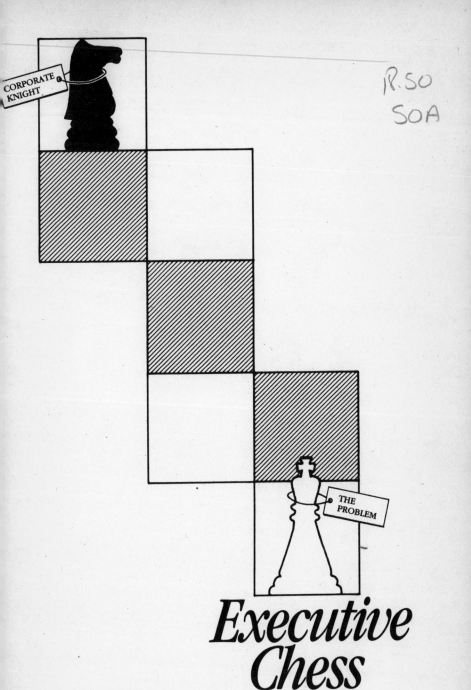

CORPORATE
KNIGHT

R.50
SOA

THE
PROBLEM

# Executive Chess

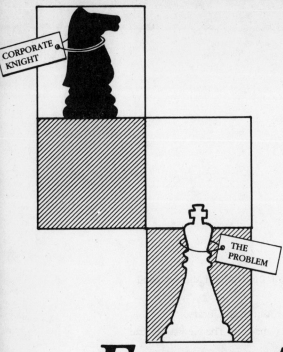

CORPORATE
KNIGHT

THE
PROBLEM

# *Executive Chess*

## *Steven J. Bennett*
## *and Michael Snell*

NAL BOOKS
# NEW AMERICAN LIBRARY
NEW YORK AND SCARBOROUGH, ONTARIO

NAL BOOKS TRADEMARK REG. U.S. PAT. OFF. AND FOREIGN COUNTRIES
REGISTERED TRADEMARK—MARCA REGISTRADA
HECHO EN HARRISONBURG, VA., U.S.A.

SIGNET, SIGNET CLASSIC, MENTOR, ONYX, PLUME,
MERIDIAN and NAL BOOKS are published *in the United States*
by NAL PENGUIN INC., 1633 Broadway, New York, New York 10019,
*in Canada* by The New American Library of Canada Limited,
81 Mack Avenue, Scarborough, Ontario M1L 1M8

Library of Congress Cataloging-in-Publication Data

Bennett, Steven J.
  Executive chess.

  Includes index.
  1. Problem solving  2. Executives—Interviews.
I. Snell, Michael.  II. Title.
HD30.29.B46  1987      658.4'03      87-1723
ISBN 0-453-00550-0

Designed by Barbara Huntley

First Printing, August, 1987

1  2  3  4  5  6  7  8  9

PRINTED IN THE UNITED STATES OF AMERICA

*Defeat is worse than death, because you have to live with defeat.*

—Bill Musselman, basketball coach

*Winners got scars too.*

—Johnny Cash, country singer

# Contents

Acknowledgments ix

Introduction xi

CHAPTER 1
Sizzle Stoppers:
*Waking Up to a New Competitor* 1

CHAPTER 2
Spy vs. Spy:
*Playing Fair in the War for Profits* 25

CHAPTER 3
Till Death Do Us Part:
*Doing Business with Friends and Family* 46

CHAPTER 4
Brain Drain:
*Keeping Key Players on the Team* 68

CHAPTER 5
Eggheads and Feathered Nests:
*Getting the Most from Salaried Professionals* 93

CHAPTER 6
The 24-Karat Mousetrap:
*Introducing the Perfect Product* 117

CHAPTER 7
**Growing Pains and Hormone Shots:**
*Surviving Hypergrowth* 139

CHAPTER 8
**The Platinum Lawsuit:**
*Recovering from a Product Liability Crisis* 162

CHAPTER 9
**Unruly Stepchildren:**
*Turning Around a Troubled Acquisition* 184

CHAPTER 10
**Greener Pastures:**
*Coping with a Boss Who Refuses to Retire* 209

EPILOGUE
**Post-Game Highlights** 229

BIOGRAPHIES OF THE PLAYERS 233

INDEX 249

# Acknowledgments

When we started this book, we thought it would be a fairly straightforward job: Design some curious business problems and then ask some unconventional business thinkers and maverick problem solvers to tackle them. But it turned into a much more demanding project than we ever imagined. Many of the executives we approached wanted to play executive chess but begged off when corporate public relations people advised them against letting their hair down in public. Others couldn't think of anything creative to say. And still others offered only formula textbook advice. Since we wanted inventive, even outrageous, solutions to tough business problems, we eventually began seeking inventive and, in some cases, outrageous people. So we ended up with an unusual collection of players, many of whom you may not recognize but all of whom bring bold, creative ideas to the everyday task of managing a business. First and foremost we must acknowledge the help and support of these "new corporate knights."

Next, since every brainchild should honor its father, we thank Joe Esposito for planting the original seed for the book. The people at New American Library, especially Arnold Dolin and Jill Grossman, patiently saw the project through to completion, always challenging us to improve and polish our work along the way. Many thanks, too, go to Peter Kinder, writer and good friend, for helping us brainstorm ideas and for offering insightful criticism of various drafts of the manuscript.

Lauren Anderson, Christopher Lohse, Jennifer Lawrence, Maureen Mahoney, Jeff Strauss, and Nancy MacDonald conducted splendid research for the book, digging deep into the annals of business history to provide us with background material and apt examples. Kathryn Nettles and Mora Rothenberg superbly juggled a lot of pesky administrative details, and Tena Martins and Helaine Gregory diligently transcribed hundreds of hours of interview tapes.

Finally, some very special people took care of us while we stayed up late and got up early to meet our deadlines: Ruth Loetterle-Bennett, Patricia Snell, and Stephan Snell.

Of course, we, like all proud parents, cannot see the flaws in our child; but for those that surely exist, we take full responsibility.

# Introduction

Imagine yourself in the following predicament. It's May 5, 1970, one day after National Guardsmen shot thirteen students at Kent State, and young people from Berkeley to Cambridge have taken to the streets to protest the tragedy. Even in sleepy Centerville, Illinois, chants of "Make love, not war!" rustle the cornstalks as students from the local university storm through the town, insisting that government offices and businesses lower their flags to half-mast in honor of the injured and the slain. Although the liberal university administration quickly capitulates to the protesters' demands in order to avoid violence, the local post office refuses. Within minutes the mob smashes windows and spray-paints angry slogans on the brick building.

Increasingly confident and frenzied, the students surge onto the highway leading into town, their sights set on the spanking new American flag flying high and proud over the parking lot of a fast-food outlet. "Half-mast! Half-mast!" they chant. When the hamburger stand's supervisor sees a rock sail from the crowd and bounce off the sign proclaiming OVER 60,000,000 SOLD, he scrambles to the phone—and calls you.

"Boss! They're going to tear the building down!" screams the petrified supervisor. In the background you hear what sounds like the invasion of Normandy. As the regional manager for this thriving restaurant chain, you try to piece together the situation and calm your distraught employee.

On the one hand, you know that your company's tough-minded CEO, Colonel "Guts and Guns" Garrett, will tolerate no deviation from the policies he's set forth, especially an act that stockholders or the media might construe as unpatriotic. If the arch-conservative Garrett sees his company's flag at half-mast on the CBS Evening News, he'll summarily fire everyone from you down to the fry cook. On the other hand, if you do not heed the demonstrators' demands, you'll be inviting the demolition of one of your newest outlets. And when CEO Garrett sees the repair bill, he'll not only fire you, he'll see that you can't even get a job mopping floors at the Centerville Chicken Shack.

How would you handle this tense dilemma? Retreat by lowering your flag? Stand your ground, hoping the National Guard will intervene? Resign before anyone can blame you for what happens? Upon reflection, none of these options appeals to you because they don't really get to the heart of the problem. Can you hatch a more creative solution, one that may buck conventional textbook wisdom but that will prove your management mettle?

Suppose you calmly ask the desperate manager, "Do you have a bakery delivery scheduled for this afternoon?"

Then suppose the manager scurries to check his logbook and replies, "Yes, boss. We've got buns coming at four o'clock. But what are we supposed to do—throw them at the kids?"

You smile. "No. Listen. Call the bakery, tell them you need the buns *now.* Ask to speak to the driver and offer him a hundred dollars in cash from the register for 'a little favor.' "

Twenty minutes later a BakeRite delivery van noses through the throng of fist-waving, chanting students. As the van backs into the parking lot it "accidentally" knocks the disputed flagpole to the ground. While cheers of triumph rise from the crowd, your embattled employees inside the restaurant breathe a collective sigh of relief. "It worked!" the manager shouts into the phone. You thank the young man and immediately report the incident to your CEO, offering personally to pay for the ruined flagpole. "I'll have a new one installed tomorrow," you say. "Our company must keep the flag flying at all costs."

Everyone wins. The students, claiming victory, not only disperse but also make the besieged restaurant their official hangout. You receive a promotion to headquarters as vice president of personnel, and the Centerville supervisor fills your slot as the new regional manager.

Outlandish? We actually based this scenario on a true story, merely changing the names to protect the innocent or guilty, whichever the case may be. We use it here to represent the kind of unconventional moves maverick managers might use to win a game of executive chess. Every day, executives find themselves in crisis situations like this one, where one wrong move can cost them their jobs or their companies. And whether they face the fire from the boardroom or production line, from the media or from a skeptical judge, they must devise the game-winning strategies and tactics that can turn a crisis into an opportunity.

We selected the chess metaphor for this book because the pieces and plays on the chessboard remind us so much of the people and maneuvers in the business world. Every corporation deploys its army of pawns who march relentlessly to the beat of the company's drums, loyally defending the firm against a host of hostile attacks. In many cases they die ignoble and unrecorded deaths in the battle for competitive advantage. Backing them up, we find more powerful pieces, the bishops and rooks, who nevertheless operate along narrowly defined paths. Their tunnel vision allows them to do their jobs effectively but without much creativity.

The most powerful piece in the game, the queen, and her counterparts, the CEOs and COOs of the business world, wield virtually unlimited power over all domains of the board. These indispensable warriors fight in the shadow of the king, the figurehead chairman, who remains aloof from the fray.

Finally we come to the knights, the mavericks who have mastered the surprise moves, jumping over their comrades to capture enemy pieces. A knight can alter the complexion of an entire game with just one lightning stroke. Likewise, when corporate knights engage in a game of executive chess, they bring to the fray an element of surprise. Whether it's converting an angry mob of protesters into regular customers, bamboozling a giant competitor into retreat, or turning today's disastrous product into tomorrow's profit maker, corporate knights prefer the unexpected to the routine.

Where can you find corporate knights? Anywhere on the business game board. Some work in large corporations. Many have started or run small- to medium-sized businesses. A large number make their moves as lone-wolf entrepreneurs and consultants. And some have moved from the business world to the towers of academia. But regardless of their turf, they share the vital ability to rewrite the rules and see problems with fresh eyes.

*Executive Chess* explores the minds of some new corporate knights by testing their wits against scenarios depicting tough business problems: competing against an upstart who has developed a superior product; deciding what's fair in the game of competitive intelligence; refereeing a fight between sparring partners who happen to be friends or relatives; keeping creative talent from jumping ship; managing scientists and other salaried professionals; figuring out when and how to introduce a near perfect product; surviving the ravages of rapid success; managing and recovering from a product liability disaster; and coping with a difficult boss who won't retire.

In an effort to make our scenarios both lively and realistic we designed each one around a specific industry, though we think the underlying issues in each case crop up in every sort of business at one time or another. All companies, be they high-tech or low-tech, manufacturing or service, wrestle with the problems of innovation, competition, and human relations that dominate our fictional cases. We have tried to highlight all the major functions within an enterprise, from finance and management to marketing and personnel. Regardless of the nature of your company or your role in it, you should be able to identify with many of the characters and issues you'll encounter in the pages ahead. We hope you'll enjoy reading our players' creative solutions as much as we did hearing them for the first time during our extensive interviews. We learned something vitally important as we watched the executive chess players' minds in action: that "street smart management" comes not only from the ivy halls of the prominent business schools or the trenches of daily corporate warfare, but also from the ability of an individual to tackle problems in a variety of creative and potentially risky ways.

We decided not to restrict our search for players to those with experience in a particular industry or functional department of business; we wanted to hear solutions from fresh perspectives. Since we wanted surprising solutions, we posed our problems to some surprising players. For example, in our chapter on marketing a breakthrough running-shoe product, you will hear not only from one of the top minds in the field, Paul Fireman of Reebok International, but also from Sally Edwards, a world-class triathlete, and Alex Randall, an anthropologist and the founder of the Boston Computer Exchange. These different perspectives offer intriguing—and at times conflicting—advice.

While the creative solutions to our fanciful problems won't provide you with any sixty-second formulas for becoming an expert problem-solver, they should spark a little of what we call "inner lightning," the flashes of insight that set the knights apart from the pawns. In the pages ahead, you will encounter a broad range of problem-solving styles and hear some startling suggestions about:

• winning the cola wars with nothing but a dead rat;

• infiltrating your competitor's war room without leaving your breakfast table;

• playing marriage counselor in an ego mine-field;

• composting your executive suite and rejuvenating your company;

• unleashing the ultimate running shoe without leaving your existing lines in the dust;

• recovering from a product liability crisis by starting a new fashion trend;

• salvaging a bungled acquisition by reviving the founding fathers;

By the end of the book you will have completed an unusual tour of corporate America, visiting along the way a number of different industries and a diverse group of business problem solvers, each with a unique style for turning a puzzling situation into a tactical advantage.

—Steven J. Bennett
Cambridge, Massachusetts
September 1986

—Michael Snell
Truro, Massachusetts
September 1986

CHAPTER 1

# Sizzle Stoppers:
## *Waking Up to a New Competitor*

## Opening Moves

It was to be a cunning public relations caper, a major skirmish in the Great Cola Wars. For years Mocha Cola and Daisyco have battled for supremacy, and far from eroding each other's market share, their head butting has increased the overall market and has virtually knocked all lesser competitors off the battlefield. Why not personify the contest at a Cola Olympics in Los Angeles, with each company sponsoring teams of professional athletes who would compete in track and field events before the cameras of a major network and millions of television viewers worldwide?

America's famous game-show personality, Roald Reel, hosts the culminating event. "Welcome, sports fans, to the contest we've all been waiting for, the grueling triathlon, where we expect the world's record to be broken today," he intones.

Six and a half hours later two international record holders, having swum three miles and bicycled one hundred, near the finish line of the concluding twenty-six-mile run.

"It looks like a photo finish," marvels Roald Reel. "Incredible! Simply incredible! Our statisticians have calculated that the lead has changed hands no less than fifteen times during this amazing race. Now here they come, Sven Jonarsson wearing the colors of Mocha Cola, with less than a one-stride lead over Daisyco's Art Scheller. Wait! I can't believe it! Scheller has started to pour it on . . . he's on Jonarsson's heels . . . he's gaining . . . he's going to pass him! No! This can't be happening! The two runners have tripped over each other's feet and have rolled through the tape in a blur of arms and legs. Oh, *my!*"

Although the judges are still studying videotapes of the startling conclusion to the Cola Olympics an hour later, Roald Reel has proceeded with the victory interviews. Instead of toasting the winners with a bottle of the victorious cola as planned, he will share a bottle of each cola with the athletes in a generous show of sportsmanship.

"Everyone wins today"—Reel beams into the camera—"but hold on, why are the bruised and exhausted runners clutching those green bottles? That's not Mocha Cola, that's not Daisy Cola, that's . . . FeelGood!"

Jonarsson nods his head enthusiastically. "Ya, sure. These colas—you cannot drink after big race. This"—he raises the sparkling green bottle—"this makes you feel *good*!"

Such a cola triathlon may never come to pass, but every day name-brand market leaders are challenged by sassy upstarts. And sometimes these Davids, armed with just a slingshot, succeed in embarrassing their bigger opponents. How should you react if that happens to you? Launch a head-on counteroffensive? Ignore the rascal? Concoct something down and dirty? To find out answers to these and other questions relating to competitive marketing, we asked a diverse group of *Executive Chess* players to tell us how the new corporate knights might thwart FeelGood!'s dastardly offensive.

## The Game: Bottling the New Kid on the Block

The CEO of Mocha Cola, Ray Sanders, was still fuming over the dirty tactics that Ambrosia Enterprises, the makers of Feel-Good!, had used at the cola triathlon, when the head of Mocha's marketing department handed him a report on the upstart FeelGood!:

Sugar-free. Caffeine-free. Minimum adult daily requirements of essential vitamins and minerals, including calcium and potassium.

Contains a complex nucleic acid that imparts a sense of physical and emotional well-being. An unusual balance of natural flavors, carbonated spring water, and colorings that makes it look appealing, taste refreshing, and satisfy a thirst without filling up the consumer. In short, the most genuine soft drink innovation in the past ten years.

Until FeelGood! upstaged Mocha and Daisy in Los Angeles, neither company had paid much attention to this new kid on the block. In fact, when Ambrosia had introduced FeelGood! a year earlier, Ray Sanders had predicted that the new drink would do little more than dent the carbonated spring water market. But after Ambrosia paid Jonarsson to endorse FeelGood!, market research surveys began showing it steadily encroaching on the turf that Mocha and Daisy had controlled for decades. Most disconcerting, however, was the rumor that FeelGood! actually inhibits the buildup of tooth plaque. If Ambrosia were to tout that fact in its national advertising, it could be a bombshell, putting dentists, as well as Ray Sanders, out of a job.

Sanders orders the company's top food chemists to determine FeelGood!'s plaque-fighting ingredient and to see how it might be integrated into Mocha Cola. But try as his scientists might, the resulting brew looks, tastes, and smells like a foul marriage of transmission fluid and cod liver oil. Apparently it's the total mixture of ingredients that makes FeelGood! such a healthful, yet pleasant-tasting, drink.

Meanwhile Ambrosia has already stepped up its attack by announcing a new product, FeelGreat!, a sweeter drink than the original brand but with a new ingredient Mocha's lab cannot isolate. Worse, its darker color makes it look just like a cola. While Ray Sanders mulls over ways to cork this effervescent newcomer, he receives alarming news that Peter Pan, the second largest hamburger chain in the country, has decided to drop Mocha Cola in favor of FeelGreat! "We love kids," Peter Pan says in its new television commercial, "and kids love FeelGreat! Three out of five dentists recommend . . ."

That does it. "This means war!" shouts Sanders at a meeting of Mocha's top executives. "While we were sitting in our trenches exchanging fire with Daisy, Ambrosia launched a predawn strike. I want battle plans from each of you on my desk tomorrow."

If you were called in to advise Mocha's leader, what moves

and maneuvers would you recommend to combat FeelGood!'s invasion into your territory?

## Strategies and Tactics

### Pulling Out All the Stops

"The first things I'm going to worry about are the deficiencies in my own company," says Philip Kemp, president of J. E. Morgan Knitting Mills. "I want to know how we got scooped in the public relations fiasco at the Cola Olympics—how we let that rat Jonarsson get in his FeelGood! plug. I want to know why my own lab wasn't on top of FeelGood! long ago and, if the product really has a market, why we didn't come up with it before everyone else did. We're Mocha, so we're the biggest and the best. Things like that shouldn't happen to us."

Once the heads stopped rolling at Mocha, Kemp, a veteran of several industries, would then sit back and wait until the dust settled. "I'd have to determine whether or not FeelGood! represents a real threat or not. Just because we got taken at the sports event doesn't mean that FeelGood! will chew up our market share."

If FeelGood! does turn out to be a legitimate threat, Kemp recommends going straight for the jugular. "I'd have my lab get a slew of rats, force-feed them ten gallons of FeelGood!, and wait until something weird happens to them or they die. Then drop them on the FDA's doorstep," jokes Kemp. "But, in all seriousness, there is a significant issue here. Anything that fights plaque involves a chemical action, and anything that's chemical in nature carries a risk. I think that it is a fair life-style statement to say that we consume enough synthetic chemicals from our diets and environments that we don't need any more, especially when there is no good reason to do it. Having been in the toothpaste business, I know that plaque is only a serious problem for less than fifty percent of the population. So why add to your chemical burden for something that may not even affect you? I think Mocha could make a convincing argument to federal agencies and the public that anyone drinking FeelGood! may be taking unnecessary risks."

The public safety gambit dates far back into corporate history. Thomas Edison used it when he found himself running afoul of impatient investors in his early days. Although Edison had made the first light bulb glow, none of his investors had gotten a dime back on their money, and they hounded him to prove electricity's profit-making potential. Eventually research conducted in his lab did lead to a salable product: the electric chair, the generators for which the State of New York bought for $8000. Ironically Edison himself staunchly opposed capital punishment and only permitted the apparatus to be developed as a means of demonstrating the danger of alternating current, which his competitor, George Westinghouse, was vigorously promoting at the time. Edison even suggested that death by electricity be called "getting Westinghoused." In August 1890, convicted murderer George Kemmler won the dubious distinction of being the first person to be executed by electrocution, an event so horribly botched that reportedly Westinghouse later commented, "They could have done it better with an ax."

More recently, the Smucker Company fired the first glop in the Jam Wars when it succeeded in getting the ads of its competitor, Sorrell Ridge, banned from New York's airwaves because of Sorrell's "no-sugar-added" claims, which Smucker's argued could be misinterpreted and therefore prove hazardous to the health of diabetics. In a similar vein, in 1984, the Sugar Association filed a deceptive advertising complaint against G. D. Searle for failing to identify its popular sugar substitutes, NutraSweet and Equal, with the chemical aspartame. Manufacturer Searle countered by claiming that the association was merely using the Federal Trade Commission to dampen NutraSweet's meteoric sales.

Kemp's point is that similar attacks could be launched against FeelGood! But suppose FeelGood! survives Mocha's attempts to disgrace or legislate it out of business? "Buy them," Kemp suggests. "And if they won't budge, get our lab to identify the key ingredients and then use our resources to buy the world supply of the stuff for the next decade."

Sound implausible? In 1981, Coca Cola actually used this tactic and its enormous buying power to protect a change in formulation. Though for years Coke had resisted using fructose instead of sugar, it decided to make the change in the late seventies. Fructose not only costs twenty percent less than sugar, but it suffers fewer price fluctuations. As a result, bottlers could save as much as six cents a gallon, reaping enormously higher profits worldwide. To make sure that competitors couldn't easily follow suit, Coke virtually cornered all existing fructose supplies and arranged for future purchases that would keep fructose production under its control far into the future.

While such maneuvers can make life miserable for upstart competitors, Kemp draws a more important main lesson from the scenario. "Don't even *think* of changing your own product to mimic the properties of FeelGood! Aside from the fact that FeelGood!'s asset may not really be in demand, you can't afford to masquerade as someone else just because they caused a little attention. Pull out the stops to give your competitor a difficult time, but don't lose your identity—it's what got you where you are today. Besides, true industry leaders don't worry about get- ting embarrassed at a Cola Olympics. They just make sure it doesn't happen again."

## Performing Corporate Jujitsu

"The worst thing you can do," insists Dr. Alexander Randall 5, anthropologist and founder of The Boston Computer Exchange, "is to follow your natural knee-jerk reaction and clobber this FeelGood! guy. That's the brawn-over-brain approach." Instead Randall recommends a martial arts approach based on jujitsu, which uses your opponent's own momentum to make him fall. "Your opponent is expecting to have your body connect with his force, and instead, there's nothing, so that he falls flat on his face. The same technique can apply to this marketing problem. Let FeelGood!'s offensive be your best defense."

How do you do this? One of three ways, according to Randall. "Maneuver number one would be to say, 'Get Higsby and Quark from Chemistry to analyze this stuff and determine its biological liability.' And this stuff is just *begging* for a liability. Follow the old maxim in consumer products these days: Whenever there's something good, there's something bad behind it. Does it cause cancer? If FeelGood! makes you feel good, then it's probably addictive. If either or both are the case, get every relevant federal and state agency on the case and feed the story to every publication, radio, and TV station in the country. Let the media kill it off. That's leveraging your energy. Maybe you could even suggest that the FDA reclassify FeelGood! as a drug; better yet, a controlled substance. In any case, the point is, let someone else do your bidding and turn FeelGood!'s strength into its weakness, its assets into liabilities."

Randall's second jujitsu strategy involves introducing two or three imitations under a new label. "The ultimate jujitsu maneuver is to not even be fighting in the same arena as your opponent," he explains. "The idea here is to flood the market with products that claim to be health drinks 'just like FeelGood!' By doing so you could reposition FeelGood! as 'juice for fruit-and-nut flakes.' In effect you also redefine FeelGood! as a niche product and let them be the leader of their niche—for a while, anyway. You probably wouldn't even have to spend tons of money to develop fully blown products. A PR campaign behind some test products alone would probably be sufficient to reposition FeelGood!"

Randall says that you might even play a Hertz/Avis game to reinforce the second maneuver, actually acknowledging that FeelGood! leads all other health colas but that your stuff sits squarely at number two. "Americans love underdogs," he comments.

The don't-stand-where-they-can-hit-you strategy has long been employed outside the cola arena, especially in politics. In 1972, for example, Richard Nixon wisely refused to debate George McGovern. Aside from his poor track record with debates, he knew that just by showing up he would make McGovern appear to be a genuine candidate.

Several of the major fast-food chains also employed the tactic when upstart hamburger chain Big Bite ran advertisements parodying popular characters such as Colonel Sanders and Ronald McDonald. Kentucky Fried Chicken, McDonald's, and Burger King exercised good restraint by not acknowledging Big Bite through competitive advertising or legal action. Wendy's International, however, stung by a parody of "Little Wendy," sued Big Bite, seeking an injunction against its infringement of Wendy's trademark. In an unusually heated opinion, the judge expressed disgust that two corporations would waste his time in an obvious ploy to gain free advertising, but he nevertheless issued an injunction against Big Bite. The suit, far from draining the fry baskets at Big Bite, merely said to the rest of the world that Big Bite was powerful enough to play in the major league.

In the case of the Cola Wars, Randall believes that the "step-aside" strategy not only keeps FeelGood! away from its main product line but that it gives Mocha a shot if it turns out there really *is* a huge market for health-type soft drinks. "In that case you don't just want to restrict our product to fruit-and-nut lovers," he says. "If there's a genuine market out there, we want to be the leader in it. Tell Higsby and Quark in Chemistry to stop looking for cancer-causing components in FeelGood and instead have them create a whole line of our own 'benefit colas.' Maybe a cola with aspirin—great for headaches and hangovers. Or a cola with antacids in it—great for overeating. Or a cola with aspirin *and* antacids—great for post-orgy blues."

Such a tactic might create for retailers what Randall calls "option shock." "If they're swimming in health colas, they might get extremely frustrated. But you've got the clout to offer them incentives that will free up more shelf space, so FeelGood! might even get croaked at the shelf level."

Whatever maneuver you use, Randall stresses that you begin with your competitor's assumptions and then do something for which it clearly has no contingency plans. Recalling a conversation with a tank commander at an army base that had retained him to teach the psychology of sleep, dreaming, and creativity, Randall graphically explains this principle in action: "If you try to attack a tank head-on, you meet its strongest part, the armor. If you try to attack the rear, you also meet heavy armor. And if you try to outshell it, you meet its artillery strength. But the average American tank can only go twelve miles on a fill-up of gas. Since gas-refueling trucks are vulnerable and less protected, knock them out and the tanks will be useless. Attacking the gas truck is in effect saying, 'I won't fight on your turf.' It works with tanks, and it works with upstart competitors."

Randall also points out that competitive exercises such as this one separate real leaders from the rest of the pack. "Real leaders are not rational," he claims. "They don't do what other people are expecting them to do. Otherwise they wouldn't be leaders—they'd be just like everyone else. Leaders shift the frame of reality in the most deft round of Executive Chess. They say to themselves, 'What is it that I wouldn't think of in this situation?' Now, I ask you, isn't that the purest essence of creative thinking?"

## Maintaining Clear Product Boundaries

Bob Savage, an independent marketing consultant, previously COO of Henson Associates, creators of the Muppets, and former advertising executive with agencies serving numerous consumer-product companies, doesn't think FeelGood! can possibly put Mocha out of business. "Would any of those beautiful people guzzling colas at the beach be interested in fighting plaque?" he asks. "I don't think so. FeelGood! is confusing something therapeutic with something designed for personal enjoyment."

According to Savage, many advertisers fall into the "mixed-messages trap." Look at the Listerine/Scope Wars, he suggests. Listerine took a medicinal approach, while Scope took a breath-freshener approach. "I think this was all very confusing to the consumer, because they weren't sure whether they were supposed to be buying taste or medicine. Same with Alka-Seltzer, although they fought a war of confusion with themselves, not a competitor. What is Alka-Seltzer? 'I ate the whole thing'; 'I have a headache.' What is this stuff for? The bottom line is that if the consumer has to ask what a product is all about, he'll be less inclined to buy it."

Perhaps that will happen to FeelGood! too, Savage suggests. "Do you drink a cola and feel like you've done something enjoyable, or do you drink it and then look at your teeth in the mirror? You can't afford to play that game. People buy your product because of the subjective enjoyment aspects, and any attempt to redefine yourself in their minds might cause them to find another product that remains consistent and understandable."

Savage explains that consumers categorize every product, with definite boundaries. "Once you cross boundaries, you stand to lose otherwise loyal customers." The makers of Cadillac crossed the boundaries and paid the price. Once high-status, luxury cars, Cadillacs took on a more run-of-the-mill image once GM started stamping them out of the same molds used for Buicks and Pontiacs, so that the line of distinction between the luxury category and the everyday sedan category blurred. To solve the problem, GM made plans to push its Avanti line in limited production runs of 5000 cars. By reestablishing its elite image with bodies from Italy and engines from the U.S., and by pricing the car at $50,000, GM hoped to compete with the high-end Mercedes Benz line and to recreate boundaries within its product lines.

In addition to maintaining clear product boundaries, Savage also suggests that Mocha keep the game on its own turf. "If you've got demonstrated strength as a market leader, don't diminish your own status. If you're Mocha Cola, *be* Mocha Cola. If you're the leading cake-mix producer, don't sell vitamin-enriched mixed products."

But if all else fails, Savage suggests a decisive ploy: "Buy FeelGood! and turn it into a carbonated mouthwash."

## Keeping a Cool Head

Marketing professor and author Rob Settle agrees with Alex Randall about the need for restraint. "As soon as a competitor comes out with a really dynamic product," he observes, "most people's knee-jerk response is to react. You say to yourself, 'How can I immediately respond to this situation?' Well, winners don't bounce off the wall like billiard balls—they play their own game."

According to Professor Settle, a knee-jerk reaction tends to obscure your long-range vision. For instance, Mocha might react by focusing on losing a little shelf space. "That's just one issue," he warns. "To get a clear view you've got to pull back and look at the long-term benefits of your products and the competitor's product. Take your time; the time horizon is irrelevant. Take six or eight months and thoroughly evaluate the situation. You can afford to take your time because you're big and have plenty of cash and staying power. That means you can approach FeelGood! from a position of strength, which is the ideal position to be in."

First of all, advises Settle, go back to the lab and do some product research. Find out why people drink soft drinks. "I think the answer would be twofold," he projects. "One, there's palatability. Two, they give you a lift, some form of stimulation. They're carbonated and tingly, and you like the feel of the stuff. So I'd go back and see what we could do along those lines to improve the product. At this point it's an R&D job.

"But be careful about just focusing on finding the right formula," he continues. "People don't buy the flavor itself, they buy the whole product. At room temperature the vast majority couldn't tell the difference between Coke or Pepsi. The same holds true for differences in coffees and beers. You not only have to have a product that's palatable, but you need one that meets the consumer's needs."

Coca Cola certainly illustrated Settle's point when it made its classic blunder with "new" Coke. Even though he thinks most people would have flunked comparative tests between new Coke and Coke Classic, the switch caused an uproar among loyal buyers because it undermined the traditional perceptions of the product. "What you see is what you taste," concludes Settle.

New Coke shares shelf space in the Hall of Marketing Blunders with other product decisions that proved to be insensitive to the consumer's needs and perceptions. Ford won its niche by enlarging the Thunderbird and Mustang. According to Settle, the decline in sales of those models can almost be correlated with their increase in size. Texas Instruments deserves an honorable mention for misreading the scientific and engineering market. Unlike Hewlett-Packard, which maintained a high price on their calculators and kept the distribution to college bookstores, computer stores, office supply stores, and other specialty outlets, Texas Instruments went the mass-market and discount route, selling basic calculators for under ten dollars. Today an HP calculator is a sign of status among scientists and engineers, much the way a Cross pen is a status symbol for business people. A TI calculator, on the other hand, is now perceived as the Bic pen of calculators.

Settle nominates two other recent candidates to the Hall: movie theaters and fast-food operations. "We used to go to the movies because it was an opportunity to be with other people, fulfilling a social need television could not match. Now that cinemas have five or six theaters shrunk down to the size of living rooms, they've misread one of their patrons' basic needs."

The same goes for fast-food restaurants. Settle points out that fast-food joints used to offer a burger, shake, and fries. Simple and quick. Now they tout salad bars and offer everything from fish and croissant sandwiches to Oriental-style chicken. Settle predicts that as fast-food restaurants become more complex, someone will probably come in and take the whole concept of fast food back to basics and start a major trend.

If the above inductees to the Hall of Marketing Blunders had carefully studied the needs of their customers, most of them would be enjoying a greater market share today. That's why Settle recommends grass-roots market research before deciding how to combat FeelGood! "Who knows," he says, "you might be fighting something that dies on its own. I'm really not overly concerned about the fact that FeelGood! has medicinal properties, and I don't think the fact that FeelGood! inhibits plaque is such a major thing. Fighting plaque is a remedial property. You can't see it working and you can't feel the results. In fact, it's really a negative property, in that you only perceive its benefit when it fails, when your gums rot and your teeth get cavities. So I really don't think that FeelGood! has such an advantage."

Given the product's dubious advantage, Settle concludes that the excitement over FeelGood! may fizzle on its own. "Every product has its own life cycle, starting with early adopters who pick up a product before anyone else does. Eventually the product becomes accepted by a greater majority, and finally by late adopters. Once it's passed the peak of the curve, the early adopters won't touch it and will begin looking for something else. A good analogy is rock or punk music. Once it filters down and becomes popular at the junior-high level, no one in senior high will have anything to do with it."

Settle recalls the great food-processor rage of the seventies. *Everybody* had to have one when they first came out, even though most people only used them as glorified blenders. Once the majority of people who would buy food processors had done so, the craze passed, and the food-processor market stabilized. FeelGood! could go the same route, once it hit the peak of its curve.

As a final caveat, Settle warns that jumping into competitive advertising would be unwise. "Why even acknowledge them? All you'd be doing is indirectly raising their recognition. Besides, what will the world think of great big Mocha Cola stepping on poor little FeelGood!? That's a no-win situation, so stay out of it."

## Bringing in the Hired Guns

Like Settle, Doug Wise, a senior vice president at McCann-Erickson, and former management representative for the firm's Coca Cola account in Japan, would sit back and size up the situation before taking any possibly precipitous action; FeelGood! may be less of a threat than it appears. "Whether I'm Mocha or Daisy, I know that a substantial number of people will drink soft drinks because of the product's indulgent nature—it's purely emotional, having to do with color and the fact that it makes me feel better, that it bubbles in my stomach. Since my product fits the indulgent qualities, I know that I still have a healthy business even if this FeelGood! guy comes in with a revolutionary new product. So I don't have to do anything in a panic state."

But what if FeelGood! does turn out to be a menace? What's the best course of action? "If you can't beat 'em, join 'em, but first you have to try to beat them," says Wise. "So my instincts would first be on the aggressive side and try to knock them off."

Wise offers three strategic approaches for accomplishing this goal. First try to beat FeelGood! by swallowing it. "You have three powerful calling cards," he maintains. "One is your money. Any upstart's major weakness is usually financial, and you might be able to name the right price. Second is your marketing expertise. You clearly know how to sell cola and have the money to advertise. And advertising is the foundation of success and failure, assuming that you have the distribution, which is your third card in the game. No new cola company can possibly have Mocha's distribution clout. You can have the best cola in the world, but if you don't have bottlers, you're dead. Seven-up has had some great advertisements but didn't have the distribution to support it, so it never became a block-buster."

Should the buyout approach fail, Wise recommends designing a new product yourself. "Don't touch Mocha Cola, though," he argues. "If it's got a special taste and heritage, I wouldn't mess with it at all." Does that mean creating a whole new product? Not necessarily. "Instead, take a weaker sister-product and breathe new life into it. This is exactly what Coca Cola did with Tab, which has been floundering since the introduction of Diet Coke. Add a shot of calcium and try to revive it."

Wise's third approach involves fighting fire with fire. Rather than sending his own gunslingers to clean up Dodge City, however, he'd hire an outside entrepreneur. "Set him up as an associate and allow him to use your distribution system," Wise suggests, "but give him the funds and all the management flexibility he needs. It's critical that you let him run his own show —if you get your corporate hands into the project, you'll muddy up the whole thing."

To augment the entrepreneurial approach, Wise would try to get a completely different perspective on the problem and the product. "Go to Japan. Get your buddies there who know the computer business to take a crack at the soft-drink business. They have a way of cutting through to the core of a problem. It may take more time, but once they commit themselves to doing it, it'll be done well. I'd have them come over here and set up shop and analyze FeelGood! until they figure out a counter-strategy."

Based on his experience in marketing Coca Cola in Japan, Wise believes a Japanese team would analyze the situation and the product in unusual ways, because they have an altogether different view of a soft-drink product. "People drink soft drinks worldwide but for different reasons. In Japan there's not the same life-style association with soft drinks that you find here. A cola's main competitors in Japan are fruit drinks. Another difference in attitudes really came out when Pepsi introduced the challenge concept. It was very poorly received over there, because people resented the idea of one product challenging another. It's a totally different way of looking at the commercial world of goods."

Whether Mocha brings a SWAT team of researchers and marketeers from Japan or fights it out on its own turf, Wise agrees with Settle and Randall that it must avoid knee-jerk reactions likely to misdirect energy to the wrong places. "Most companies tend to react to a new competitive situation in terms of the effect it will have on the pocketbook," he concludes. "The afterthought is, 'Did my actions turn the consumer on or off?' In other words, they think from the company point of view, not the consumer's. When you do that, you really don't acknowledge your customer, and you risk losing their loyalty. And loyalty is like virginity. Once it's gone . . ."

## Protecting the Southern Front

Jim Quest, president of advertising agency Posey Quest Genova, Inc., and a former account-management executive at an agency involved with Coca Cola, agrees with Settle that the medicinal properties of FeelGood! may not make it a world-beater. "Colas are part of an indulgence category," says Quest, "and as helpful as decay prevention may be, it's not health that drives the category. I doubt that in our lifetime it ever will. The major cola companies have done 'need-state research' that determines when and under what conditions people will consume soft drinks. When the need-state is health, soft drinks would not be the product of choice. So FeelGood! might cause some erosion of the cola market but not nearly as much as its inventors probably imagine.

"Besides," he continues, "by going the no-caffeine route, FeelGood! has already tossed out more than half the business. Studies show that more than half of the people who drink soft drinks do it because of the caffeine or caffeine-sugar combination. Eliminate caffeine and you eliminate half the audience. The major cola players discovered that they misread the market on this score—the noncaffeine products have turned out to be dogs. They total less than a few percent of the market."

Although Quest thinks FeelGood! already has two strikes against it, he would not take any chances and suggests a battery of "normal and dirty strategies that should be deployed against any competitor, not just those purporting to have a revolutionary product."

Comparing Mocha to Coke, Quest would use most of his marketing funds to protect his Southern business. "Our heartland is south of the Mason-Dixon line," he explains, "where per capita consumption of Coke is ten times what it is in the North. That's what is referred to at Coke as the 'Southern strategy.' I can step up my advertising or do specials in the Southern states and let Daisy know what we're doing. Let them fight it out up North."

But wouldn't the FTC frown on that kind of collaboration? "Oh, you don't have to sit down at the table with Daisy," Quest answers. "We'd publish all sorts of promotional materials that explicitly give our advertising strategy down South. Someone from Daisy would be smart enough to pick up on it and run a similar strategy in the North." And if Daisy doesn't want to play? "Great!"—Quest laughs—"let them get creamed. I get rid of a major competitor, and then I can begin my own Northern conquest against FeelGood!"

Specifically Quest would protect the South by dominating retail shelf space: "Offer Mocha at so low a price that you're in effect subsidizing the dealer. Pack the shelves with so much of your product that there's no room for FeelGood! That's how Coke originally dealt with the Pepsi challenge, lowering its price in some areas to twenty-five cents for a two-liter bottle. There's enough profit margin that they can sustain such price wars over a long period of time, six to twelve months. Maybe during that period you could even go back to a nickel Coke. Of course, during such a pricing campaign you'd increase advertising, but most of it would be in-store promotions."

If Mocha wanted to supplement the shelf-space gambit, Quest

suggests using the political clout Mocha has gained as a soft-drink giant. "The soft-drink industry is one of the greatest money machines in history," Quest says, "and has raised a lot of money for political causes. Use your political muscle to get the FDA, FTC, and any other agency you can push to attack whatever sweetener is in FeelGood! That's what the sugar lobbies did when artificial sweeteners came out."

Another of Quest's tactics would play off the emotions of cola drinkers. Coca Cola and Pepsi have both done brilliant jobs of convincing Americans that drinking Coke and Pepsi is wholesome and patriotic. "While we can't come out and say Feel-Good! is un-American, we can reinforce our American image by donating money to some patriotic causes, such as the Statue of Liberty renovation a few years ago. We can make it feel un-American to drink anything else. We can do the same thing with the macho image too. Just as Coke and Pepsi project themselves as 'young macho,' we can make FeelGood! look wimpy through our ads. Also, since we probably own a major motion picture company or two, we can subtly reinforce these things by putting FeelGood! in the hands of weak or un-American characters in the movies."

Quest moves on to suggest several "guerrilla-type tactics" that might pour sugar in FeelGood!'s engine. "In the analysis of FeelGood! I see that it has a nucleic-acid base," he observes. "Now, there's a chance to undermine the product if I've ever seen one. Just mention to the press that a product has something called 'acid' and you'll set off a storm. Just credit the product's own formulation."

But how do you get the media to cooperate with something so obviously self-serving? Under-the-table PR, responds Quest. Shifting gears from the CEO of Mocha to the head of Mocha's PR firm, he proposes the following tactic: "Go to the ten labs on the leading edge of nucleic-acid research and find out what's happening with the chemical. Is it used to make fertilizer? Kill rodents? Strengthen asphalt? Then write an article, saying here's the revolution going on in nucleic acids. It's legitimate news. Of course, in that article, you're going to mention that the same stuff used to bring bats down from the sky is also a key ingredient in a popular soft drink. The article gets published in the context of 'Here's What's New on the Medical Front.' Cable picks it up, and so on. It's just a good old misalignment of facts."

Quest next turns his attention to the issue of the Peter Pan hamburger chain adopting FeelGood! "If Peter Pan has indeed copped out, and we can't afford to lose the distribution, we buy Peter Pan, no matter what it costs to do it. That's not just a fanciful idea—you're talking about 'mega-economics' here. Given the industry's enormous profits, a soft-drink company can buy a fast-food chain or anything else it wants. To build a war chest in this business, all you have to do is charge an extra nickel per gallon of syrup. You'd raise $30 or $40 million overnight. You could double that if you asked the bottlers to pitch into the cause. They could recoup their investment; they just might pass the cost onto the consumer. Price isn't the issue with colas. Who thinks about the fact that a six-pack of Coke can be more expensive than a six-pack of beer?"

## Creating the FeelGood! challenge—for FeelGood!

Herbert Baum, president of Campbell, USA Division, joins earlier players in recommending that Mocha Cola try to buy Ambrosia Enterprises. "You've undoubtedly got more resources," Baum says. "How long can they afford to fight a giant like you? You could probably win through a war of attrition, but why chance it? Buy 'em and get it over with if you can."

Should that strategy fail, Baum would deploy two others: preempt or neutralize FeelGood!'s dental claim. "You can fight fire with fire without going to the enormous expense of creating a whole new product," Baum suggests. "All you have to do is to tout one of your existing sugar-free products in a new way. If it's sugar-free, it's the kind of stuff dentists like and endorse. Make a big deal of that. I don't think that people would differentiate your message from FeelGood!'s. After all, good dental health is good dental health, whether it results from fighting plaque or from lack of sugar. With your advertising resources, your own general dental-health claim can probably preempt FeelGood!'s more targeted claim."

To neutralize FeelGood!, Baum says, all you need to do is challenge its claim. "Even if it turns out that the claim is correct, once it's been challenged, people will always wonder about it. The questionability never leaves their minds. You could issue your challenge in the press, or you could file a complaint with the National Advertising Review Board of the Better Business Bureau. The more controversy you can stir up, the more people will doubt the FeelGood! plaque story."

Ideally, in Baum's view, the best thing that could happen

would be for the Federal Trade Commission to step in, as it did with Listerine. After claiming to fight colds, Listerine received the strongest punishment short of being taken off the market. In addition to having to print disclaimers about Listerine's cold-fighting prowess on the packaging, the manufacturers of the product were forced by the landmark action to spend a princely sum on an ad campaign that retracted the earlier claims. Although FeelGood! does sport an impressive professional endorsement, Baum suggests that Mocha may be able to prove that FeelGood has stepped over the line with false or deceptive claims.

Regardless of the outcome of such preemptive strikes and neutralization efforts, Baum believes that although Mocha shouldn't overreact, by the same token it mustn't be complacent. "You need to be proactive whenever you can," he advises. "When you get blindsided you have to act quickly and effectively." Baum tells how Campbell Soup was testing various plastics and papers for its microwavable trays, when all of a sudden Banquet and DelMonte appeared with their own plastic microwave dinners. "We were only in our second test phase and we saw there was a lot of hot press about the competition's new products. So we decided to safeguard ourselves and went from test to national rollout in six months. Normally we would do that in two years. But we did it calmly in six months." What happened? DelMonte got out of the business, and the new trays boosted sales of Campbell's Swanson microwave dinners.

## Outflanking the Competition

"The first, second, and third options are to try to buy out FeelGood!" says Gary Kreissman, corporate vice president of VAL-PAK, the largest network of cooperative direct-mail distributors in the country, and former marketing director for Rémy Martin Amérique, the premier Cognac maker. "If FeelGood! has no interest in selling, Mocha's best bet would probably be to try to preempt as many benefits as possible, preferably using an existing product."

Assuming that options one, two, and three failed, Kreissman would offer option four, ordering a detailed market research study about FeelGood! customers, particularly those who have switched from Mocha to FeelGood!. "You need to get more information about the type of personality that is switching to

FeelGood! and find out among loyalists why they aren't switch-ing. It's also important to reinforce the people who stuck with your product. You need to use them as a base before you go out and try to combat the benefits that the competition offers.

"Taste is the ultimate factor," he continues. "All the benefits are terrific, but if FeelGood! drinkers really prefer Mocha's taste, you have nothing to worry about. You can always outspend them, sponsoring taste tests and running advertising that plays heavily on the taste issue."

What if FeelGood! drinkers really *do* prefer the taste of FeelGood!? Not to worry, says Kreissman. Even if you lose the taste test, you can still sell the *idea* of good taste. "You can also use your heritage," Kreissman suggests. "After all, you've been around for a hundred years and can create a comfort level that an upstart can't. Many American consumers feel brand loyalty. You want to make them think that they must be loyal, that they'd be traitors if they switched: 'Hey—you've loved this product since you were a kid. Why change now?' "

If your research indicates that customers really have switched to obtain the health benefit, Kreissman still doesn't recommend that Mocha try to duplicate the formula. "There are other ways of tying health to taste without actually adding an ingredient. Associate Mocha with credible health. Maybe use Arnold Schwarzeneggar as a symbol of health. Or perhaps some-thing warm and fuzzy with no definitive message. From an ad standpoint that might be something more interesting for the mass consumer. The consumer might even respond better than through a straight health claim. Whichever you choose, the idea is to use the sleight of hand of advertising to duplicate Feel-Good!'s effect without touching your own product."

Kreissman also offers a variation on this idea. "Use your main brand as a gold standard, and try to preempt the competition with a 'flanker' or line extender. Maybe a variation on a diet or caffeine-free cola. Put a lot of money behind your trademark with the flanker, then let the line extension get all of the bene-fits of your standard product: taste, an implied association with health, and the comfort and trust that comes from a tried-and-true product."

The flanking maneuver has become quite popular in the spar-kling water industry, with Perrier and other brands creating flavor spin-offs from their original "gold standards." According to *Beverage Digest,* an industry trade magazine, the sales of flavored waters tripled between 1982 and 1985, and they should triple again over the next three years. Perrier alone reported a fifty percent increase after it introduced its flavored line. Wine coolers, too, have borrowed the tactic, with new offerings ranging from the basic wine and nondescript fruit juice to raspberry, peach, and strawberry delights. The extensions seem endless.

Line extensions, sleight-of-hand imagery, these all make sense in the fight against FeelGood! But isn't there a downside? "Yes," responds Kreissman, "you can blow it by referring directly to FeelGood! Never acknowledge an upstart competitor, because that just raises doubt in the consumer's mind. Sure, it's very tempting for management to say, 'Let's go stomp those guys!' but you have to resist those temptations. You're much better off outshouting them and diluting their message. You also don't want to dispute or test FeelGood!'s claims. Take the high road and let the new guy do the competitive advertising. The old guy is a fool if he does."

Kreissman's advice and recommendations come from first-hand experience on the battlefield. During his stint at Rémy Martin, more than a few pesky upstarts tried to bore their way into Rémy's turf with offbeat marketing schemes. "Remy has a reputation for making the most premium of cognacs," he says proudly of his former employer. "That's an envious position others wanted to usurp. In one incursion a competitor attempted to outprice us on the high end. This concerned us, because we wanted to maintain a premium price of at least five to ten percent above the competition. Fortunately, when the competitor came out with their new product, they had insufficient advertising and were unable to sustain a test. I think they were caught up in corporate politics; someone there said they had to succeed by a certain time. Chances are they would have died trying to compete with us, but they might have been able to make a middle market, like Sunoco's blended gas. At any rate, they withdrew the product and came out with a lower-tier product. Without firing a shot we remained the premium cognac."

If the would-be premium cognac hadn't withdrawn from the game, Kreissman recalls contemplating a clever countermaneuver during the competitor's test. "The idea was to get people to

stock up on Rémy now, at a special price. The message was that
it's still the best and most expensive, but we just happen to be
having a sale. No denigration of image . . . just a matter-of-fact
sale. I think it could have worked."

Kreissman's "buy-now" technique has been successfully deployed in other marketing counteroffensives too. In fact, it represents the cornerstone of what may be one of the greatest
maneuvers in the history of Executive Chess. The case involves
entrepreneur Wilson Harrell, who in 1967 bought the company
that manufactures Formula 409 spray cleaner. Harrell knew that
he was invading the territory held by giants like Procter &
Gamble, and sure enough, the Goliath of household products
prepared to launch a test of its own spray cleaner, Cinch. Knowing how big companies typically introduce new products, Harrell began his offensive by bamboozling P&G's marketing
machine into thinking that Cinch would be a surefire winner.
He cleverly cut off the supply of his own Formula 409 in the
Cinch test cities, and with no Formula 409 on the shelves,
Cinch outperformed P&G's wildest expectations. Then, when
Procter & Gamble took its apparently unbeatable cleaner national, Harrell crammed the shelves of the nation's stores with
special bargain-priced, king-size bottles of Formula 409. What
customer could resist the opportunity to get a three- or four-
month supply for less? Procter & Gamble's surefire, heavily
funded winner flopped, and the company gave up on it altogether.

Not all marketing offensives and counteroffensives go so
smoothly. But, as Kreissman is quick to point out, if you're
confident about your product and you understand your customers and your competition, the dice are loaded in your favor.

## Lessons from the Game

1. Avoid the knee-jerk response to a new competitor or a new
   competitive product. Sit back and assess the situation. Does
   it pose a real threat, or will it evaporate as just another flash
   in the pan?

2. Don't tinker with a winner. You'll only mess it up.

3. Beware of trying to pitch a product as all things to all people
   when compensating for a competitor's new feature. If you

don't communicate a consistent message, you'll confuse and possibly lose your customers.

4. Never engage in competitive advertising with an upstart. Every dollar you spend will merely boost the competitor's recognition.

5. Let other forces—the media, the public, the government— do your bidding when trying to cork an upstart. You can gain tremendous leverage by stirring an outside force to disgrace or ban a competing product or company.

6. Remind yourself what made you successful in the first place. If you know your strengths, you can put them to good use when fighting any competitor.

7. In any competitive situation that demands a high level of creativity, ask yourself, "What *wouldn't* I normally think of next?" Remember, if real leaders thought in ordinary ways, they would be just like everyone else.

CHAPTER *2*

# Spy vs. Spy:
## *Playing Fair in the War for Profits*

## Opening Moves

At six o'clock on weekdays a familiar scene repeats itself in a major U.S. city, as expensively tailored men and women, their briefcases and attaché cases securely tucked beneath their chairs, crowd into The Vault, a leather and mahogany and fern-studded bar close to the heart of the financial district. To the accompaniment of piano music and the tinkling of ice cubes, they dissect the deals of the day, paint rosy portraits of future profits, and share their deepest secrets, all in an atmosphere of camaraderie, celebration, and can-you-top-this? competition.

But wait a minute. See that striking blonde on the left, the one who keeps leaning toward the table where the executives of Flagship Foods are toasting their latest weapon in the Video Dinner Wars? She bears an uncanny resemblance to Deborah Ann Fountain, former Miss New York, who was disqualified from the Miss U.S.A. beauty contest in Biloxi, Mississippi, for padding her bra during the swimsuit competition. No, that can't be Deborah Ann, but if, as the pageant official did in Biloxi, we were to march this eavesdropper backstage and conduct an investigation, we'd discover more inside her bra than the gifts with which nature endowed her—we'd find a highly sensitive microphone and a miniature Japanese tape recorder.

A clip from the latest James Bond movie? Hardly. Such cloak-and-dagger corporate espionage occurs every day in popular executive watering holes and resorts from Wall Street to Nob Hill. In fact, for less than the cost of dinner for two, you can snap up your own stereophonic brassiere from any number of mail-order catalogues. And, if it's a business expense, it's tax-deductible.

Not all corporate eavesdropping and espionage involves such exotic devices. The first industrial spy simply relied on good memory. In 1789, Samuel Slater, an apprentice of a British textile mill, surreptitiously memorized his employer's layout and then hightailed it across the Atlantic for the New World, where he set up the first American mill, in Pawtucket, Rhode Island. That little stunt effectively ended Britain's monopoly over the textile business.

Today, some corporate spies may simply masquerade as fire inspectors, utility workers, or telephone repairmen to gain access to a competitor's plant. Others may pay the cleaning staffs of competitors for trash from the executive suite. Whatever the method, losses from such espionage activities total more than $100 million a year, and the problem seems to be growing. According to some investigators, as the pressure to gain competitive information increases, so do the limits on what people are willing to do to gather it. When Procter & Gamble introduced its Duncan Hines cookies, for example, it claimed a Keebler employee had taken aerial photos of P&G's unfinished cookie factory, that a Frito-Lay employee had sneaked into a secret P&G meeting, and that a Nabisco employee had wormed his way into a top-secret area of P&G's processing plant.

Questions of business ethics come in many shapes, sizes, and colors, but seldom black and white. Some activities, such as trespassing, theft, and blackmail, can clearly put you behind bars, but what about sifting through a competitor's trash at the city dump? Or how about conducting fake job interviews with a competitor's employee when you really don't have a job to offer but just want an opportunity to pick the employee's brain?

Where would you draw the line? How would you react if you found yourself the victim of corporate espionage? Would you discipline your own employees if you knew they had resorted to unacceptable market-research techniques to steal the march on your competitors? When we posed these and other tough ethical questions to our panelists, we heard some fascinating answers.

## The Game: The Case of the Stolen Sushi

Gourmet "video dinners" have captured the fancy of affluent young consumers who want to serve something quick but special to guests gathered to watch vintage films on their VCRs. Your company, Flagship Food Corporation, has invested $2 million developing "Candle Light Cuisine," $5.95 video dinners packaged in handsome gold metallic boxes and containing napkins and dinnerware created by a famous Italian designer. Each dinner also comes with two tapered candles that fit into molded bases in the corners of the elegant serving tray. The menus range from Chicken Cordon Bleu and Sole Almandine to Veal Oscar and Coquilles St. Jacques. You've even got a sushi version in the wings (just thaw and eat) and a Sunday brunch package complete with Eggs Florentine and Crepes Diane, not to mention an assortment of vitamin supplements and stress pills.

A week before your Candle Light advertisements are due to hit the airwaves, you almost choke on your own dinner when, despite ongoing competitive intelligence efforts, you see a surprise commercial during the World Series that advertises Intimate Cuisine, a video dinner from Ambrosia Foods, your archrival. How did Ambrosia keep that secret? The product looks exactly like your own, from the designer packaging and candles right down to the Sunday $B_6$ pills. You watch as two handsome couples offer a toast to their hostess's good taste.

Stunned by Ambrosia's preemptive strike, you call an emergency meeting of your own key managers and eventually conclude that a spy must have stolen your blueprints for Candle Light Cuisine. Either an agent for Ambrosia has penetrated your security, or one of your own people has committed treason. Perhaps both. Your lawyers inform you that Ambrosia's product differs enough from your own, and the concept behind Candle Light is sufficiently generic that you cannot successfully seek a court injunction to stop their campaign. As your security staff works around the clock to plug the leak and ferret out spies, you wonder how you'll regain the lead that Ambrosia has stolen.

To your surprise, one perspiring and pale-faced Richard

Becksworth, the product manager for Candle Light Cuisine, rushes into your office to confess that he's a spy—not against Flagship but against World Food Inc., another of your major competitors. It started innocently enough when an ex–World Food employee interviewed at Flagship, Becksworth explains, but the skulduggery quickly spiraled out of control when one of his own people volunteered to "quit" and join World's research department. Then came the chance to buy photographs of World's packaging designs, memos from the trash cans of World's key officers, and actual samples of World's test products, chemical analyses of which revealed the details of secret sauces and proprietary preparations. "I felt pressure to perform," Becksworth says with a sigh. "World was working on its own version of Candle Light Cuisine long before we started."

You sadly conclude that Ambrosia has simply stolen an idea you yourself stole from World. According to Becksworth, World's management suspects that Ambrosia, not Flagship, has been conducting corporate espionage, but as soon as you announce Candle Light Cuisine, you'll find yourself in a legal free-for-all that might permanently damage your image and balance sheet. You've invested far too much to turn back, yet going forward spells certain disaster. How would you maneuver in this situation?

## Strategies and Tactics

### Searching for the Mundane

"Strategically Flagship could roll out its product," says Leonard Fuld, president of Information Data Search and world-renowned authority on competitor intelligence. "They might have to wait a month or two and come out as a 'me-too' product. Or their counsel might decide that they could win a court case. But that sidesteps the issue; even assuming that there is no legal retribution, there is still the big question of conscience and what Flagship did to discover the product."

Fuld believes that situations such as Flagship's need never happen, because the best competitor intelligence gathering comes from plain, hard-nosed research involving such mundane sources as newspapers, trade magazines, and data bases. Smart companies also know how to tap their own sales force. "The best information gatherers are savvy listeners who aren't afraid to ask questions," he claims. "Hardly anything in industry can be kept secret, and the salespeople are the ones who will hear things on the street.

"Wherever money is exchanged, so is information," Fuld continues. "And I don't necessarily mean espionage. Take the situation in your scenario. I'm Flagship Foods, and I have this new dinner that I'm about to manufacture. I may need a custom-designed conveyor belt for the new product, so I call up my conveyor-belt supplier and tell him we need another belt. 'What's it going to be used for?' the belt person will ask. 'A new frozen dinner.' At that point someone outside the company knows that Flagship is going to introduce something new. I might also call up the freezer company and tell the salesman that I need a new freezer. 'What's it for?' he'll ask. 'A flash-freezing process that can do $X$, $Y$, and $Z$,' I answer. Okay, now *two* people from the outside world know that something is up. No company is so self-sufficient that a new product can be kept completely under wraps."

Obviously someone in the conveyor-belt or freezer company could sell the information, but Fuld says the company will more likely just amass it with other information about World generally "known on the street." But can a company actually profit from nonspecific information? "Absolutely. If you go to the right source, whether it's the press or your sales force, you can get the information you need to make strategic decisions. It won't be perfect, but that's not what business is all about. Perfectionists don't do well in business. The fact is, you don't need to know everything about World. You just need to know that they're retooling for something. Talk to your sales force and your ad agency, and you'll be surprised to discover how much can be found out without espionage."

According to Fuld, any manager contemplating espionage must ask two questions. One: Does it pay? Two: Is it necessary? "I've already talked about why it isn't necessary," he says, "and I don't believe that it ever pays off. In your scenario, Becksworth will wind up costing the company a lot of money, because Flagship may delay or drop the product, or wind up in expensive litigation. It's just not worth the risk."

Fuld's point proved more than valid in the infamous Hitachi case, which began when two Hitachi engineers handed an FBI agent a wire-deposit receipt for nearly half a million dollars. To their surprise, instead of receiving secret IBM documents, they listened to law-enforcement agents read them their rights. As the scandal unfolded, thirteen Hitachi employees were indicted, and the company wound up paying a $300-million settlement to IBM. No company can afford such a huge cash penalty, but equally important, it may never repair the damage to its reputation and credibility.

Beyond the monetary losses that a company stands to incur when caught with its hands in a competitor's cookie jar, consider the psychological costs and the message that it flashes throughout the rest of the company. "Why should employees be loyal to a company that's corrupt?" questions Fuld. "If senior VP Big John can do it, employees will say, 'Why can't I step over ethical boundaries too?' "

Fuld believes that companies must assume responsibility for guiding their employees through the murky waters and gray areas of competitor intelligence. "Some people ask, 'Why do adults need to be told what's right and wrong?' The answer is that at certain times, under stress, people do have to be told that there are limits. And sometimes adults aren't always adults. They may breach ethical barriers because of ambition and drive. And if they're caught up in a whirlwind of working ten to twelve hours a day, they might lose track of how their actions fit into the bigger picture. I think companies need to remind their employees of what the big picture looks like."

Fuld counsels companies to issue specific guidelines about various types of behaviors. These policies, he says, must transcend the traditional ethical considerations, such as antitrust, price fixing, and other issues that seldom filter down to the line level. "The key is to be specific. Say what your staff can and cannot do at a trade show, what's fair when interviewing a potential job candidate who's currently working for a competitor, and so on. In each case you have to explain the repercussions of stealing an idea. A rough analogy I like to use is that a bullet in your pocket won't hurt anybody. But put it in a gun and it can kill someone. It's the same with an idea. You can carry it in your head for years and it can't do anything. Put it in a competitive context and you can harm the company you got it from."

Fuld believes moral guidelines can keep organizations out of embarrassing and costly predicaments, and wishes more companies would publicize them because the overall image of business sorely needs bolstering. "I believe that business and industry really is 99.9 percent pure in terms of intelligence gathering," he asserts, "but purity doesn't make for good press. Look at the size of the GNP. Look at how many millions of stock transactions take place during the course of a business day. What tiny percentage of them makes the news? You could say that there are not enough reporters, but the truth is that most of it is very dull stuff. What defines the laws and sells newspapers are the extremes, the outrageous, the microphones in brassieres. And those cases represent a very small part of what business is all about."

Given the public's poor perception of the business world, Fuld believes that companies have a pressing responsibility to deal swiftly and strongly with employees who engage in unethical information-gathering practices, employees like Richard Becksworth. "In the real world of Executive Chess," he concludes, "Becksworth's superiors have only one disciplinary move: 'Checkmate . . . you're fired.' "

## Settling for Number Two

Marketing Professor Rob Settle agrees with Fuld that the pressure to perform causes many people to play loose with their ethical standards. "Things like your scenario do happen," he says, "because people get caught up in a whirlpool of pressure. We want employees to maintain the cutting edge, but we don't tell them how far to go."

In Settle's mind, quite clear-cut boundaries do exist in the area of competitive intelligence. "I don't think there are really any gray areas when it comes to ethical behavior. I don't steal; my employees don't steal. My rule of thumb is simple: Would I be ashamed to tell my parents and children about what I did? If so, then there's my answer. In this case there's no question that what was done was clearly wrong."

Given that orientation, Settle believes that Flagship Food would be wise to sit back and let the originator take the lead. "There are two advantages to this approach," advises Settle. "First, we would still have a clean reputation, and we wouldn't compromise our image. Second, it might improve our positioning in the market. The customer is really seeking variety. I don't think either of the two competitors will be able to satisfy the whole market. Depending on price and distribution, the market share will vary."

Starting off as number two has certainly served others well, the Japanese being a case in point. While the Japanese seldom originate an idea or a technology, they've turned the art of imitation into more than a sincere form of flattery; they've beaten the pants off American innovators who created markets the Japanese could sweep with products that simply improved on original technologies. For instance, International Harvester's first tractor stands sedately in the Smithsonian, while Komatsu tractors are plowing cornfields in Iowa; Clark forklifts once hoisted all the crates in warehouses from Kalamazoo to Timbuktu, but Toyota, Nissan, Komatsu, and Mitsubishi now shoulder those loads; and Xerox may have pioneered the field of photocopying, but Ricoh, Minolta, and Canon practically duplicated the originator out of the small-copier market. Americans may pride themselves on getting there first, but the race often belongs to the competitors who wait and watch before springing.

If Flagship does jump into the market, it will have to marshal what Settle calls a "pull strategy" behind Candle Light Cuisine. "We're going to have to use a lot of heavy advertising to pull the product down through channels in supermarkets," he points out. "And in order to get adequate display, we'll have to spend a lot of money. So why not let the other guy prime the pump for us? Then we can push our knockoff product through the channels he has opened up."

Some "wait-and-see" competitors might worry about consumers viewing them as mere imitators, but Settle doesn't think the public looks at products that way. "Picture yourself at the supermarket; you're going to try something new. If you see another new brand, you'll try that too. You won't think, 'Gee, that's an imitation.'"

If, as head of Flagship Foods, you lack the courage or patience to sit back and watch your competition initiate a market you've hankered to create yourself, Settle advises looking to the FTC for arbitration help. "You might try to work out some arrangement with World regarding product licensing and royalty fees," he muses. "Obviously there would have to be some limit in terms of time or percentage. In short, World should be compensated for having originated the idea. On the other hand, if our employee had not stolen the idea, World would have enjoyed an initial advantage; but if they were successful, we would have followed suit and developed our product as soon as possible."

This option, Settle thinks, would put tremendous pressure on Ambrosia Foods. "Ambrosia would come out stinko," he says with a chuckle. "They'd have to join in that consent or they would come off looking like a real villain." Despite that sweet revenge, Settle says to think twice before going to the FTC for help. "We might get a very adverse reaction. The royalty percentage could be astronomical, and we might get blocked altogether from entering the market. It could also look very bad from a PR standpoint. Everything really depends on how people react because one of our employees really screwed up. Whether they would react favorably depends on the tenor of the business community and the mood of the public at large."

Given the up-side and downside possibilities, Settle would lean toward the first strategy, putting your plans on hold, during which time you could do your homework and find out everything you must know to win shelf space when you introduce your own product.

But what about the internal issues? What should Flagship do with Becksworth? "In business school we have mandatory expulsion for cheating," says Settle. "It should be the same way in the business world. Send security down to Becksworth's office and have him thrown out of the building."

Settle agrees with Fuld that leaders should inform their people about the moral, legal, and social implications of their behavior. "As we get deeper into the Information Age," he observes, "we have to redefine the rules, because we assume that information is fundamentally different from other products. If you steal my car, I'm angry because I can't go to work, the grocery store, or whatever I use it for. But if you steal my idea, I still have it—I'm not deprived in the sense that I am when you've got my car. What you've gained is an unfair advantage over me. So we have to establish a set of rules on the transmission of information. Otherwise people who normally wouldn't dream of stealing, shoplifting, or cheating will become tomorrow's thieves."

## Trading Off for Success

Pamela Alreck, executive director of Associated Business Consultants, expands Settle's marketing strategy by looking for ways to turn the situation to Flagship's advantage. "Assuming that we don't dump the product, we must first overcome the problem of confusing the consumer," suggests Alreck. "There is already one similar product out there, and one more on the way, so we have to factor in that the consumer might lose track of who's who in this game."

The answer? Differentiate. "But don't change the physical product," she warns. "Change the *promotion* for the product. We know that there are two similar products out there, and we've got some idea about the kind of promotion strategy they're using. We really benefit from that knowledge. While World and Ambrosia fight it out with similar products, we can create a much different image for our product. Maybe make it more playful or sexy, so the consumer sees it in a different light. The only modification I'd make is to take out the vitamin $B_6$ pills. Nutritional concerns wouldn't match with the kind of sexy, romantic image of the campaign."

Alreck also recommends waiting until both World and Ambrosia have introduced their versions so you can monitor their sales to see how well they're doing. "Perhaps wait six months, then trade off the delay for the fact that they've done all the promotion for the concept. Since the consumer won't differentiate your entry from the established lines, you'll benefit from World's and Ambrosia's pioneering efforts."

As an example of how well this trade-off strategy can work, take a gander at Geno's Pizza. Jeno's Pizza (with a *J*) had been around for many years and had carved out a strong niche in the frozen-food market. Along comes Geno's (with a *G*), which naturally benefited from the work and effort of its sound-alike competitor. Ethical? Perhaps. To the consumer it's all just another offering in the Frozen Pizza Wars.

Whether you're in pizza or gourmet dinners, everything you need to know about the competition is sitting right there in the frozen-food counter. Like competitive intelligence expert Leonard Fuld, Alreck believes that the most useful information is right out in broad daylight for everyone to see. "You always want to monitor the marketplace," she says, "and, in particular, monitor other people's tests. All you have to do is send people out and count how many products are sold every day. There's nothing illegal, unethical, or shady about that."

Monitoring someone else's test market can indeed pay off, as

General Mills proved when it allegedly observed Lever Brothers' Mrs. Butterworth's pancake syrup with butter during its one-year market test. Borrowing the idea, General Mills created its own Log Cabin brand before Lever went national. And it did it without sending a single spy into a Lever Brothers plant.

But what do you do about employees who take a shortcut around counting and observing ad campaigns? "Written policies are certainly in order," Alreck says, "but equally important, you've got to deal strongly with people who jeopardize the future of the company through unethical or illegal actions. Becksworth must be fired immediately. There's a positive approach, too, and that consists of rewarding honest innovation. But in the end, I don't think a company can bring about dramatic changes in employees who behave in unethical ways, because people have a pretty strong sense of right and wrong by the time they're adults. And in the end, it's the morals that people bring to the job that count."

## Graduating from Business Disneyland

Paul Fireman, president and CEO of Reebok International Ltd., agrees with Alreck's final point: People bring their own ethics to the job. "Every person is going to be able to justify in their mind why what they're doing is right or wrong," says the head of the wildly successful shoe company. "It really depends on the circumstances and their motivation. If you have a culture that condones unethical behavior, then the justification becomes easier."

Fireman believes that exciting, creative companies thrive in ethical environments, where leaders embody the highest standards of conduct. "Once people start seeing corporate shenanigans being condoned or done by people at the top, they see that the company's culture is really based on compromises, and the really creative ones tend to shut down."

Given this view, Fireman believes that Flagship must dump its product line. "I would imagine that if Flagship's counsel says that Ambrosia's product is sufficiently different that you couldn't sue them, your own product could be made different enough from World's to stay out of court. But that isn't the issue. I think the only course of action is to dismiss the guy who did the espionage and go to World. Tell them what happened and that you are dropping the product. And make a big story out of it to the rest of the industry and your own people. This will give them an incredible morale boost. And chances are that they'll exceed their personal expectations and come back with an even better and more creative product than Candle Light Cuisine."

Fireman thinks that incidents like the one in our scenario happen because American enterprise embraces two types of ethics. "One is an ethics of convenience. If it's convenient, it's time to be ethical. Another one is 'survival ethics.' Confronted with a threatening problem, many businessmen will operate by survival ethics. That means they can take the less ethical route in a situation and justify it by saying, 'It wouldn't make any difference, anyway,' Those are the six most powerful words in business. As long as you keep saying them, anything is possible."

In addition to desperation, Fireman cites the thrill of carrying out a "secret mission" and beating the system as one of the reasons that some people get involved with espionage. He supports this observation with an incident that occurred in the mid-1970s at a trade show, when he was a sales rep in the electronics business. "A friend of mine represented a company that had just developed a revolutionary microprocessor, which was a major event at the time," recalls Fireman. "They were at a trade show and had heard rumors that another company had also developed a similar product but with more features. At twelve-thirty one night they were sitting in the suite of the CEO of their company, who motioned them to a door in the bedroom and said, 'Watch this.' They walked through the door into another bedroom, where the CEO handed an employee from their competition an envelope that supposedly had $25,000 in cash. In return the employee gave him the blueprints for the rumored machine. No one could believe it!

"As it turned out, the other system didn't come close to the one produced by my friend's company. At first my friend thought his CEO was paying $25,000 to remove any doubts. But then everyone realized that the product was irrelevant. He was playing 007, a game that he enjoyed more than worrying about whether the product was good or bad. His adrenaline was probably so charged with meeting this guy in a clandestine way. That's what they think he was truly playing for—the opportunity to be in the Disneyland of business espionage. Incredible!"

For those who want to play Agent 007, the opportunities abound. In one feat of daring, a competitor of DuPont hired two pilots to fly over DuPont's top-secret methanol plant in Beaumont, Texas, before the roof was built and photograph the naked processing equipment. Employees jotted down the number of the airplane, which enabled DuPont to win an injunction and suit against the flying duo. In another mission, a Dow Chemical employee celebrated his last day on the job by dipping his handkerchief into a vat of a proprietary anti-tuberculosis drug, Rifamicin, and then selling it to a South Korean buyer.

Another celebrated espionage tale involves Dr. Robert K. Aries, who taught chemistry at Brooklyn Polytechnic Institute. Aries allegedly duped some of his graduate students, who happened to work for drug manufacturers, to procure secret formulas that he then sold to other parties. Pharmaceutical giant Mercke & Company later filed for an injunction when Aries licensed Mepyrium, a drug used to kill parasites on poultry, to a French chemical concern. Mercke claimed that Aries had purloined its own parasite killer, Amprolium, through a graduate student, but Aries moved to Europe and retired on the Riviera, insisting that *he* had been ripped off by Mercke.

Fireman says that there is sometimes a fine line that separates acts of spying from acts of ingenuity. "Clearly the CEO's payoff in the hotel to the employee was unethical and probably illegal. But the next day, something else happened that makes for an interesting comparison. My friend put a prototype of his computer out the next morning under a glass case. And, of course, all the foreign and American constituencies instantly came over to see the product release. They couldn't physically touch it, but no one could stop them from taking pictures at a distance, or from making notes of what the thing looked like.

"The following morning, two major companies at the show did their own release—under glass, of course—of a product almost exactly like theirs, quoting a delivery time some three months later and offering features that didn't exist on the original. He found out from someone later how it was done. What was in the glass case was a clay model built the night before and painted."

Wasn't the creation of the clay impostors an unethical act on the part of the competitor? "No," answers Fireman, "that ploy was just smart marketing. The worst that could happen was that they'd default on the delivery of the actual machines. They were gambling that if they could discover how the product worked between the time of their release and the time they had to ship, they'd win big. I don't have a problem with that. A public release had been made, and their imitation was fair game. Whether or not they could make the technological leap, that was their risk."

More than a dozen years later Fireman continues to encounter dirty tactics. He says that until recently, every time his company attended a trade show, someone had broken into his booth. At first the thieves stole samples of Reebok's new products, presumably for reverse engineering. Later, when Reebok had become an industry leader, the break-ins were meant to disrupt Reebok's display. Today, Fireman deploys a solid defense against this unethical behavior. "We now have two armed guards at the booth."

## Minding the Store

Adding a legal perspective to the discussion, intellectual property specialist and attorney Bruce Sunstein considers who can sue whom and for what reasons. "Let's start with the obvious issue," he begins. "A trade secret has apparently been stolen. I say 'apparently,' because there may be a possibility of arguing that what World offered really isn't a trade secret. If people nosed around the table, they might have been able to put the Candle Light Cuisine idea together themselves. In other words, World's 'ideas' might have already been publicly available."

Flagship, however, shouldn't feel too confident about proceeding with its release of the product; Sunstein suspects that the courts might be sympathetic to World, given its substantial investment of time and money. "A trade secret is more than just an idea," he explains. "It can also be a business plan, a marketing strategy, sales projections, and other kinds of information particular to the project. In addition, there's the issue of what we call 'trade dress'—the design, the look, the coloring and shape of a package, the general typesetting. If the appearance of these things is likely to confuse consumers, you lose."

By the same token, World couldn't just sit back and cry foul because it would have to prove that it took reasonable measures to protect its idea. "If they're a company of any size, they should have identified all confidential materials, preferably with rubber stamps. All employees involved with company secrets and the new product also should have been made to sign confidentiality and noncompetition agreements."

Sunstein believes that the existence of contractual elements would likely affect the outcome of World's case against Flagship and/or Ambrosia. "Usually where there's a loss of confidential information, it's not a matter of a Batman-like crook sneaking in, picking the lock on the safe, and photographing the plans. It usually comes from a breach of trust, and where there is broken trust there is often an agreement that has been breached. In this case, it's the breach of the ex–World employee. Becksworth himself will probably be liable under various laws that protect against unfair business competition."

Clearly a company of Flagship's standing cannot tolerate such illegal and unethical conduct and must restrain the zealousness of any employee with ethical and legal measures. "Becksworth must be disciplined in some way, and the company should immediately develop a code of ethics to eliminate future mishaps of this nature. Perhaps a policy is needed to spell out what kinds of competitive conduct are legitimate."

What kinds does Sunstein find acceptable? "If you stick with information that's publicly available, you're okay. There's certainly nothing wrong with monitoring a competitor's sales or buying one of his products and exploring it through 'reverse engineering.' In fact, reverse engineering not only gives companies good food for thought, it forces them to keep competitive."

Just about every product maker reverse-engineers its competitor's offerings, and sometimes they do it with spectacular results. Look at how Xerox profited from reverse engineering when it made its comeback in the small-copier market. After years of concentrating on large machines for large businesses, Xerox lost market share to the smaller, more affordable machines made by Savin and a slew of other manufacturers that understood the needs of small businesses. To accelerate its return to the market, Xerox dismantled every competitor it could get its hands on and quickly discovered that it could use more plastic, which would reduce costs, lower the weight, and extend the life of its machines.

In our scenario, the ambitious Becksworth could have accomplished his goals by waiting until World released its product, says Sunstein, and then reverse-engineering it through spectrographic analysis or other means. But since he jumped the gun, he's got to go. "First, interview him concerning the incident and find out what other unethical activities he might have engaged in. If the facts check out, fire him. If he signed an employment agreement, you can still probably fire him, because an employment contract generally can't protect an employee against breaking the law."

Of course, getting rid of Becksworth still doesn't solve Flagship's dilemma, and Sunstein suggests three basic courses of action. "First, you could go ahead with the product launch and run the high risk of a suit. Not a good idea—I counsel against it. Second, you could avoid the launch altogether and not come out with the product. That means eating $2 million in development money. But there's a third approach, an intermediate approach. Delay the launch for the amount of time that would be sufficient for a company of Flagship's size to have independently developed a similar product line of its own. In the meantime, World might sue Ambrosia and succeed in keeping Ambrosia's product off the market. During that time it may be possible for Flagship to negotiate a license from World. A delay in entry, by the way, is the kind of court remedy that World might get if it sued Flagship for theft of trade secrets. So if World sued Flagship at a later date, Flagship could argue that World already had the time benefit that its trade secrets promised. Just be careful about the 'trade dress' issues we discussed earlier."

Sunstein believes that corporate espionage will continue until our society alters some fundamental beliefs. "It's a problem with our society's values. When intellectual property is stolen, people often don't see it as theft, because they don't see any tangible harm. Also, when a corporation is the victim, the absence of a face makes it easier to rationalize the wrongdoing. A business doesn't scream when it's attacked."

## Rebuilding Corporate Trust

Corporate ethicist Dick Sanner, who holds degrees in industrial management and theology, says the Flagship scenario represents a violation of basic trust. "One of the important things about doing business is the values that are manifested in an organization. And one of the basic values is structured around 'judicious trust'—we don't take unnecessary risks in organizations. We have a conceptual map of the business world which says there are certain things we can and can't trust. In this particular case, that trust has been broken, and if I were Flagship's CEO, I'd call in the key people and say, 'Folks, we can't operate like this. If our research people aren't able to develop products and be creative without resorting to stealing other people's ideas, then we need some new research people in here.' "

As for releasing the product, Sanner believes that once World and Ambrosia have slugged it out, Flagship's product introduction would not run counter to ethical standards, because "the cat is already out of the bag," and Flagship presumably could have developed it on its own once the rivals went public. "I don't think coming out with the product at some point is a major ethical issue," Sanner says. "The more important task is seeing that the situation never happens again. But the problem is that people usually don't sit around thinking about ethical issues until a crisis strikes."

General Dynamics certainly proved that when the government charged it with defrauding the Pentagon. GD responded by establishing a Committee on Corporate Responsibility, with a steering group and a hot line. In addition to providing training seminars to employees, the company drew up easy-to-understand guidelines for managers, which include such ideas as: "Am I willing to make my decision a general rule for the company?" and "Would I be comfortable explaining my decision to my family or on *The Today Show*?"

Whereas General Dynamics went all out, hiring professional ethicists and giving them a blank check, most companies do not go to such lengths. In fact, Sanner suggests that many do not even know what to do when it comes to ethical repair. "Companies constantly make boundary decisions. They establish geographical boundaries, product boundaries, financial boundaries, and any others that have to do with a market niche. But it seems that when they come down to ethical issues, they're reluctant to establish lines of demarcation."

Sanner cites two reasons for this: Ethical issues look "fuzzy"; and most executives do not know how to undertake an ethical analysis, which involves evaluating activities in terms of their behavioral implications and impact on the business. "It's not that executives aren't ethical," he adds, "it's that they don't have a method or framework for dissecting ethical problems."

As for the "fuzzy" issues, most businesspeople are used to thinking in concrete terms, and ethical issues run toward the abstract. The farther up you go in the firm, Sanner says, the more likely you are to find people thinking abstractly. "Typically you find more people at the top concerned with ethical issues than at the bottom. That's one reason that any attempt to create an ethical policy will probably happen at higher levels. Top management can then try to get the middle levels to start thinking in new ways."

An issue related to the problem of abstraction centers around the fact that most people who teach ethics come from a philosophical background and want to turn businesspeople into philosophers. "That doesn't work," Sanner criticizes, "for the reasons just cited. Businessmen and businesswomen should be taught through examples of situational or contextual ethics. That means the correct behavior is not only determined by principles, but by situations in which the principles have to be realized."

A new wave of ethics training programs, instituted at companies such as General Dynamics, McDonnel Douglas Corp., Chemical Bank, and American Can Co., are taking Sanner's approach. At training sessions sponsored by these companies, men and women discuss hypothetical dilemmas ranging from deciding what to do when a manager asks an employee to do something illegal to dealing with situations involving nepotism and stolen confidential documents.

Sanner sees these seminars as an encouraging sign and notes that once top management starts tackling ethical issues, it must eventually issue explicit policies that guide the rest of the company. "The critical aspect," he maintains, "is to make sure that the policies aren't vague. Although the contexts may vary, the principles can be clear-cut."

More important than creating any document, though, top management must set role models. "You have to act like you talk," Sanner insists. "In the recent literature concerning corporate culture, one of the aspects is the value structure. When you have a value structure that permeates a firm and that value structure is based on integrity, people will act according to it. That's why I wouldn't fire the people who perpetrated the espionage. As CEO, I'd have to take some of the blame for not making my expectations clear. I need to clarify the values of the company before I can expect anyone else to follow them."

To designate honesty as a prized cultural attribute, Sanner believes you can provide rewards for ethical behavior, although most executives find it easier to reprimand or punish unethical behavior. "Why not reward the Flagship team if they were to do their work honestly? Why not come out and say, 'In this day and age, when so much industrial success is attributable to questionable practices, it gives me great pride that you people have done it cleanly and honestly.' I think that kind of verbal reinforcement would go a long way to keeping the issues active in people's minds."

In the bigger scheme of things, Sanner believes that we need to reorient our attitudes toward success at any cost. "As a society, we need to understand the implications of the behaviors we induce. "If we uphold success as the major motivating factor, then we have to pay the price. There will be more pressure to produce more and produce it faster, and people will take shortcuts to achieve these goals."

The cure? Says Sanner with a grin, "Well, if we can't adjust our priorities, we can all move to Australia. People are more relaxed about business down there."

## Curing a Sick Culture

Social psychologist Signe Dayhoff agrees that Flagship's top management may be to blame for the problem. "Since people tend to follow the cultures of their company, I'd want to make sure that there isn't something in the culture that was giving them a green light to do this sort of thing."

How do you give your company's culture an ethical checkup? "Oh, there are litmus tests for ethical issues and honesty," Dr. Dayhoff says, "but I wouldn't use them. Instead I'd do a survey, based on the 'Mach' [Machiavelli] scale, asking what is really allowable, and what ends justify what means. I'd administer this from the top down, so as to get a general feel for how people perceive the culture. I'd also want to identify, without mentioning names, whom people perceive to be the role models for the culture. One of the good things about surveys is that if they're done right, you can figure out who the respondents are talking about even if they aren't named."

Once you've completed your survey, Dayhoff would urge you to get everyone in the company involved in formulating and enforcing ethical standards, from the CEO down to the custodian (remember, emptying the wastebaskets can be a lucrative job if you have the right connections). "While top management should preside, every division of the company should be represented on an ethics committee. And it shouldn't be a SWAT team, either, disbanded after a little booklet is produced and distributed. That will just lead back to business as usual. The committee should have the ongoing responsibility to report ethical breaches. I don't want to create a secret police state. It's more peer pressure. But I do want to generate a sense of ongoing ownership and responsibility."

Dayhoff believes that the concept of ownership, more than any other, can forestall some of the primary justifications for unethical behavior in large organizations. "Research clearly shows that when people tend to see something in a depersonalized way, like taxes, they are less likely to feel guilt about doing what they feel necessary to create equity. This is especially true in large organizations where people often feel that they have no control, and no investment."

You can induce a sense of ownership even without giving away actual stock, if you create "psychological equity." Says Dayhoff, "Being made part of an important company-wide policy-making effort that has the stamp of top management can create that vital sense of ownership. And when you do that, the system becomes less depersonalized. So you've accomplished three goals. One, you've made a statement about the integrity of the culture; two, by promoting a sense of ownership you've gotten people to feel more sympathetic about the real costs of actions like those of Becksworth, and to realize that what hurts the company hurts them; and three, you've put in place a means of checks and balances that can prevent future incidents."

One company that benefited from employee involvement in ethical issues, the Caterpillar Tractor Co., developed a comprehensive set of guidelines for dealing with uncomfortable situations in parts of the world where bribery was a customary way of doing business or a rampant problem. Caterpillar's "A Code of Worldwide Business Conduct," which was reviewed by fifty managers in various functional areas, covers such topics as product quality, sharing of technology, differing business practices, competitive conduct, observance of local laws, and relationships with public officials. Under the latter category, Caterpillar explicitly states: "Company employees are also required to make good faith efforts to avoid payment of gratuities or 'tips' to certain public officials, even where such practices are customary. Where these payments are as a practical matter unavoidable, they must be limited to customary amounts; and may be made only to facilitate correct performance of the official's duties."

Perhaps Flagship should put Becksworth in charge of writing a similar ethics policy. "On the one hand, that would be a fitting exercise," says Dayhoff. "But I think at this point, making an example out of him is more important. No more frozen dinners for him. We have to show people that our new concern with ethics is deadly serious. But before he's canned, I'd want to know what other proprietary sauces he's got his fingers in, and what it was about the culture that he felt sanctioned his behavior."

As further demonstration to the employees that Flagship takes its commitment to ethical behavior seriously, Dayhoff would advise the company to abandon the Candle Light line. "Even if we could survive it legally," she concludes, "it would be so counterproductive to our educational efforts that it wouldn't be worth it. Besides, I'd want the people who had invested a year of their lives to be angry at seeing the fruits of their labor tossed away because of the reckless behavior of one person. It's a hard lesson, but it will go a long way toward creating peer monitoring systems."

An alternative approach to dropping the Candle Light line is to use it as the basis for an original Flagship product. "I don't think it would compromise the goal of the ethics program to say, 'Look, folks, we aren't going to sell this product as is. I don't care how good it is, either. Let's go back to the generic TV dinner and recreate something using our own ingenuity.' When the new product is finished, you might want to give some kind of conspicuous award to the team that did it, noting how they proved that the goals of the company can be accomplished without resorting to illegal or unethical practices. Make sure the whole company sees it, and issue more awards for other products in the future."

For Dayhoff, the decision about what to do with the Candle

Light line is of secondary interest. The primary issue is whether Flagship can help people make a connection between their behaviors and consequences in the real world. "You really have to reverse the thinking that in a large organization little acts of cheating and unethical behavior can be hidden. People have got to be made to realize that one act of one person can bring the whole company down. And when that happens, everyone loses."

## Lessons from the Game

1. Do everything you can to keep abreast of trade activities in your field: Read newspapers and trade magazines, and tap your sales force. You should be able to piece together everything you need to know to make an informed competitive decision.

2. Explain to your employees the high costs of unethical business behavior. Companies must help people make the connection between their actions and the reactions of the outside world.

3. Explain the power of a stolen idea. Employees may not be aware that the theft of information is just as devastating to a business as the theft of property and equipment.

4. Encourage originality. The intellectual property laws say there is no such thing as a free ride, and protect the independent innovator.

5. Check the ethical level of your corporate culture. If people perceive that unfair business practices and behavior are okay at the top, they're okay for everyone else.

6. Devise codes of behavior that address the real issues. Lofty discussions of antitrust and other issues have little impact on people. Talk about what's fair on the playing field.

7. Don't try to turn your employees into philosophers. When running ethics seminars or training sessions, be as concrete as possible, and frame issues and dilemmas within an everyday context.

8. Don't wait until a crisis strikes before developing a set of guidelines for ethical behavior. Education is your best defense in the war against espionage and unfair practices.

9. Make ethical behavior a way of corporate life for everyone in the company. Swiftly and strongly punish those who transgress ethical boundaries, and reward those who stay within them. Ethical behavior must be incorporated as an everyday aspect of doing business.

CHAPTER 3

# Till Death Do Us Part:
## *Doing Business with Friends and Family*

## Opening Moves

One hot Friday evening in August, management consultant Jerry Parnette joins his old college roommate and war buddy George Ashley, a research chemist at Cal Tech, for a reunion dinner at The Wharf. The annual dinner has become a ritual, and the two greet each other like long-lost brothers before they settle down for the feast.

"I'll have the bluefish special and a glass of Chablis," Jerry informs the waiter.

George grimaces. "With or without the carcinogens?"

"Wha . . . ?"

"I'd order the Norwegian salmon," George suggests. "Bluefish can be loaded with PCBs."

After the waiter takes their salmon orders, Jerry laughs. "You sure know how to spoil a guy's appetite. Why don't you hotshot scientists *do* something about those toxic pollutants?"

"Funny you should mention it, but I've been working on that problem in my spare time, and I think I'm close to patenting a process for degrading PCBs into harmless sludge. If I'm right, my method will turn the hazardous-waste-disposal industry on its head."

Jerry gets that faraway look indicating he's once again calculating the business angles. For the first time in fifteen years, talk of wine, women, and song takes a backseat to business as the two discuss George's process and its money-making potential. By dessert, they hatch a plan for an entrepreneurial venture that could make them both rich.

Does such a scenario sound farfetched? Hardly. Every day, friends and family members form enterprising partnerships. Many of these will fail miserably, leaving the participants with shattered dreams and relations, as well as strong negative feelings about doing future business with people they know and love.

On the other hand, those who have successfully combined family, friendship, and business argue that the commitment close relations bring to an endeavor can make an enterprise flourish. Besides, they say, if you can't trust those you love, whom can you trust?

The annals of business history are filled with stunning and heart-wrenching examples of the consequences of doing business with loved ones and friends. When it works, it works wonders, but what happens when an initially successful arrangement among tight relationships begins to falter because of human friction? Can you salvage the business and the relationship? In the following scenario, scientist George Ashley and entrepreneur Jerry Parnette seem to be heading for divorce court as success strains their former bond of friendship. Let's watch the new corporate knights try to untangle the problem.

## The Game: Here's to Good Friends . . .

Imagine yourself as the president of Silver & Silver, Inc., a successful venture-capital company headquartered in New York. Over the years your decisions to back technical geniuses who have developed important new processes and patents have struck pay dirt: a Harvard/MIT—based group of bioscientists formed the nucleus for a firm that now supplies a third of the world's interferon; a physicist from Texas has turned his work with gravity-free crystallization into a company that may someday give the major drug manufacturers a run for their money. And this new venture, launched by two of your old college fraternity brothers, could turn Silver into gold.

Although you have always followed the rule of not bankrolling undertakings involving friends or relatives, you couldn't resist the enthusiasm, not to mention the windfall opportunity, that Jerry Parnette and George Ashley have offered you. It looked like a dream deal: George had hit upon a simple, yet extremely efficient and cost-effective, way to render PCBs harmless, and Jerry brought plenty of business experience to the party.

In fact, the business plan they submitted looked so good that you invested $250,000 of your own money in TekChem Systems, Inc., before you kicked in an additional $950,000 from Silver & Silver's coffers. In return for the capital, Silver received forty percent of the stock and a seat on Tek's board of directors.

Jerry scraped up $25,000 and could earn the rest of his share in the company with sweat equity, actually managing the business, while George could earn his cut by contributing his process and directing research and development. Both started off with fifteen-percent interests, which could expand handsomely through a performance and stock-option plan.

Within eight months Tek unveiled a working prototype of its PCB degradation system, and private companies, towns, and hazardous-waste firms began lining up to buy it. A year later Tek's device was regarded as the state-of-the-art means for the economical and safe disposal of PCBs, propelling the company's annual revenues to $15 million, with earnings of nearly $1.5 million. The usually conservative Jerry projected annual revenues of $60 million within three years.

Just when you thought you could forget your uneasiness about doing business with friends, conflicts begin to pollute Tek's waters until what started as a trickle of discontent cascades into torrents of anger. In the beginning, businessman Jerry had wanted to bring the product to market as soon as it met EPA standards; scientist George argued for a seemingly endless series of tests first. Then Jerry insisted on moving the company to New Jersey, where tough state laws forbade businesses from selling their properties before safely removing any PCBs. George left Pasadena kicking and screaming, and evened the score by hiring his new girlfriend at $42,000 a year as his personal "executive assistant." Jerry wanted to curb expense accounts; George bought the company a Mercedes and talked about leasing a private jet. The frictions finally reached critical

mass with George's insistence on a bigger office, a teak cre-
denza, and a double parking space for his new car.

This afternoon George calls you to deliver an ultimatum: it's
him or Jerry. If you won't issue Jerry his walking papers, George
will bail out of the company and return to California. You're
alarmed because George has displayed a rare flair for developing creative ideas and coming up with workable, lucrative solutions to complex technical problems. You're also not sure
whether you can hold him to the buy-back and noncompetitive
provisions of the articles of incorporation.

On the other side, Jerry's done a brilliant job of managing
and marketing the company and has charted a solid course for
the future. Your mission is to protect Silver & Silver's investment while minimizing the damage to lifelong friendships in
the process.

## Strategies and Tactics

### Isolating the Problem Child

"This really isn't a problem resulting from friends getting together to do business," remarks attorney and business consultant Arnold Goldstein. "It's a simple case of two business
partners drifting apart only to find themselves at each others'
throats. The fact that they started off as friends just makes the
aftermath more gory."

Goldstein should know. In the process of writing twenty-two
books on small business, including two on crisis management,
he's become an expert in the trials and tribulations surrounding
start-ups. Over the years he has encountered more than his
share of business conflicts involving friends and family. His conclusion? "As a policy, I don't think relatives should do business
with each other," Goldstein advises. "Family relationships are
far too important to be sullied by something as insignificant as
money."

Yet few heed Goldstein's advice. Take the legendary wine-
making Sebastiani family. After his father's death in 1980, Sam
Sebastiani became head of the winery that bears his family's
name, but six years later, because of a falling-out with his
mother, Sebastiani found himself kicked out of the company,
deeply embittered by the experience. Another family-owned

winery saga also ended in bitterness when the Mondavi family took their grievances to court. After a lengthy legal battle they settled their differences out of court, but the late Cesar Mondavi's two sons, Peter and John, each left to start rival companies.

Of course, such family-business traumas aren't limited to the spirits industry. Take the classic case of Adolf and Rudolf Dassler, who opened a slipper and track-shoe factory before World War II, then, after a bitter fight, went their separate ways. One brother started Adidas; the other launched Puma. After the breakup, neither spoke a word to the other for the next thirty years. The same goes for the Revson brothers of Revlon fame, one of whom wound up denying the other's existence because of disagreements surrounding business dealings.

While such horror stories cause Goldstein to caution relatives about the problems of doing business together, he does appreciate the instances when friends bring a certain magic to their business endeavors. Citing Hewlett-Packard as a shining example of such magic at work, he wonders whether the company started by two college buddies could have turned its electronic tinkerings into a corporate giant if it hadn't been able to rely on the friendship to get them through the rough times any fledgling operation encounters. Both Robert Hewlett and Donald Packard remain active in their firm today.

Goldstein stresses, however, that such success stories typically involve friends who bring complementary talents to the endeavor. "In the case of TekChem, the two friends started out with complementary skills, but when the business really got rolling, they got into each other's hair by getting too involved in each other's areas. It sounds like Jerry wanted to dictate scientific goals, while George wanted to call more of the business shots."

In many cases, Goldstein goes on, people go into business with friends because they like them or because they're comfortable with them. "They somehow feel that those characteristics will make a successful business relationship. That's seldom the case, though."

Goldstein notes that manager Jerry and scientist George probably joined forces for the wrong reasons. "They get together once a year to catch up on women and sports—what do they really know of each other's business skills? Nevertheless, they did start the company, and now that they are at each other's throats, what can you do to resolve the crisis? It's especially complicated here, since a third friend has bought an equity stake in the operation."

Given these circumstances, Goldstein advises to try to mediate first. "Work out compromises—you've got nothing to lose. This case, though, sounds like it's gone too far for that, so you've probably got to go right to step two: isolation. Keep the warring partners away from each other and have them report independently to someone over their heads. Above all, make them feel as if they're operating autonomously."

The advantage of the isolation technique, Goldstein says, is that the firm can still benefit from both partners' talents and creativity. They'll simply forget about their "opponent" and go back to work. After all, when grown-ups behave like children, they think like children, too: out of sight, out of mind.

"The final move is the old heave-ho—one or both," Goldstein concludes. "No one is irreplaceable." History certainly bears him out. Whiz kids can be bounced, as Apple's Steven Jobs discovered when John Scully booted him out of the company he had cofounded. Even luminaries can be canned. After Lee Iacocca brought Ford back from the grave by wrapping new sheet metal around the Falcon frame and creating the Mustang, he received his reward in the form of a pink slip.

But if both Jerry and George are dispensable, which one should go? According to Goldstein, while the manager probably deserves to stay on, it would be harder to replace the scientific brainpower. But even if you act on that fact from the start, he cautions, you should still try to make George feel as dispensable as possible. "You have to shake up the scientist's idea that he's one of a kind. Otherwise you lose all your leverage and you can forget mediation or isolation."

So you save the business. What about saving the friendship? "Doubtful," Goldstein says, shaking his head, "but that really can't enter into it—they're in business to stay in business. If that isn't their primary goal, why bother?"

## Forcing Accountability

Charles Levin, president of Sandler & Worth, Inc., a $30-million-a-year family-owned carpeting and Oriental rug company, agrees with Goldstein that you must protect your business from family intrigues at all costs. "It's very difficult for a friend or family member to detach business problems from personal relationships," Levin claims. "George and Jerry obviously have this problem. George's going wild with expenses is mainly a statement of resentment, perhaps a challenge. These two people don't understand that the business has to take precedence over the individual relationships."

As a solution to this dilemma, Levin recommends that all three friends take a vacation together where they can relax and clarify their personal and corporate goals. "Hopefully," he says, "something would be accomplished by putting them in a context where they can relate to each other as they used to. Some shreds of the original friendship may still be intact."

And if this gambit fails? Disagreeing with Goldstein, Levin insists that you should get rid of George. "The scientist is creating the most problems, so if you can't get him to behave himself and work to the benefit of the company, try getting him on retainer as a consultant—that way you can still draw on his knowledge. But if worse comes to worst, he's really the more expendable of the two."

But what about Goldstein's point that while thousands of managers emerge from business schools every year, gifted scientists only come along once in a blue moon? "You already own the invention," Levin explains, "so you bring in other R&D people to refine the product and develop spin-offs. You really don't need top-level scientific talent to do that. The most important function at this point is marketing, and Jerry is doing a great job, so he's the more valuable person. Besides, a lot of bright people in the sciences only make one major discovery in their lives, usually when they're young, and then never do anything else really significant. George may already have had his big hit. Why put up with him?"

Although Levin would pick Jerry's business sense over George's nonsense, he places blame for the present predicament squarely on the head of the third friend who funded the enterprise. "He should have insisted on a more solid business plan, with tighter financial reporting and controls," Levin insists. "That would have made it more difficult for George to go to such excess. The problems might have manifested themselves in some other way, but at least George wouldn't be doing things that financially harm the company. The third friend should have also established a strong board of directors or an advisory board that would be responsible for developing a solid growth plan and enforcing expense control, and that could overrule either or both of the feuding partners."

Levin, who runs Sandler & Worth side by side with his in-laws, sees weak planning as the biggest potential pitfall whenever closely knit groups, especially families, do business together. One planning area that receives far less attention than it should in such situations is compensation, which smart managers should project far into the future for several different growth scenarios. "Compensation issues must be explicit from the beginning," he warns, "and they should be taken seriously. Otherwise you're headed for certain disaster."

Another key planning issue, which particularly plagues family businesses, involves succession. "Who's going to be running the show two and three generations down the line?" he asks. "Succession probably tears apart more family businesses than any other issue."

By the same token, you should clearly and decisively answer the question: "Who really holds the cards here and now?" According to Levin, a surprisingly low number of family-owned businesses survive the first generation. "The first generation is primarily interested in preserving what the business has. The second generation, which is usually younger and looking toward the future, is more willing to take risks in favor of growth. That's where the problem comes in, because the second generation can't make any moves without the first generation, which may not want to move in that direction at all. If the two generations lock horns, the business will stagnate or, worse, go under."

The first generation of Hansen Juice, Inc., probably wished it had heeded Levin's advice. Vincent Hansen, a Los Angeles supplier of fruit juices, who had barely survived the Depression, made a conscious attempt to keep the company small and local, operating purely on a cash basis. Taking the opposite view, Hansen's son, Robert, an entrepreneur who didn't share his father's abhorrence of debt, envisioned a national market for their products. Robert split off on his own to start a company that grew to $25 million in sales the first year, while his father's firm took in a mere $1 million in sales.

Of course, the second generation can make mistakes, too, as the case of King Arthur Flour aptly illustrates. Shortly after the young Frank Sands graduated from Harvard Business School in

1963, he took over his family's business, the Boston-based Sands, Taylor and Wood, producers of King Arthur's Flour. Hoping to propel the 200-year-old firm from its stodgy $3 million a year in sales, Sands started acquiring other companies: Allied Bakers Supply, Joseph Middlebury, H. A. Johnson, and Goodhue Products. Although combined sales soared to $45 million by 1978, profits evaporated to the point where ST&W faced almost certain bankruptcy. Luckily, Sands reverted to the family's old reliable strategy of selling a high-quality natural flour and divested the company of all its acquisitions by 1985. Sales now sit at a mere $3.5 million, but the company is alive and well, a testament to the fact that sometimes "father knows best."

Whether the old guard retains control or the new guard usurps power, Levin maintains that closely knit businesses too often make decisions in an emotional, rather than a businesslike, manner. "The odds are really stacked against you when you do business with friends or family," he continues, "because you're less likely to use sound judgment. You tend to just assume everything will work out all right because you know the other people so well."

Levin goes on to stress the notion that a business must have a life independent of the owners' family or personal lives. "It's critical for any group of people in business to agree on *why* they're in business. A lot of people feel that their companies exist solely to serve their own needs, so they skim cash whenever they can. In a family setting this is especially dangerous, because it's impossible to control cash when everyone has his hand in the till. If that happens, the company will in all probability fail, because its owners are guaranteeing that it won't be able to finance the future."

Can Levin think of any good reasons to mix family and business? "I suppose the main strength you get from doing business with friends or family is trust," he concludes. "You go into it with the sense that these people aren't going to steal from you, which is one of the major things in the back of the minds of most business people. Perhaps that means you also get a stronger sense of loyalty and commitment."

## Letting the Brain Overrule the Heart

Dr. Max Tesler, chairman of PharmaControl Corp., would strongly dispute Levin's last statement. Some years ago, one of his business associates, who also happened to be a relative, was convicted of conspiracy to make false statements to a federal agency and tried to implicate Tesler.

"Never, never, *never* do business with friends or relatives," Tesler says emphatically. "You assume that because someone's your best friend or brother-in-law you'll never get screwed. Wrong! Anyone can screw anyone, regardless of whether or not they're related. It just depends on the people involved. But you're more likely to get taken by friends or family because you let your guard down."

For Tesler, business, like Gettysburg, can be a battlefield where brother takes up arms against brother, father against sons. And history certainly bears him out. Consider the familial skirmishes of William K. Kellogg, of boxed-cereal fame. William and his brother, Dr. John Harvey Kellogg, accidentally invented cornflakes during their employ at the Battle Creek Sanitarium in the mid-1890s while experimenting with a new food for the patients. The brothers had been boiling wheat and left a tray of it to sit overnight while they responded to an emergency. When they resumed their experiment the following day and pressed the wheat through a roller, to their surprise they were left with a tray of wheat flakes, which became an instant hit at the sanitarium. William bought the rights to the flakes from John and, in 1906, started what was later to become today's well-known cereal giant. In 1925, William named his son, John L., president of the company, but later fired him on moral grounds after John L. abandoned his wife for an employee. William Kellogg had even hoped John L.'s grandson would one day rule the company but wound up driving him out and later suing him for using a Kellogg process.

The reverse happened at shoe manufacturer Genesco, started in 1924 by James Franklin Jarman. When James died in 1938, his son, Maxey Jarman, took over. Like Frank Sands of Sands, Taylor and Wood, Maxey embarked upon an acquisition binge that resulted in a bloated portfolio of shoe and apparel companies. In 1972, Maxey's son, Frank, forced him out of the company and began rapidly divesting many of the firms his father had blindly devoured.

To this gallery of rogues Tesler adds the following recent account: "I know of a family-owned drug company in which a father and his two sons were literally having fistfights in the halls. One week a court granted an injunction that put the father in business and the two sons out on the street, and two weeks later the court reversed itself, and the two sons were running the business and the father was out on the street. It all came down to the fact that the father's first wife died and there was a general disagreement as to what happened to part of her estate when the father remarried. This was a fine company that was making a good, solid profit and was unfortunately sold for a song to another company that stripped and ruined it."

While misplaced trust causes its share of problems, Tesler sees misplaced objectivity as the primary culprit in the Tek-Chem case. Agreeing with Arnold Goldstein, he points out that the scientist and the manager were too close to know that they couldn't work together as business partners and that "unless they can sit down and work out their differences, one of them will probably have to go." Which one? That depends on the company's needs at the moment.

"You really can't categorically say whether the scientist is more valuable than the manager, or vice versa," Tesler explains. "If there's more creating to be done, you'd better put the scientist in a box and let him create. Managers are a dime a dozen. If, on the other hand, the managerial guy is really terrific in his field and the creative guy has done his creating, buy out the scientist and send him back to California to contemplate his navel."

Tesler pins blame for the problem on the venture capitalist friend, who should have recognized that George would eventually pour kerosene on Jerry's fire. He lists the liabilities that attend business dealings among people who are too close to one another: "It's just like a physician trying to treat a member of the family or a best friend. As a healer, I try not to do it because I know my judgment is colored. I might tend, for example, not to order a test that might be inconvenient or painful because I want to spare the person. Yet that test may be critical to the correct diagnosis and treatment, so I'd ultimately be doing them a disservice. It's the same thing in business—when you're dealing with people who are close, you tend to respond more through your heart than your brain, overlooking things you shouldn't. You might turn your back on serious blots in someone's past or accept behavior that you wouldn't accept for five seconds from someone else."

## Balancing the Team

Venture capitalist and scientist Fred Nazem, whose firm, Nazem & Company, has funded more than sixty successful start-ups, challenges the basic definition of the problem in our scenario. "Don't worry about whether friends should go into business together; worry about whether they *become* friends once they *are* in business," he says with a smile. "A friendship must develop along with the essential entrepreneurial bonds."

Nazem admits that friends do tend to overlook each other's weaknesses, and nine times out of ten, he would rather see strangers become friends rather than friends become strangers as a project unfolds. In either case, he offers "preventive maintenance" as the key to binding people together. "All companies fail because of human frailties, and those frailties lead to friction. You can head off that friction by being aware of potential clashes among the partners."

For Nazem, preventive maintenance means carefully monitoring people and numbers. "You have to look at the 'dollar shadows.' If managers are consistently optimistic, but the numbers don't come through, something may be wrong. Firsthand visits are important too. If a company has a beer and pretzel session on Fridays, I attend and keep my eyes open and start talking with people. I want to know who's not happy and why, so I can help defuse problems before they explode and cause irreparable damage."

What tactics can you deploy if the friction between partners does become explosive? "Bring in someone above them. We've done this numerous times, with great success," he says, beaming. "The way it works is you tell the partners, 'Look, you've come a long way and have really done a great job. But the reason you're having problems now is that the company has new needs, and we must get in someone whose experience will take us to the next stage.' Then you find someone whose authority would not be in question, someone whom everyone can look up to. Last year we brought in new CEOs in half a dozen of our companies, and they worked phenomenally well."

What happens if the sparring partners don't buy the idea? "That's easy," Nazem responds. "All you have to do is remind them that even though they each own twenty or thirty percent of the stock, it's worthless if the company doesn't work out. I tell them that if they want to make a real return, they have to think like owners, not like employees. That means someday they will have to step down, sideways or whatever, and give the reins to someone who can take it to the next level. This concept of ownership is something I discuss very early on when I finance a company—it's critical.

Like Levin, Nazem pins the blame for the problems at Tek-Chem on the friend who funded it. He should have set up a different structure, Nazem says, holding back stock until Jerry and George had proven their compatibility. "Entrepreneurs are very hopeful people, but they perform because of two things: incentives and fear. Many sit across this table from me and say they want six million dollars and forty percent of the company. I say, 'I'll give you fifty or sixty percent. But you're going to get ten percent now and ten percent next year, and so on, as milestones are met.' That provides continual incentives. Many venturists don't agree with my approach—but my track record proves me out."

As for the second motivator, fear, Nazem argues that you can use the natural fear of failure in a healthy way. "We don't want anyone walking away from the table saying, 'We got a lot of money. We succeeded.' That's the wrong orientation. We want people to stake their self-worth on what they're trying to accomplish with their company. When that happens, money just becomes a scorecard because they have something infinitely more valuable on the line, something that they'll fight hard to protect."

In addition to providing the right incentives and maintaining the right level of fear, Nazem insists that the fate of a start-up hinges on whether the people involved bring complementary leadership to the undertaking. He uses the word *leadership* rather than *management* because the latter implies "guiding a herd," and he strongly believes that you "can't build a company with cattle." Specifically Nazem seeks to forge what he calls a "balanced team approach," which means assembling a group of people with proven experience and expertise in four areas: product development, marketing, finance, and overall direction. If you erect these four pillars, Nazem says, the strong foundation can help the company weather even the stormiest events.

Some companies implement Nazem's balanced approach through the use of "smart teams," which enable leaders to draw on the diverse skills of a group of managers to make important decisions and resolve problems. Smart teams work remarkably well at high-tech companies, such as Compaq, that recognize their markets are too volatile for one person to be calling the shots. This approach differs from the early days of high-tech hegemony, when daring pioneers could create and maintain empires by virtue of their talents and personal flair. Other fast-paced industries, such as biotechnology, are likely to experience the same growing pains and might look to collective brainpower as a means of achieving solid growth and development.

But whether you're talking about balanced teams or smart teams, can you really persuade rough-and-tumble entrepreneurs to buy them? Nazem ponders that question. "Entrepreneurs unfortunately tend to think they can handle all aspects of a business when, in fact, most can't. When you're building an enterprise, you don't have the time to learn everything. That message is very hard to get across, and it can be even harder when friends or family members are involved, because they tend to see themselves bigger than they really are in life. So if a group of friends comes to me and wants to start a company, I'll first try to balance their leadership experience."

Many people seeking venture capital from Nazem express surprise when he tells them they're missing one of the essential pillars of a balanced team. "One common scenario is that a couple of engineers have a great product and believe that they need a CEO to worry about the business. We tell them that they need a marketing person and they're shocked, because they just figure that the product will sell itself. They really don't know the difference between selling and marketing."

And the result of this ignorance is, "Sadly the product or company goes nowhere."

## Caging the Creative Talent

Arthur Lipper III, a venture capitalist and publisher of *Venture* magazine, suggests a different strategy for resolving the situation at TekChem. "It's very simple," Lipper points out. "You let the scientist go back and live in Santa Barbara and be a consultant to the company. You create an entity for the scientist to use, and the entity gets a percentage of earnings. The scientist carries his own expenses and he owns the new company, but he can't sell it without your permission."

Lipper believes this approach creates two advantages: "First, you take care of the competition problem in a way that works. I don't believe in inhibiting competition through contracts—I want to inhibit competition through fear of financial loss. You let the scientist pay himself a salary from the new entity, but if he goes into competition with you, then the revenues stop. Second, the scientist gets to be leading the life-style he wants, but you still have him locked in. There's nothing he's doing that can't be done with the use of Federal Express or a facsimile machine. Most important, you get him out of the M.B.A.'s hair."

If shipping George back to Santa Barbara does not work, Lipper would reluctantly get rid of him. "The master of the relationship has to be the company—it is the entity to which loyalty is owed, not the individual who happens to be involved in creating it. Frequently the individual with the skills necessary to create does not have the skills necessary to manage and, consistent with the issue of loyalty to the company, has to be removed. You see this problem in any field where creativity is required for product development. And it's not just high-tech. You can see it just as much on New York's Seventh Avenue, which is the antithesis of high-tech. You desperately need a designer to get the business off the ground, but in most businesses you sure as hell don't need him to run the show. It's like letting the director in a play determine how much the actors will be paid or what size theater will be used."

Lipper goes on to say that the problems at TekChem should never have happened in the first place. "It's a silly structure," he insists. "George should never have had a decision-making role. He should have been treated like an artist and kept in a pen." In fact, Lipper sees as the main lesson from the scenario the conclusion that you should never let scientists or engineering types get enmeshed in management. "The manager is concerned with profit margin, and the scientist or artist is concerned with recognition, which is what George's buying a Mercedes and hiring his girlfriend is all about. The manager's job is essentially a function of saying 'no.' The scientist's is a function of saying 'yes,' so the two couldn't possibly live together in a framework where they have equal voice. The real problem with this structure is that there was no boss, and the only management structure that I believe works is the pyramid —*one* guy makes the decisions. It's certainly demonstrable in most successful companies during their formative stages. Look at Ford, IBM, and General Motors, for instance."

Lipper, in contrast to Nazem, doesn't recommend deferring stock or money as a tactic for creating incentives and protecting his investments. "The only precaution I would have built into the arrangement is a mechanism to get control of the company if the entrepreneurs failed to meet their objectives. I wouldn't withhold anything up front—I'd want them to make a lot of money. I wouldn't fool myself by paying a $150,000-a-year guy $30,000 and predicate my financing on that number, because when he gets hit by a cab, I'll have to pay $150,000 to replace him. People should be paid what they're worth, and that should be budgeted. If the business can't afford that, you'd better think about refinancing the business."

Lipper maintains that you should almost always avoid doing business with friends and family. "The downside is that you fire them more slowly than you should when you discover their incompetence. You're also considerably more likely to overlook that incompetence before you go into it, because there's a loss of objectivity. Then there's the problem of making too good a deal with them going in—you give them too much of the company or pay them too much. You're too interested in their welfare as opposed to the welfare of the enterprise."

Unlike most of the players in this chapter, though, Lipper worries less about family members doing business with each other. "By definition you like your friends and have affection for them," he says. "No one is forcing you to like your family members." Indeed, although the odds against them may be terrific, some family businesses do extremely well. Take Mary Kay Cosmetics, started by retiree Mary K. Ash and her son. Today, Mary Kay Cosmetics fields a sales force of more than 250,000 women who ring up $450 million in annual sales. The business not only began with family, it still functions like one big family, with a reward system that includes handsome cash bonuses and pink Cadillacs.

Harper & Row is another example that proves family members can do business with each other and still survive. The company was founded by four brothers who stuck together for nearly fifty years, managing an entity that became a major force in the publishing world. On a larger scale, Dayton Hudson, the retail conglomerate; Loews Corp., of movie theater, tobacco, and insurance fame; and the E. & J. Gallo Winery also prove that blood and money can mix.

But what about the less fortunate family business? Can the

kind of contractual and succession planning that Charles Levin discussed earlier forestall failure? "Not likely," Lipper retorts, "especially if an entrepreneur is involved. Take succession planning. That's almost oxymoronic when it comes to entrepreneurs. None of us are going to die. We don't need successors. Nor do we really care what happens. I would dare say there's a higher percentage of entrepreneurs walking around without wills than executives of equal estate."

Are there any precautions that friends or family members might take to minimize the chances of disaster if they are insistent about going into business together? Lipper points to the blend of skills. "If they have opposite and complementary skills, then it might work," Lipper says. "It's what I depict in *The Larry and Barry Guide to Venture Funding,* which I wrote several years ago. Larry is the outside marketing guy, and Barry is the inside operating guy. That combination works well as long as they're supportive and complementary. If they become intellectually competitive, though, they're heading for sure disaster."

## Playing Marriage Counselor

Christina Darwall, president of New Venture Services, Inc., which helps start-up companies find funding and develop marketing and growth strategies, brings a different perspective to the problem. "If I had been the person in charge of Silver & Silver, I'd be feeling a little shamefaced at this point for having let the situation get so far out of hand," she says.

Darwall likens TekChem's difficulties to the kind of communication problems and power plays that can crop up in marriage. "One of the things that struck me is that Jerry is the one who wanted to move to New Jersey. Jerry's deciding to move unilaterally and pulling George behind him would be like one spouse saying, 'We're moving. Period. I have a better job in New York, so we're moving to New York.' Those things happen less these days, but when they do, it often ends in divorce. So for me, the fact that Jerry apparently made this unilateral decision was justification for George's erratic and seemingly selfish behavior. It's as if the spouse who was pulled along said, 'Well you've gotten to further your career, so I'm going to get even in my own small, but very irritating, way by building a bigger house or whatever.'"

Continuing the metaphor, Darwall defines the role of the

venturist or funding party as that of marriage counselor who should detect problems at an early enough stage for the partners to ventilate their high emotions before pressure builds to dangerous levels. The sensitive and experienced venture capitalist should constantly reinforce the fact that frustrating situations are seldom as bad as they seem. He also needs to spend a lot of communication time with the partners, leveling molehills that could eventually make mountains. "For example," urges Darwall, "Jerry may think, 'George is really irritating me with that double parking space, but I don't want to bring it up with him because it's not a big deal.' So Jerry keeps it inside, and it adds fuel to the fire. Later, when he's complaining to George that the product development schedule is behind, he may be really voicing his anger about the parking space. George will be harboring similar things. The Silver guy should be able to make sure everybody is open and voicing their feelings."

According to Darwall, once you've dug down to the roots of the problems, you should sit Jerry and George down and discuss how each has been distressed by the other's behavior. After both have aired their feelings you should tell them, "A lot of the things that both of you have done may just be matters of style, and you guys are going to have to agree on what matters of style you can live with. We've gotten big enough now that we've got to start making major decisions together about how we're going to run this company, or else we're all going to lose it."

Sometimes it's hard for the venturist to use this approach, Darwall admits, recalling a situation in which the business partners actually called in a *real* marriage counselor to help everyone sort through their feelings. "That sounds a little bizarre," she says with a laugh, "but sometimes partners get to the point where they need a very structured intervention to get them back on course." Considering our scenario, though, Darwall believes that the former strength of the friendship and the relative good health of the company should make it fairly easy for the three friends to defuse the ticking bomb.

Part of the solution is to make the three friends aware of how the most petty-sounding things can carry great symbolic weight. "The size of a desk, the size and location of a parking space—these are symbols of value," Darwall points out, "and one of the things you look at in a start-up situation is how similar are the partner's values. I think the guy from Silver should have realized that although Jerry and George were friends, they have very dissimilar values and perhaps were going to have clashes when they started working together." In social situations, Darwall continues, good friends may tolerate, even joke about, their idiosyncracies. But when they find themselves working shoulder to shoulder, even minor quirks can become major irritants.

Since Darwall ends up with an equity position and a board seat when she takes on a client, she always makes a point of spending a lot of creative time with any prospective partners, especially in nonbusiness settings: "I think taking potential partners to dinner, and not necessarily together, is a very good way to begin to understand their value structure. On those occasions I don't just want to talk about the business itself—I want to figure out their styles and feelings. The more I do this, the easier it becomes to zero in on hidden attitudes that are likely to manifest themselves once the business is started."

Darwall thinks that friends who have worked together before usually encounter the fewest hidden problems, while families, especially husband-and-wife teams, are a more risky proposition. "Husband-and-wife teams either work out terrifically well or absolutely horribly," she says. "I think it's a fifty-fifty shot. I wouldn't dismiss a husband-wife team out of hand, but I'm a lot more suspicious of potential trouble. Being around each other all the time in the intensity of a business situation can be an overload for spouses—they have no one to go home to and vent their frustrations. I also think that the bits of courtesy that people give one another in the workplace, the veneer of politeness we expect, is often gone because spouses can be *so* honest with each other. That just makes it more difficult to work well together."

The saga of Tago Laboratories sheds light on Darwall's position. Started by scientist Helga Johnson in 1973, Tago produced diagnostic testing kits for research labs, from which it wrung annual profits of $10,000 to $40,000 a year. That modest level of business continued until Helga's husband, Bob, a former manager of G. D. Searle's European divisions, joined Tago and convinced her to expand. After plowing some of their own cash into the operation, they watched sales climb from $150,000 to $600,000 a year, with profits reaching $80,000.

With such success the Johnsons wondered if the business could be expanded even more by an injection of the plentiful venture capital that seemed just waiting to be soaked up by technology-related companies in the early eighties. To find out, the Johnsons gave up two seats on their board in exchange for a $900,000 outside investment. Unfortunately, while the strategy worked wonders for sales, their marriage suffered under the strain of dramatically increased business and a public offering, and the new board used the marital conflicts as an excuse for kicking both Johnsons out of the company.

Ironically the Johnsons' fight to save their company, though it wiped them out financially, brought them closer together and strengthened their marriage. Few such cases, however, wind up with happy endings. More often they end in bitter dispute. In 1976, Lore Harp, who had no prior marketing experience, took the computer add-on board that her husband designed and within six years was running a $36-million-a-year company. The company began faltering in the early eighties, and while the lawyers struggled in bankruptcy court, its husband-wife founders were busy settling up in divorce court.

Darwall concludes that while human friction and value clashes occur every day in big companies, they produce more harmful effects in smaller ones where you can afford so few foul-ups, especially in the formative stages. "Little problems get magnified to the point where they can really take you down. In a big company that has two thousand cogs and wheels, if two or three get broken, you're still manufacturing something. But if you have only ten cogs and you lose two or three, you're out of business."

## Clearing the Vision

Entrepreneur Geoffrey Rappaport would take a hard-nosed approach to the situation. "No one is irreplaceable," he says, "and if the scientist and the manager can't get their acts together, then one or both must go. The business simply cannot withstand the kind of petty bickering you describe."

Rappaport also agrees with Goldstein that friends who decide to go into business together quite often fool themselves into believing that a good relationship is justification for starting a company. "A lot of people have unrealistic ideas about starting a business," he says. "They see old Hollywood movies where a

group of buddies are crouched in a trench with shells explod-
ing all around, talking about how they'll start a bar or restaurant
or car dealership when they get back home, and how they'll
stick together through thick and thin. That kind of fantasizing
might get John Wayne through tough situations, but it's destructive in real life. You need more than a friendship to make
a business work—you've got to have a viable idea and a vision
of how to make that idea succeed. And that vision has to be
regarded as absolute truth—you can never deviate from it."

Looking back ten years, when he cofounded the highly successful Supercuts haircutting chain, Rappaport recalls how both
he and his former teacher, Frank Emmett, contributed to what
turned out to be a phenomenally successful concept. "I had half
of a good idea, and Frank had the other," Rappaport says half
jokingly. "We looked around and saw that there were few alternatives in haircutting. Either you went to an expensive salon
where you were told, for an outrageous fee, how to look, or
you went to a conventional barbershop where your options
were limited. We each knew that it was possible to create a
third possibility, where you could get the best kind of cut for a
reasonable price. That's been our shared goal for the past ten
years, and since we've both been dedicated to a common goal,
we've never had any problems working together."

Rappaport and Emmett's shared formula for success—a passion for perfection—can go a long way toward smoothing the
wrinkles in friend- or family-based businesses. Take the case of
computer-board manufacturer AST Research, started by Tom
Yuen, Albert Wong, and Safi Qureshey, who in the early days of
the microcomputer revolution gambled that there would be a
huge aftermarket for add-on products that enhanced the IBM
PC. Their bet was a winner; from a low-key, garage-based business that grossed less than half a million dollars its first year,
AST grew to $140 million in sales within six years. What im-
presses people the most, however, is not the tremendous
growth or spanking new corporate headquarters—it's the fact
that success has not gone to the heads of the founders. Ac-
quaintances claim that their friendship and style is still the same
as in the days when family members gathered together and
helped package and ship the fledgling company's products.

What AST and Supercuts show is that money doesn't *have* to
corrupt the bonds of friendship. "It all depends on your expec-

tations," Rappaport says. "If you're going into a business to make as much as you can as fast as you can, like the guys in your story, then people aren't going to matter very much. But if you're doing it to create the best possible product or service you can, then ties with people around you are likely to grow as the business grows."

## Lessons from the Game

1. Be objective. Try to deal with loved ones the same way you'd deal with a stranger you've just hired.

2. Accept the fact that no one is indispensable. In many business situations you can best solve the problem by removing its source.

3. Pay attention to complementary skills among friends and family members. Any business, regardless of the relationship of the owners, must have people with expertise in the key areas of management, or it is doomed to failure.

4. Allow the corporate entity to overrule all personal relationships. In many cases it makes sense for an outside party to assume the top job and solve problems objectively.

5. Establish crystal-clear rules governing compensation and succession. Think both short-term and long-term about who gets what, when, and why.

6. Define, promote, and maintain a shared vision of what the business should be and where it should go. If partners have the same goals and passion for the company, they can weather the stormiest seas and enjoy the greatest chance for success.

CHAPTER 4

# Brain Drain:
## *Keeping Key Players on the Team*

## Opening Moves

Marsha Bulfinch and John Holstrom sit across from each other in a secluded booth of Les Poissons, the light from a candle reflecting off John's Harvard class ring. As he spells out his tantalizing offer, all of Marsha's carefully rehearsed rebuttals vanish from her mind. Yes, she fears letting this opportunity slip away. Yet John's proposition to finance her own management-consulting company makes her feel as if she's perched on the edge of a precarious cliff. Even with the assurance that three of her current employer's most lucrative accounts will follow her, she agonizes over the risk. But her own company! It would take at least ten years for her to rise from her present vice presidency to head of the firm. But imagine, too, the look on her employer's face when Marsha breaks the news.

Torn between loyalty to the people who gave her a chance to establish a reputation as one of the sharpest strategists in the industry and her urge to strike out on her own, Marsha debates the pros and cons, then accepts John's offer. Now all she has to do is resign.

Marsha's boss will soon join the ranks of executives who must wrestle with one of the most difficult problems facing business today: "brain drain," when today's key personnel become tomorrow's arch-rivals by starting their own firms or joining the competition. While advertising, publishing, consulting, and other service businesses that can be started on a shoestring most frequently fall victim to this phenomenon, almost every company in every industry will suffer from it at one time or another.

Ever since the first M.B.A.s matriculated from colleges, brain drain has plagued American corporations, but today it has grown especially acute. Do today's M.B.A.s differ somehow from those of previous generations? Are they more entrepreneurial? Less loyal? More ambitious and less patient? Some say that the "information generation" practices its own breed of greedy self-interest. Others believe that the economic pressures on those born during the baby boom make it unrealistic for executives to expect their creative talent to remain loyal when other opportunities arise; after all, unlike their parents who could afford a family, a house, and two cars on one income, young couples today must rely on two hefty incomes and defer having children just to make ends meet. Finally, others cite the simple demographics of the information generation. With too many M.B.A.s and too few high-level positions available, young managers can hardly resist the blandishments of headhunters and venture capitalists.

Whatever causes brain drain, its prevalence in today's business requires executives to approach it with the utmost creativity. To learn about some imaginative remedies we asked our panelists to put themselves in the shoes of Marsha's boss and stave off a serious defection of valuable talent.

## The Game: Fatter Carrots, Shorter Sticks

Some things haven't changed in the twenty-two years since you began A. R. Lothrup & Associates, a $25-million-a-year general management-consulting firm now employing 150 professionals. Mary Smith still supervises the typing pool, Harry Thompson still empties the wastebaskets, and you still work late hours trying to catch up on your paperwork.

Mary left hours ago, Harry has already vacuumed your office, and you're busy reviewing recommendations for promotion. As the clock strikes eleven, you pause and ask yourself if you'll be condemned to doing promotion reviews for the next fifty-eight years of your life, too. Suddenly a shadow crosses your desk, startling you and interrupting your musings. You look up and see your niece nervously twitching the handle of her briefcase and digging the heel of her running shoe into the carpet.

You smile. "I thought you had a date, dear."

Marsha blushes. "I lied, Aunt Alice. It wasn't a date, it was a business dinner with John Holstrom."

"Holstrom? I thought I warned you about him." Indeed some things never change. That vulture Holstrom has lured away some of your best people over the past several years, but you really hadn't thought he'd have the nerve to entice your own niece away from the firm that bears your name.

"You did warn me. But he's a wonderful man—he's convinced me I'm ready to start my own firm. I know the risks, but as you taught me, I'm going into it with a little insurance. I'll be taking Thurston Hotels, TekChem, and Execor Industries with me, as well as Larry Brown from R&D and John Weston from Finance."

You shake your head. "He's wonderful, all right, a wonderful pain in the butt. After all this company did for you! Why, you could be sitting at *this* desk in a few years. And Brown and Weston—I gave them their first real jobs. This is how you repay me, by joining Holstrom?"

Your harsh words merely mask the pain of Marsha's betrayal, not to mention the knowledge that if Marsha leaves, you'll really feel the loss of the business she takes with her. You can't keep Lothrup on top with Mary and Harry. Be calm, be objective, you remind yourself. You've planted the seeds and nurtured crops of whiz kids before, and this isn't the first time some pest has tried to pluck the fruit first. Your mind flashes over the scores of people who have announced that they were leaving A. R. Lothrup to become independent consultants or to join your rivals. Since you convinced half of them to stay by offering them more money and more perks, you offer Marsha the same: a raise, a new BMW, two extra weeks' vacation—just about anything she wants.

Marsha sighs and tries to smile. "You don't understand, Aunt Alice. I appreciate your offer, but maybe I'm more like you than you realize. After all, you did the same thing when you left

McDougal & Company to start Lothrup. I don't want to go through life succeeding because I'm the boss's niece. I need to find out if I'm really as good as you are."

If you were Aunt Alice, how would you keep your own niece from walking out the door?

## Strategies and Tactics

### Composting the Corporation

According to Alex Randall, founder of The Boston Computer Exchange, the now classic approach to Aunt Alice's problem would involve giving her niece access to the resources of the whole company, letting her run her own "mini-show" from within. In other words, Aunt Alice could establish an intrapreneuring program.

"It won't work, though," cautions Randall, "because Marsha is an entrepreneur, and intrapreneuring tries to ritualize and bureaucratize a process that's by definition spontaneous. Besides, intrapreneurship is just a hollow form of manipulation that any real entrepreneur can see right through."

Many people share Randall's conclusion that intrapreneuring is a sham, benefiting one party: the employer. Look at what happened at Prentice-Hall during the 1950s. In one case it worked beautifully. When the aggressive young Prentice-Hall editors James Leisy, Richard Etinger, Jr., and Charles Jones decided they'd learned enough to start their own company, they accepted Prentice-Hall's financial support and started Wadsworth in California. Wadsworth thrived and eventually spun off, after which it grew to more than $30 million in annual sales before being acquired by Thomson Ltd. Flush with this experience, both Prentice-Hall and Wadsworth let bright and eager editors start a whole flock of new publishing houses: Reston, Brady, and Winthrop, among others by Prentice-Hall, and Dickinson and Duxbury, among those by Wadsworth. When, as so often happens, some of the brilliant editors failed to become brilliant business executives, the parent companies folded some of the fledglings back into the nest, quite often benefiting the parent companies with a number of perennial best-sellers and saving quite a lot of overhead by letting some of the "intrapreneurs" go their own ways. Manipulative? Surely not. But ask those who started their own companies only to lose them after investing gallons of sweat equity, and you might get a different opinion.

In our scenario, if Marsha did suspect intrapreneurship to be a trap, what should Aunt Alice do then? Something radical, Randall suggests. "Get out, give Marsha the company," he insists. "Say, 'Hey, blood is thicker than the bottom line. It's all yours. *You* be president and I'll be *your* junior partner. Just let me devote myself to creative projects.'"

What's the benefit? The business stays in the family, the accounts and brainpower stay in the business, and Aunt Alice enjoys an early semiretirement if she wants it. She also gets instant relief from the administrative headaches that keep her at the office till the wee hours of the morning. "It's a Machiavellian maneuver," Randall says with a snicker, "but Aunt Alice gets the best of all worlds."

Aunt Alice might, however, go even further, as former IBM engineer Gene Amdahl did. Amdahl made significant contributions to the famous "you bet your company" line of IBM 360 machines. After leaving Big Blue to set up Amdahl Corporation, he eventually grew frustrated with the control being exercised by Fujitsu, the Japanese company that was holding the financial umbrella over his company. So he retired from the company that bears his name to start Trilogy, the most heavily funded start-up in the history of American business.

Aunt Alice could carry out a similar escape-and-retrench maneuver. Drawing from her many years in the business, she might *sell* Marsha the company and start a new one herself. Who knows, consulting might be even more lucrative the second time around.

But let's assume that Aunt Alice elected to stay on in a junior capacity, as Randall suggests. Could this technique for combating brain drain actually work in a setting other than a small, family-owned or close-knit firm? "It would be complicated," Randall admits, "but I think there are variations that could be applied to giant companies. Remember, the key is to do something that radically upsets the expected order."

He could envision a situation, for example, in which a company continually promotes worthy junior personnel to senior level and demotes senior deadwood to junior levels for rejuvenation. "It's kind of a corporate composting system," Randall suggests. "It might smell lousy at first, but holy cow, it would stimulate growth!"

## Turning Traitors into Ambassadors

Venture capitalist Fred Nazem sharply disagrees with Randall: not only must Aunt Alice let Marsha go, she also should throw a bon-voyage party to celebrate the event. "Brain drain is a natural phenomenon," asserts Nazem, "you can't stop it. Bright, creative people have to follow their own course."

That's the bad news. The good news, according to Nazem, is that smart executives don't lose sleep over brain drain because it can actually lead to profitable new opportunities. Recalls Nazem, "I had a guy in my own organization who came to me with trepidation and said he had an offer from another venture-capital firm. I said, 'Go! And if you need money in between, I'll give you some. And later on I'd like to do some deals with you.' "

Nazem knows that ex-employees can open doors wherever they go. Assuming the turncoats did a great job for you, chances are they'll do a great job down the street, winning the confidence of their new bosses and thinking of you as a potential collaborator rather than a competitor. Even if they start their own firms, they'll owe you a debt for having taught them the ropes. The key? Parting on amicable terms. "I've never forgotten anyone who's taught me a lesson," Nazem says, beaming. "We all like to think of how something was added to our lives through the fortunes of others. So if I was the aunt, I wouldn't fret over the niece's leaving at all, because I know she would remember the mentor relationship we had developed. And if I didn't hinder the departure, I know that the niece will develop into a confident business ally and, most importantly, a good friend."

Nazem goes on to say that he hopes all his former employees would want to create an organization like his own. "A successful business is like a religion—it propagates itself. Treat people right and they'll remember you as a good person to do business with. They'll also spread the word about you."

By recognizing the power of goodwill, Nazem joins some illustrious company. For example, William O. McKinsey, grand patriarch of McKinsey & Company, used goodwill to build an international management-consulting empire; whenever a key employee left to join a major corporation, McKinsey extended his heartiest approval. Guess who that former McKinsey employee hired when he needed consulting help?

Many law firms use a variation on the McKinsey maneuver to garner new clients. This involves hiring platoons of associate lawyers who are willing to work forty hours a week, but not the sixty or seventy hours necessary to become a partner. But since a forty-hour week is more acceptable for a corporate lawyer, many of these associates move on to corporate settings. If treated well by their first employer, whom will they turn to when they encounter problems that require outside legal savvy?

Clearly, generating goodwill with departing employees makes sense in every type of business. And for the venture capitalists, Nazem claims, it carries some fringe benefits: "You start a company, you invest in a group, and they want to go somewhere else. That can work out fine, because it's not always good to have the original crew taking the company into later growth phases. It's the wrong part of the growth curve for them, and they can actually disrupt the company. You need managers at that point, not entrepreneurs. Some of the original people might transform into managers. Others need to start fresh with a new project. So you invest in them again if they've done well. They create new products and you create an investment in their group."

Don't you run some real risks by sending people off with your blessings, possibly even your money? "No one is really defeated by others," Nazem answers. "You're only defeated by yourself. People who are really creative, who think free and *are* free, are not under this overwhelming suspicion that other people can do them in."

But what if the person who leaves is the linchpin of your organization? Again, Nazem recommends that executives stop thinking in terms of what other people can do to them. "If someone is solely responsible for the greatness of a company, then the company isn't great. It's a fluke."

## Separating the Managers from the Professionals

Joe Raelin, a recognized authority on managing professional workers, latches on to one of Fred Nazem's key points. Aunt Alice, he suggests, should invite her niece to think long and hard about whether, at heart, she wants to be a professional or a manager, whether she wants to devote her career to the science of strategic thinking or to the administration of an organization.

Raelin argues that if Marsha really wants to be a manager (just as the Prentice-Hall and Wadsworth editors mentioned earlier wanted to be executives), then Aunt Alice has little choice but to let her niece test her wings at being a boss. If Marsha truly loves consulting, however, and would rather solve creative problems than boss people around, then Aunt Alice should focus on enhancing the creative possibilities at Lothrup.

"I talk a lot about transition to management because I'm constantly surprised that when you take professionals and make them managers, they usually begin 'bossing.' Marsha may, in fact, be more interested in the perks she sees but not in the management game. Maybe she just wants to get the most out of her career."

If so, then Aunt Alice didn't offer the right perks when she held out the raise, the car, and the extra vacation. Instead she should try to uncover her niece's most deep-seated desires and ambitions. Assuming Marsha feels drawn to managing her own firm for the perks and the self-esteem, give her the perks, but work even harder on the self-esteem. Let her design her own creative projects, perhaps ones that will take Lothrup into a whole new market. If the projects really succeed, Lothrup might even fund a subsidiary or two.

Lotus Development Corporation did something like this when Ray Ozzie, the mastermind behind the *Symphony* program, finished his work and wanted to develop his own ideas. Lotus founder and software guru Mitch Kapor agreed to spin off a new company, Iris Associates, headed by Ozzie, whose products Lotus would distribute and market. This maneuver benefited both parties; Ozzie enjoys the blessing of a major player in the field, and Lotus solves one of the biggest headaches in the software industry: keeping valuable programmers from jumping ship to reap fortunes through their own operations. (Kapor was all too familiar with the problem, having worked for VisiCorp before starting Lotus. He later bought his alma mater after Lotus's 1-2-3 program virtually drove VisiCorp out of business.) In keeping with the trend, Lotus also spun off a similar company, Arity Corporation, to keep some of its artificial-intelligence wizards working happily in the fold.

In our case it may not be necessary for Aunt Alice to pull a 1-

2-3 punch and fund a spin-off company for Marsha, says Raelin. She can just reverse Alex Randall's suggestion: Don't give Marsha the company and take early retirement yourself, but keep the company and award Marsha "early retirement" in the form of creative exploration. Suddenly Holstrom's offer might look more like an invitation to seventy-hour-a-week managerial drudgery than a chance to fly in new creative directions.

Once again, Raelin points out that Aunt Alice must force Marsha to clarify her goals before she goes any further: "If she's a professional, then the idea of managerial drudgery will be a nightmare, and she'll have second thoughts about wanting to run any firm. If the career ladder is what she wants, then maybe late nights of paperwork will be perfectly acceptable. In that case it doesn't matter whether she does it as head of Aunt Alice's firm or at her own firm. Either way she's best off staying right where she is. Aunt Alice just has to make that clear."

## Turning All of Nothing into Part of Something

As Joe Raelin pointed out, many employers would try to use money and other tangible incentives to keep talented people from leaving. New venture consultant and McKinsey graduate Christina Darwall agrees that a fatter carrot at the end of a shorter stick will not necessarily do the trick. "Money is definitely *not* the issue here," she says. "The way to make a lot of money today is to go into investment banking. Those M.B.A.s who go into consulting are going to make a lot less, so it tells you something about what they're looking for."

Just what *are* they looking for? According to Darwall, these M.B.A.s long for intellectual challenges that let them exercise their creativity. If those opportunities begin shrinking at their present place of employment, which is quite common at companies that have expanded rapidly, today's "gold-collar worker" begins to look elsewhere for job satisfaction. "It's kind of a catch-22," Darwall explains. "As your [consulting] firm gets more successful, it will take on more people and will probably become more structured and bureaucratic. When that happens, the vibrancy that characterizes a small organization becomes diluted, and people move on."

Is it possible for an executive like Aunt Alice to solve this apparent paradox? One solution is the "matrix organization," pioneered by TRW and other companies in the mid-fifties. Within a matrix organization, people from various departments are assigned to work on specific projects and report to a project manager. This approach enables employees to participate in a variety of projects, while the company maintains order through traditional departments. Both benefit from the cross-fertilization of ideas and talent.

Matrix organizations have been successfully used in the defense and high-tech industries, the most well-known example being the Eclipse team at Data General, which developed the Eagle computer and were featured in Tracy Kidder's Pulitzer Prize–winning book, *The Soul of a New Machine.*

Another alternative is the mysterious lattice structure, which at first glance appears to be nothing more than a free-for-all lacking titles, ironclad positions, or other traditional forms of business hierarchy. On closer examination, however, it often contains a hidden structure that nurtures creativity. For example, at W. L. Gore, the highly successful manufacturer of waterproof fabric, everyone in the company operates as an "associate," free to create his or her own special niche. After a period of observing, each new associate finds the equivalent of a big brother or sister who will serve as a mentor. This approach appeals to employees because it extends almost limitless possibilities for choosing stimulating and fulfilling tasks.

Does the lattice sound more like an induction into a tribal culture? Perhaps, but it works, even on a very large scale. At the lattice-based Honda plant in Marysville, Ohio, for example, all employees function as associates, wearing identical white work suits with their names stitched above the pockets. You cannot tell the professionals from the managers and the line workers. The result? One of the most efficient manufacturing plants in the country.

Obviously, even mammoth operations can use such techniques to give people options for exercising their creativity, but sometimes, according to Darwall, even these creativity-nurturing environments can't retain bright, ambitious people who have been bitten by the entrepreneurial bug. Marsha may be one of those people. If so, Aunt Alice can play the game in one of several ways, depending on her emotional investment. "Unfortunately," Darwall says, "in these situations an employer sometimes feels betrayed and may feel that the person leaving is a traitor or acting out of malice. When this happens, they'd rather have all of nothing than part of something."

Yes, Aunt Alice could rant and rave and get nothing as Marsha cleans out her desk. Or she could go for "part of something" by telling Marsha that she understands her need to seize the helm and that she sympathizes with Marsha's impulse to start her own company. Darwall suggests that Aunt Alice then give Marsha genuine insights, drawn from her own start-up experience, that will give Marsha a feel for what it's like to put together a company. She could even go one step further, offering Marsha full authority over some aspect of Lothrup's business, helping her draw up a strategy for expansion, and providing reasonable capital to help her achieve her goals. If the unit does perform as expected, and Marsha proves her executive ability, Lothrup might then spin off the unit.

Darwall acknowledges, however, that such an approach might not satisfy someone as driven as Marsha, in which case she recommends that Aunt Alice help Marsha determine which she wants most—her own operation or more creative assignments. She might say, "Look, I know you're interested in information technology, and the hottest thing in strategy today is how you link information technology back to the core structure of a company. I'd like to propose that we put aside some money for an R&D fund and explore what that linkage really means to the best and the brightest of the companies out there. You can go to these companies and bring them into the project. You can't do this kind of thing on your own—you just won't have the resources. Since I'm established and have the ability to fund R&D, we can do something state-of-the-art together rather than selling just what we know."

If the R&D gambit doesn't work, Darwall thinks Aunt Alice should go all out and propose a joint venture, in which she funds Marsha's company, *loans* her Brown and Weston, and sits on the board in an advisory, nonvoting capacity. The catch? Since Marsha's departure will leave a hole in Aunt Alice's organization, she would probably urge Marsha to stick to her specialty at first, rather than trying to branch out immediately into general consulting. But if Marsha agrees, she and Aunt Alice can end up referring clients to each other, matching their respective strengths to clients' needs.

With such a joint venture Aunt Alice comes out a winner on several counts, Darwall says. "First, Aunt Alice gets a friendly deal. It's a good investment, since consulting firms often make the most money in their early growth phase. Aunt Alice also gets to see what Marsha is up to, and if Marsha grows in her specialty, the joint referrals could become lucrative. Finally, and most importantly, if all goes well, Aunt Alice winds up with part of a deal, rather than an empty desk in Marsha's office."

What if Aunt Alice were running a high-tech company? Would the same principles apply? Darwall, some of whose clients are high-tech players, insists that they do. "About the only thing you can do is set aside one or two million dollars for a research fund to back the guy who's ready to leave. Even though you'll have more overhead by funding a new operation, and you might not have the guy working on the right product line, at least your technology won't walk out of the door into a competitive company."

Darwall admits that such maneuvers are really last-ditch efforts. But what's the option? All of nothing.

## Handcuffing the Golden Talent

If Katherine August, former McKinsey consultant and currently executive vice president of First Republic Bancorp, were Aunt Alice, she'd have thoroughly prepared for a possible defection beforehand. "Aunt Alice should have anticipated this was going to happen," observes August. "She should have set it up so that the top people she really wants to keep are locked in with 'golden handcuffs.' "

August suggests that as people rise within the ranks, they should be rewarded with a combination of partnership/ownership positions. But you must take care, she cautions, that the plan forces them to stick around long enough to earn the carrot: "Offer stock options or strong profit-sharing incentives, but structure them as *deferred* compensation so that it becomes very expensive to leave."

Some companies, for example, pay out seventy percent in current compensation, keeping fifteen to thirty percent in deferred compensation that pays out gradually over five to ten years, so the pot keeps growing. Some consulting and investment-banking firms, August claims, have even refined the deferred compensation maneuver to a high art, keeping current remuneration to sixty-five percent or less of total compensation.

With such well-run plans August believes you can overcome all but the strongest urges to leave. "I know someone at an investment-banking firm who'd love to start his own firm," she continues, "but he'd give up more than a million dollars in deferred compensation to do it. And a million dollars is a pretty big price tag for the thrill of starting one's own firm."

Perhaps such a plan would retain Marsha, but would it really serve Aunt Alice's best interests? Could she really depend on someone who feels an overwhelming itch to be elsewhere and chafes under her present employer's manacles? August wouldn't worry about that: "I think deferred compensation largely works to keep people happy where they are. I believe that in the financial district [of San Francisco] there's about a thirty percent turnover rate. In our company we're expecting a voluntary turnover rate of two to three percent. *Every* employee in this company has stock options and participates in an employee stock-ownership plan and a pension plan. They're paid what they could get on the outside, but there's an up side that may be from one to ten years' worth of compensation at some point in the future as this company's stock value increases. So when a secretary is typing a loan application at seven o'clock on Friday night, she's not sitting there thinking what a lousy job this is—she's thinking, 'Wow, we processed so many loans this week, our profit-sharing plan will be strong.' "

Nevertheless, August acknowledges that although deferred compensation offers a powerful disincentive for leaving, you've still got to give people a positive reason for staying. "The job has to provide the kind of stimulation that brought them to the firm in the first place," she says, "but in any company there are ways to give people new areas of responsibility. Aunt Alice could step aside and become chairman of the board, letting Marsha become chief operating officer, and if she's successful later on, chief executive officer."

Obviously, though, in any company there can only be one COO and one CEO. The solution? Create new profit centers around your best people. As they feel the need to exercise their executive muscles, create new centers, moving other eager beavers into the vacated ones. Such a maneuver can create a situation in which employer and employee both feel they've won.

"In a consulting firm you can set up specialty industry practice groups that go after new markets or develop entirely new products to offer clients," August says. "In our [mortgage] business I could see developing an insurance subsidiary or a savings and loan or a mortgage banking subsidiary. There are many possibilities for setting up operations that people here can run."

But what about the entrepreneurial itch? Can any system of incentives and disincentives really scratch it? Like all other players, August believes that the true entrepreneur may never be happy working for someone else, a fact supported by a recent *INC* magazine survey of why people start their own companies. Seventeen percent of the executives surveyed said they struck out on their own because they wanted to make money; twenty-three percent felt frustrated with big companies; forty percent simply wanted to be their own bosses, and fifty-five percent sought control over their own lives.

Those statistics don't intimidate August, though, because she doesn't believe the entrepreneurial spirit runs that high among professionals. "These 'gold-collar workers,' as you call them, have trained for professional careers and aren't looking to be entrepreneurs," she asserts. "They go for high-challenge, low-risk jobs, and most are actually scared of risk. Knowledge workers—analysts, lawyers, bankers, consultants—tend to be satisfied when they're in situations that allow them to take pride in the quality of their work and that give them the kind of income they're looking for. And they're not seeking greatness, either; very few lawyers feel they have to go out and become F. Lee Bailey to make a great living."

## Wildcatting for Innovation

As the head of a new start-up in the biotechnology area, Jim Stanchfield, CEO of Betagen, Inc., *does* lose sleep over the problems of keeping his creative people happy. "Aunt Alice has a real problem," he advises, "because *no* environment she creates will meet Marsha's needs. So the only thing to do is back a new entity for Marsha and form a relationship. And negotiate for the clients she's trying to walk off with. I don't see what else you can do."

Stanchfield goes on to say that while this basic solution might satisfy an M.B.A. type in a consulting setting, it seldom works with engineers and scientists, who require a different approach. "Running a company is the last thing that scientists or engineers want to get into. Their chief concern is to be in situations that allow them to do the kind of work that uses their talents and fires their imaginations. So I think that if the scenario involved an engineering or scientific setting, your goal would be to create an environment in which Marsha's equivalents could pursue the kind of work they want to."

This theme has come up so frequently in our players' interviews, it's worth emphasizing again. Yes, Gene Amdahl started a successful company when he left IBM, but he never could translate his scientific genius to the boardroom. Eventually his lack of administrative expertise forced him out of his own company, and it contributed to the spectacular fall of Trilogy.

Sheer ambition plus state-of-the-art expertise in your field— be it advertising, computers, high-fidelity sound equipment, consulting, publishing, or automobile manufacturing—does not add up to managerial ability. Adam Osborne, the computer wizard who introduced the first fully powered portable computer, discovered this fact. So did John DeLorean, who may have possessed more than enough ambition and automotive know-how but who made disastrous business decisions that culminated in bankruptcy and massive litigation.

The moral: You can get the requisite business decision-making ability two ways: on the job or in school. But the former takes so much time that few impatient entrepreneurs will sit still for it. The latter may be quicker, but such purely theoretical training usually boils down to little more than what H. L. Mencken once called "a wheelbarrow full of burnt oyster shells."

Can the so-called "intrapreneuring" programs fill the gap? Some say yes, pointing to highly successful examples. There's Charles Kettering, for example, perhaps the first intrapreneur. Kettering, a genius working at General Motors, fathered a big family of innovations, including four-wheel brakes, long-lasting colored paint, crankcase ventilators, and vibration dampers, to name but a few. But his main claim to fame came when he discovered that leaded gasoline eliminated engine knock. GM, quickly deciding that it didn't want to get into the chemical business, formed a joint entity with Standard Oil of New Jersey, called the Ethyl Corporation. As Ethyl's first president, Kettering went down in history as the man who put leaded gas in filling stations across the land.

Of more recent vintage is 3M's Art Fry, patron saint of the modern intrapreneur. Fry, originally seeking a better bookmark, serendipitously stumbled onto an adhesive that didn't stick very well but formed the basis for the ubiquitous Post-It notes, which bring in over $100 million in sales a year. Hewlett-Packard, Xerox, and other leading technology companies can also thank dedicated intrapreneurs for spearheading projects that have yielded highly successful products.

All of the companies that reap the rewards of intrapreneurship share two common traits: an environment conducive to the process of innovation, and a genuine understanding of the creative psyche of the intrapreneur. Stanchfield points out that without those elements, intrapreneuring becomes "a meaningless buzzword. A lot of companies have gotten on the intrapreneuring bandwagon these days," he notes. "They set up big programs and print manuals on policies for it. But as soon as it becomes a set of policies, the people who are supposed to be involved realize that it's just a manipulative management ploy, and it won't work."

According to Stanchfield, "sincere" intrapreneurship means a clean break from the parent company, rather than a new layer of bureaucracy. In fact, he recommends keeping management as far away as possible from the "skunk groups," as Tom Peters, coauthor of *In Search of Excellence,* calls them. "If possible," he continues, "you'd even get the intrapreneurs off-site. I think it's important psychologically for them to feel that they're physically not working under the shadow of the sponsoring company."

Although Stanchfield acknowledges that some forms of intrapreneuring can work in large companies with the right cultures, he cautions leaders of fledgling enterprises to avoid initiating them. Instead Stanchfield believes it makes more sense to try to keep the environment as stimulating as possible. "We have an idea for a very exciting new product," he says, beaming, "and I'm not about to say to my engineering staff, 'Hey, guys, how'd you like to start a new company based on this idea?' Instead I put together a 'wildcat' group that can take pride in the fact that they've played a major role in developing this new product."

Many excellent products have come about with such a rallying effort. Apple Computer, for example, chose to develop the MacIntosh as part of the company, rather than spinning off a new division or a separate operation. Though some critics cry that an important cash cow, the Apple IIe, suffered because the company poured so much of its resources into developing the Mac, no one can argue with the results. While the Mac "pirates" enjoyed some unusual perks, such as on-site masseuses, nothing outweighed the satisfaction of developing an earthshaking new product.

"Isn't that enough?" Stanchfield asks.

## Thinking Like an Entrepreneur

Jim Gregg, president and CEO of Applied Immune Sciences, Inc., places the blame for the problem squarely on Aunt Alice's head, who he believes simply failed to anticipate the problem and must now pay the price. "When you're managing good people you have to be entrepreneurial in *your* thinking," he says.

Such entrepreneurial thinking includes development of a creative succession plan. While it won't satisfy anyone's immediate urge to hit the exit door, it does hold forth the vision of a future in which they can take the helm. The succession plan of Billye Ericksen-Desaigoudar, head of Capsco Sales, Inc., an electronic components distributor, demonstrates how you can creatively design seating assignments in the future executive suite. When Ericksen-Desaigoudar turned fifty, she decided that once her company reached the $10 million mark, it would require controls and systems that weren't her management style. So she appointed a board of directors made up of hotshot managers from the electronics industry who agreed to train five of her own managers (three of whom are her children) during six-week stints over a two-year period. If the scheme works, Ericksen-Desaigoudar will cultivate a team of super managers capable of buying the company from her through a leveraged buyout. It's a win-win maneuver that gives the next generation of managers strong incentives to stay with the company.

Beyond planning for who will run the company tomorrow, an entrepreneurial boss also keeps his or her vision sharply focused on today's working environment. "Aunt Alice just wasn't listening or observing other people," Gregg concludes. "After all, Marsha didn't just wake up one morning and decide to bolt." A strong adherent of Peters's "management by walking around," Gregg believes that a truly good manager tunes into *every* level of the business. "Probably the best manager I ever met was Marion Saddler, president of American Airlines. Three or four times a month he'd get on a regular passenger plane and just fly somewhere. It was really 'management by flying around,' and it gave him a bird's-eye view of what the people in his company were really doing."

What if you can't afford to walk, or fly, around your company? "Step aside," Gregg insists. "You really only have two assets— money and people. Money resolves itself on the bottom line. People management is different, and if you're having trouble, say a high turnover rate, then you have to wake up and say, 'Either I'm going to run this company or I'll bring in other people who can.' "

Aunt Alice? At this stage Gregg feels she has few choices, but she might try to determine the real basis for her niece's departure. "Marsha's leaving with a strong support network of colleagues and clients," Gregg observes, "so maybe she's not so confident about her plans. Maybe she's really asking Aunt Alice to reaffirm her value in some way. If so, Aunt Alice might talk her into accepting more responsibility and being brought into the executive fold, with some kind of equity as a reward. Or perhaps a freestanding business sometime in the future would be in the works.

"But it all might fail," Gregg cautions. "If you have people who are real entrepreneurs, you'll never be able to structure the organization in a way that allows them to use all their talents. The bottom line is that you can't keep a hundred percent of the people in your company. You can't go around living in fear of losing talented people. What counts is the turnover rate. If it's larger than you'd expect, then it's time to find out what *you're* not doing right."

## Breeding an Entrepreneurial Environment

Herbert M. Temple III, chairman of Temple, Barker & Sloane Inc. (TBS), a general management-consulting firm with four hundred employees and offices in three major cities, believes that a consulting firm must not only tolerate entrepreneurs, it must cultivate an environment that spawns them. "Loyalty is certainly an important attitude, but it won't do you much good if it comes without brilliance," says Temple. "But with brilliance you're going to get a certain degree of egoism and eccentricity, and you have to be prepared for that. All of our staff are super-educated people who take themselves quite seriously. They want a career here—they don't want to be sublimated."

He continues, "The trick is to build a suitably strong policy structure that can hold everybody in at the outer edge, but within it can give them the freedom to do what's necessary to get the wash out and do their own distinctive thing. The structure really has to allow the barons to live within the larger fiefdom."

Temple explains that TBS fields three separate businesses: general management and economic consulting; market research; and investment management and investment banking. "Within each of those businesses we have sub-businesses," he says. "We give the people in them an industry or a specialty for which they have cognizance. We also give them what is called a charter, and say, 'That's your piece of cake. You can go out and make it just as big as you want to.' Of course, we try to make sure before we commit to it that there is a market out there on which a business can survive over the foreseeable future.

"We currently have around a dozen barons in our business, each of whom runs a part of the practice that is either industry-specific or functionally specific. They have P&L accountability and do the hiring, but they have to work within a policy framework. It's up to them to be as entrepreneurial as possible to develop their practice areas. That's why we try to get people to start the businesses and grow them here, so that they are bringing a longitudinal perspective to the business. They find growth for themselves, too, in doing that."

But if you're breeding entrepreneurs, why would they want to stay with the firm over the long haul? "This gets into the concept of equity," explains Temple. "We try to give them equity that can appreciate at a rate that when they think about it in the dark of the night, they think, 'What the hell, how much better off am I going to be taking a hundred percent of the risk than here, where I take a much smaller percent of the risk?' We provide them the equity, but if that equity is growing, we participate in the growth. Besides, we can fund a new practice area with an equity financing program that is attractive to our professionals and makes it a low-cost acquisition for us. If employees go off in businesses of their own, they're going to have to put a hundred cents in for every dollar of equity they get."

To create an atmosphere where employees will think like entrepreneurs but stay with your organization, Temple recommends a number of incentive/disincentive policies. In fact, he believes Aunt Alice's basic problem stems from her not developing such policies when she started the company. Therefore, he says, Aunt Alice should pass on the operation of the company to her niece or someone and become a real CEO and spend her time developing a policy framework that will keep valuable brainpower from walking out the door.

"The generic solution, I think, to holding people—and this is not only in the consulting business but in any professional service business—is making sure that a piece of the ownership is available to them. I do not know of any consulting firm that will long endure and grow that does not spread the ownership."

Temple says that if you want people to work at their peak in a professional services business, you have to compensate them well. So in a firm like Aunt Alice's, you would expect to find a stock-ownership program that extends ownership to the key contributors in some meaningful way.

Temple cites McKinsey & Company as an extreme example of trying to dole out equity on a proportional basis. McKinsey recuts the ownership pie every two or three years to increase people's incentive to stay on. Regardless of how frequently you redistribute the wealth, Temple advises that the essence is to try to keep the equity interest "roughly proportionate to economic contribution over some period of time. People need to see their rewards as a direct function of their labor."

In addition to dividing the pie in an equitable way, Temple suggests that Aunt Alice design a very generous bonus program, in which a bonus for key contributors can run as high as 100 to 150 percent of one's base salary. "Total compensation for key performers in a consulting business must be very attractive as long as the business is up and growing," he says, "but it has to be flexible, because if business goes sour, they'll have to be cut back."

Temple mentions the Boston Consulting Group's bonus formula as the extreme in flexibility for trying to keep people happy, yet on their toes. The up side is virtually unlimited, with almost no bounds as to what you can earn in a year. On the downside, however, if you had little applied client work, you could find yourself earning very little money because the formula has minimal base guarantees.

Whatever formula Aunt Alice uses to reshuffle the deck, Temple recommends that she adopt a reasonable noncompete agreement and a "rights and confidentiality agreement." Finally she can build a buy-and-sell feature into the stock-ownership program. Explains Temple, "The buy-sell agreement should have a yin and a yang in it. In situations of death, disability, or retirement, there should be provisions to repurchase shares of the stock of the individual. If he leaves of his own volition, it's quite a different arrangement though—possibly an option, but no obligation, to buy. And if the option is exercised, the firm should watch the terms of repurchase. This is not in any way to penalize the individual if his leaving is what might be termed an 'honorable departure.' If the guy wants to go into business for himself and he says, 'I'm leaving and I'm going to set up a business, but I'll respect the buy-and-sell agreement,' the firm might say, 'Fine.' But if he appears to be playing games, the firm may do differently to defend itself and strengthen its position for any violation of the noncompete agreement."

Are such methods airtight? "Nothing is airtight," Temple says, "and that's the issue. If a person wants to compete with you, you can't stop them in the long run. But the business is tough enough as it is, and you can put up with a person who wants to be elsewhere just so long. So you must ultimately say, 'If you don't like it, my friend, let's work out a departure.' "

## Anticipating the Unthinkable

Speaking from years of experience in operating a consulting firm in the Silicon Valley, Michael Killen believes that knowl-edge workers basically desire independence. "They spend their time developing their minds," he says, "and people develop their minds for one reason: to get control over their environment. That extends to the workplace as well."

Killen believes that creative people will naturally want to strike out on their own at some point, and any scheme you devise to keep them will merely run contrary to their natural impulses. "You have to take a fatalistic attitude," says Killen. "If people want to flow with me for a while instead of being inde-pendent, that's fine. When they're ready to leave, I know there are plenty of other smart, creative people in the river who'd like to flow with me too. So I can select those people who seem like they will immediately pay for themselves. If I misjudge, it's back into the water. There's no point training someone when you know that they'll probably be walking in two years max."

Killen didn't always accept brain drain so fatalistically. As

August did, he tried profit sharing and other incentive plans in his early days, but he eventually found such measures too expensive and cumbersome to maintain. Worse, they led to disruptive internecine wrangling. "I had four vice presidents," he recalls, "and they constantly fought for resources because of the profit-sharing incentives. There were horrendous internal conflicts. For instance, vice president A would argue that he wouldn't get his bonus unless he got X amount of resources. Meanwhile vice president B would want the same resources and would argue that he needed two times X, and so on."

Killen continues, "Only in a large firm that has the infrastructure to manage the details can such programs possibly work. The other advantage that a large firm has in controlling this brain drain is that knowledge gets diluted in a large organization —no one ever gets a total grasp of the big picture, which means they'll never be a major threat to you if they try to compete. So there's more incentive to stay on and less confidence in being able to leave."

Killen believes that although Aunt Alice does face a critical brain-drain crisis, she can resolve it the same way she'd resolve any other business problem, by applying one of a handful of core strategic maneuvers. Advises Killen, "In your story Aunt Alice would begin with what I call the Principle of Economy of Resources. That means don't apply time, money, energy, or other resources to something that you can't control. Don't knock yourself out swimming against the current."

Okay, so Aunt Alice shouldn't lose any sleep over her niece walking out the door. What next? "The Principle of Concentration," Killen explains, "which means focusing all of your mental resources on the key decisive point. When this niece comes to you and announces that she's leaving with your best accounts, concentrate on discovering the weaknesses in her situation: her possible exposure to lawsuits; the fact that her financial resources may not come through; the potential fickleness of her sponsor; her need for credibility; the security of her operation; and her ability to keep the members of her own team together."

Once Aunt Alice discovers the weaknesses in Marsha's plan, her next step would depend on her temperament. "Aunt Alice could certainly use them to blow her niece away," Killen says, "or, less drastically, she might use them as a threat to get her niece to adjust her actions."

Many companies attempt to "adjust the actions" of would-be turncoats by striking fear into their hearts, usually by suing former employees who have left. The tactic has spawned a subspecialty in the legal profession, and the courts are flooded with cases of individuals being sued by former employers for allegedly stealing ideas and materials that undercut their business.

Merrill Lynch and E. F. Hutton, for example, both undertook suits against brokers who jumped ship with client mailing lists. In one case Merrill Lynch won punitive damages from a former employee. In another case, IBM successfully sued Cybernex, winning an injunction that prohibited their rival from manufacturing certain computer products for three years, not to mention a fine requiring some of the former IBMers to return a portion of the salary they earned while working at Big Blue.

Texas Instruments similarly tried to sue the founders of Compaq for allegedly pilfering trade secrets, but Compaq, arguing that it had used no proprietary TI designs in its line, promptly countersued TI. And when Steven Jobs announced he was starting Next Computers, talk of lawsuits and trade secrets immediately began flying.

The trade-secret issue doesn't just affect the high-tech industry, as demonstrated by a lawsuit between the two auto rental giants, Hertz and Avis. After Hertz's president, Joseph Vittoria, changed driver's seats to become Avis's vice president and later its president, Hertz went to court claiming that trade secrets had left with Vittoria. The judge, however, questioned the value of trade secrets in the car-rental business, and Hertz could not stop Vittoria and other former employees from working across town.

Sound silly? Perhaps. But when a company loses such valuable brainpower, it not only mortgages a piece of its hope for the future, it writes off a significant investment in time, training, and energy. It also risks losing the turncoat's comrades and valuable technologies that it may have spent years developing.

While Aunt Alice could resort to drastic actions such as lawsuits, she'd probably be better off using the holes in Marsha's plan to force the same kind of cooperation outlined by Nazem and Darwall. "This could lead into what I call the Principle of Interworking," explains Killen, "in which both parties coordinate their resources to magnify the effectiveness of their efforts.

Using this principle, Aunt Alice might strengthen her position by saying, 'Okay, you're leaving. Fine. But leave in six months instead of thirty days. And keep your hands off my accounts and key employees. Do that and I'll help you refine your game plan.' The niece, realizing that Aunt Alice could patch up her deficiencies, might agree. Perhaps a beneficial long-term cooperative arrangement might even come out of it."

Killen concludes his advice with the Principle of Being Prepared. "Anticipate the unthinkable," he insists. "And be ready to act on it."

## Lessons from the Game

1. Be prepared. Use all the formal and informal means at your disposal to detect and deal with early signs of defection.

2. Treat your departing employees as ambassadors, rather than rebels. Every departing employee represents a potential client or partner downstream.

3. Always take part of something over all of nothing. Remember, if someone leaves, the departure does not necessarily reflect badly on you.

4. Never throw away the key when you slap golden handcuffs on someone's wrists. Disincentives seldom work without equal or greater incentives.

5. If key employees announce their departure, try to find out what they really want. Determine whether they're leaving from a position of weakness or strength, whether they're fleeing or trying to bargain. Many professionals fail as managers, and most creative people need to be shown that they're appreciated, whether in the form of cold cash or responsibilities.

6. Never attempt to bureaucratize or ritualize the entrepreneurial/innovation process; otherwise, you will blunt it. Creative people will see any halfhearted attempts at sponsoring creativity as a sham. Instead build a bona fide culture of innovation.

7. Offer ownership as an incentive to stay. Be sure, though, that the equity doled out is proportionate to the contribution the employee makes.

8. Accept the dynamic nature of the workplace. Unless you anticipate and accommodate yourself to the people flowing in and out of your organization, you'll lose creative talent.

CHAPTER 5

# Eggheads and Feathered Nests:
## *Getting the Most from Salaried Professionals*

## Opening Moves

The 17th International Congress of Molecular Biology convenes in Stockholm, luring scientists from all around the globe to hear papers on everything ranging from the latest techniques for extracting interferon from mouse genes to using yeast cells to mass-produce insulin. During a luncheon banquet at the Thurston International Regency, six scientists who have never met before find themselves sitting at the same table. Their quick introductions reveal that three conduct research at academic institutions, one works for a hospital, and two are employed by the giant pharmaceutical company, Alpha Biomedical. Amid talk of tumor necrosis factor, monoclonal antibodies, and other esoteric topics, the hospital-based scientist blurts out, "Hey, forget that stuff, I wanna know what it's like working at Alpha: huge research budgets, complete freedom to pursue promising leads. That must be heaven!"

One of the Alpha scientists laughs. "Well, I know it sounds too good to be true, but so far they've given us everything they promised. Virtually unlimited funds. No pressure to produce, and best of all . . ."

"It *is* too good to be true," says one of the academic scientists with a snort. "Just wait—some executive will get impatient for results, then the heavenly choir will start playing a different tune. Mark my words."

"Not likely," insists the other Alpha scientist, a Nobel laureate. "Our top management will never compromise an R&D program that's put so many long-range dollars on the bottom line."

"Watch your tail feathers," the academic says with a smirk, "or you may experience a very different sort of bottom line, the kind that comes with a swift kick in the seat of the pants."

Although we might chalk up the academic scientist's comments to cynicism or jealousy, clashes between scientists and bottom-liners date back to the day that the first fruits of scientific research turned a profit. Some observers have defined the gap as a basic clash between the culture of science and the culture of management. If the relationship between the two deteriorates into open hostility, a company can find itself fighting for its very life.

Is it possible to promote a greater understanding between the two cultures? Can creative executives work out compromises between their conflicting demands? Can they help their scientists understand that short-term, marketable research is vital to the immediate survival of the company? And can they convince bottom-liners that long-term research is a road to large-scale success?

To find out the answers to these and related questions, we asked our players to assume the role of the Alpha scientists' boss. Let's see what happens when the scientific and management cultures collide in Alpha's boardroom.

## The Game: As the Yeast Rises

You practically burst your vest buttons with pride when you saw your picture on the cover of *Corporate Weekly,* the nation's most prestigious big-business magazine. At last *CW* has bestowed on your company, Alpha Biomedical, the ultimate bouquet, dubbing it "the most progressive and imaginatively managed pharmaceutical company in the country." The feature article, "Alpha's 'OMEGA': Our Medical Dreams Come True," explains how, under your leadership, the company has invested nearly $450 million (200 percent of its pretax profits) for non-goal-specific research into how the human body works, what

makes viruses tick, and how bacteria and yeasts can be har-
nessed to produce miracle drugs cheaply.

It took all of your persuasive power to sell Alpha's board on
the OMEGA project, but the opposition softened when you
described the long-range bottom-line results that the research
would generate: breakthrough pharmaceuticals for the treatment of Alzheimer's disease; new tools to combat a variety of
human cancers; and possibly a vaccine or a cure for AIDS.

To ensure OMEGA's success you enticed top scientists and
physicians from prestigious universities and research institutes
by promising the best facilities, unlimited funds, and no pressure to produce short-term results. With three Nobel laureates
now heading up your all-star teams, you feel like you've just
bought a round-trip ticket to paradise.

Unfortunately, after reading the *CW* article, one of Alpha's
major stockholders, Winslow Rumsford IV, sees red, not roses,
and would rather send you a one-way ticket to hell. Rumsford
kicks off his anti-OMEGA campaign with a press conference
during which he outlines his plans for cutting the project's
budget back to the industry R&D average, returning the difference to the stockholders as a dividend. Then, after engineering
nominations for himself and several like-minded shareholders
to the board, Rumsford initiates an aggressive proxy battle on
his insurgent slate's behalf. "Unconscionable! Irresponsible!" he
shouts to an army of scribbling reporters.

Although the Rumsford slate does not win any seats, it does
attract thirty percent of the vote, creating extreme anxiety in
Alpha's top-floor offices. At first you attempt to placate Rumsford with the same argument you used to convince the board,
but to no avail: He responds by filing a shareholder's derivative
action accusing Alpha's management of wasting money. An av-
alanche of press releases detailing his forthcoming suit attracts
so much attention that *Corporate Weekly* prints a story entitled,
"Turmoil in the Lab of Eden?"

When Diversified Financial, which holds seven percent of
Alpha's stock for institutional clients, calls to express concerns
about the soundness of the OMEGA program, and as the news
of the anti-OMEGA campaign spreads through the company,
causing Alpha's research staff to unite and threaten to resign if
you renege on your promise of unbridled support and freedom,
you know you must act swiftly. Your dream of eternal bliss has

suddenly become a hellish dilemma. On the one hand, you cannot ignore a mounting effort to thwart OMEGA's mission; on the other, if you knuckle under, you'll risk losing Alpha's valuable brainpower. What would you do to restore peace to paradise?

## Strategies and Tactics

### *Balancing Long-term and Short-term Expectations*

Dr. Max Tesler, CEO of PharmaControl Corporation, which holds the world's only patent on water-soluble aspirin, can empathize with the plight of Alpha Biomedical's leader, having himself placated disgruntled shareholders, board members, and staff scientists over the years. "I remember one of the worst board meetings of my life," Tesler recalls with a grimace, "one of the members got up with a yellow pad and grilled me for about an hour. He wanted airtight answers and predictions about the research that no one could precisely answer. We finally convinced him that we were spending money wisely. On the other side, I've also had to bring scientists down from the clouds and enlighten them about where their paychecks come from. Sometimes they act as if the money well has no bottom."

In both cases, Tesler explains, you must convince each party that you share their goals, and that takes a lot of concentrated communication. "Look," he says, "if you were capable of selling the OMEGA program in the first place, you can sell it again. And again and again. You never would have proposed such a program unless the company could afford it, so you have to go back to that point and stress the company's strengths first, then explain how the program builds upon those strengths and how the company has nothing to lose and everything to gain by carrying out the research. This is very important in getting dissident people thinking in the right direction."

Next, says Tesler, you want to convince everyone that you're not just running an open-ended think tank and that the research has already obtained "positive results," even though you may not have yet put a tangible product on the shelves. In other words, you invite them to imagine profitable products that will eventually result from the research.

To do this, Tesler suggests talking with the dissidents in a language they can understand. "Too often," he claims, "an executive, especially one who has scientific training, assumes an unrealistic level of technical knowledge on the part of the investors and lets their imaginations run wild. Unfortunately wild imaginations tend to run toward the negative rather than the positive. So you've got to use the plainest possible language, demystifying technical concepts with accessible metaphors and analogies. The worst thing you can do is to make the board feel like you're trying to hide behind a shield of technical expertise or that you're looking down on them from an enlightened position."

One effective tactic Tesler has found involves assessing whether you're the right person to argue the case. If Alpha's CEO is a scientist by training, it might be best to bring in another executive whose background will enable him or her to sing a tune more harmonious to dissenting ears. "My own area is medical and scientific." He explains, "That's why when I walk into a board meeting I let my financial VP do the talking. He speaks everyone else's language and does such a great job that no one can argue with him—his presentation just becomes overwhelming."

But what happens if the message still falls on deaf ears? Then you should consider asking the scientists to go along with a modified agenda. "Again," Tesler stresses, "it's a matter of building confidence and alliances through effective communication. And choosing the right person to deliver the message is critical —you need someone who will be perceived as an ally, a partner in crime. If you're not the kind of CEO who can talk to these guys without making them run scared, find an intermediary who can. Find a liaison who can get down in the trenches with these guys and say, 'Hey, there's some dissatisfaction at the boardroom level and there's some pressure coming down. If we want to keep our budget, we've got to come up with a plan for bringing a marketable product on-line earlier.' "

Sometimes, Tesler admits, you must resign yourself to the fact that you can't keep your researchers from leaving, in which case you must prepare yourself to recruit new talent. Tesler himself recalls the time he formed a company with a scientist who held a Ph.D. and three master's degrees. "When I picked the guy up at the airport, I said to him that I only have one problem—I'll go out and raise a million dollars for you, and you'll go down in the basement and putter around, then the trapdoor will open at the end of a year and you'll poke your head up and say, 'Max, I need another million,' then disappear for another year."

Just as Tesler feared, the trapdoor shut, and no products popped out of that basement. When the company went public, the board realized that the stockholders were bankrolling alarmingly open-ended experiments, so they told the scientist to put his pet project on a back burner while he concentrated on more profit-oriented projects. As a result, he left the company in a huff.

"That was emotionally very difficult for him, as if his children were being taken away," Tesler says, "but he pulled himself together, sold his stock for about $1.7 million, then bought a motel in Big Sur."

When Tesler's board members complained that his scientist was taking too much time to achieve tangible results, they joined some noteworthy company. Consider the case of self-taught inventor Stanford Ovshinsky. Since 1964, his company, Energy Conversion Devices, has raised more than $200 million and received more than two hundred patents for gizmos ranging from photovoltaic cells to flat computer screens. Unfortunately most of these items remain on the lab bench, causing skepticism in the investment community and the eventual pull-out of a key backer, Standard Oil Co., which had invested $86 million in the company.

The list of inventor-scientists who thumbed their noses at the bottom line includes Edwin Land, founder of Polaroid, who reportedly told an angry stockholder that the only bottom line is "in heaven," and Henry Kloss, founder of Advent and creator of brilliant new electronics technologies, who waved away the losses of his latest failing enterprise by insisting to a *Forbes* reporter that financial figures are only one way to measure a company.

But the plastics and rubber industry has almost single-handedly populated the "Damn the Profits, Full Speed Ahead on the Pure Research" Hall of Fame. High awards go to Drs. J. C. Patrick and Nathan Mnookin, two Kansas City chemists who in 1927 stumbled across a smelly new synthetic rubber substance that they called "thiokol" and waited until 1941 for the stuff to turn a profit. By 1986, Morton-Thiokol was pulling in $350 to $450 million a year from the space-shuttle contract alone. Of course, that may not continue in the aftermath of the *Challenger* disaster.

In 1908, Belgian chemist Leo Backeland developed the first synthetic plastic while searching for a shellac substitute that would put the Indian lac bug out of business. Instead he invented Bakelite, which made other companies a fortune when they used it in telephones, costume jewelry, pump impellers, decorative laminates, cafeteria trays, buttons, knobs, pot handles, and helmet liners.

Another award goes to John Hyatt, who in 1869 created celluloid while searching for something else, an ivory substitute for which a billiard-ball manufacturer, squeezed by an elephant shortage, had offered a huge prize. Though Hyatt's celluloid made lousy billiard balls, it quickly appeared in combs, artificial teeth, piano-key coverings, clock cases, Ping-Pong balls, hairbrushes, and eyeglasses. Like Bakelite, celluloid became a miracle substance from which others eventually profited.

But perhaps the highest honor in the "Damn the Profits" Hall should go to Charles Goodrich, who spent a lifetime experimenting with ways to "cure" rubber and prevent it from becoming brittle in winter, sticky and smelly in summer. Ignoring the bottom line, he hocked his wife's best linen and sold his children's schoolbooks to obtain a few more dollars to fund his research, but he didn't get results until he accidentally dropped a wad of sulfur and rubber on the kitchen stove. The discovery bounced like a ball, and "smelled like a rose." Using his vulcanization process, Goodrich introduced a variety of products at the Prince Albert Exhibition in 1851: bracelets, knives, opera glasses, corkscrews, and surgical instruments. But despite the enormous potential of these and other innovative products, when Goodrich died in 1860, from a lifetime of exposure to toxic chemicals, he left behind $200,000 in debt.

Such cautionary tales offer two morals. One, the inquisitive mind will pursue its quest regardless of the expectations of investors; and two, the patient investor can eventually reap tremendous rewards from the monomaniac's obsession. Must investors simply accept this phenomenon, or can they find ways to focus a scientist's attention more firmly on the bottom line? Max Tesler thinks you can, if you offer them bonuses for developments that lead to marketable products. "I don't care if the guy who works for me earns more than I do. If he makes it as a result of his contribution to the company, and that's reflected in the overall net worth of the company and the value of the stock, he's making me a rich man. And he's making the shareholder a rich man too."

In fact, Tesler has seen a new type of researcher emerge in recent years. "The image of the scientist as the fellow with baggy pants and the pipe is no longer accurate. Sure, some still operate in an academic environment where making money is less a consideration than publishing esoteric papers, and where nothing really terrible happens to them if they don't get results, but we're seeing a lot more financial sophistication in these people because they realize they won't change the world, get the best labs, or get the biggest paychecks unless they go about it in a businesslike way. I think that they really understand that a profit orientation is not necessarily a restriction of their freedom."

If you can find this new sort of bottom-line-conscious scientist, fine, but if you can't, Tesler suggests you place an intermediary between the scientists and management, a person who can act as a buffer, a teacher, and a catalyst for both sides, not just as a pressure valve. "Sometimes that requires hiring someone from outside, if you can afford it. Otherwise it demands that the chief executive learn how to bridge the natural gulf between long-term research and short-term profits. Whoever acts as go-between, though, must function in an atmosphere of trust and respect. Otherwise people will see him as a spy, and if that happens, you can forget about getting products out the door quicker—you'll be lucky to get them out at all."

## Brokering for Dollars

Dr. Thomas Okarma, senior vice president for research and development at Applied ImmuneSciences, Inc., agrees that academic scientists have become more product-conscience. "Even academic scientists must have products that satisfy their administrators and attract new talent to their departments," Okarma points out. "It might not be a tangible product or process but a bit of information that eventually leads to some concrete diagnostic or therapeutic application. In a way, what you call a product is a matter of semantics. But one way or another, everyone is working to make something."

Nevertheless, Okarma acknowledges, academic scientists often do find it unnerving when they must adjust to an industrial setting. "First, they have to get used to sharing operational hegemony with nonscientists and to accept the notion that the budget is a pot of dollars that must be divided up among the research, manufacturing, and executive branches. In other words, they aren't the center of attention anymore. Also, academic scientists are very isolated from the administrative components of the university—I never had to worry about the operational aspect of the university. Here, however, their daily lives are very much influenced by those concerns."

Can academic scientists make the jump and work productively in a setting such as the one at Alpha Biomedical? "Absolutely," insists Okarma, who is responsible for recruiting scientific talent at Applied ImmuneSciences. In his view, Alpha's problem is not the scientists themselves but the way the scientists *aren't* being managed properly.

"What's clearly missing is a scientist-manager who can orient the staff scientists to the practical needs of the organization," Okarma maintains. "A good scientist-manager must be able to convince his staff scientists that their work has real-world value. And he has to do it without boxing in their creativity. This is done by being very up-front with them and explaining how the system works. If you do it right, they feel a sense of responsibility for the organization as a whole, rather than just their own work. When I hire scientists, they know exactly where the money is coming from. In our case it's all venture capital. We had some base inventions that had some value in the near term; now their job is to take the base technology and create applications."

Beyond orienting the staff scientists, a good scientist-manager can also strengthen a company's money-raising efforts, especially when the company plans to risk that money on highly speculative ideas. "It's not so much dollar raising in the traditional sense," he says, "but an ability to demonstrate that you have a concept worth selling." If you have developed something like celluloid for which you can't dream up any immediate uses, you might do what Patrick and Mnookin of thiokol fame did, structuring a co-venture with a company that can concoct applications. Over the years Patrick and Mnookin worked out relationships with Standard Oil of Indiana and, later, Dow

Chemical, to insure that their discovery found its way into a useful product.

Okarma sees the "concept-brokering" approach as being particularly valuable for start-ups that have "application-rich technologies" but do not have the resources to develop them into marketable products by themselves. "Say you find someone who has a system that works in lab animals, but it can't be done in humans because it lacks a critical piece of technology, one that you have developed and can bring to the table. If that marriage of products leads to a new way of solving a major problem, your original concept suddenly takes on significant dollar value in today's marketplace."

Okarma cites his own company as an example of concept brokering in action. "We've developed a means of removing abnormal molecules and cells from blood," he explains, "and it is a novel approach for treating autoimmune and malignant disorders. The principle of our company's strategic plan is to utilize biologicals produced by recombinant DNA technology in a novel way that avoids their introduction into the body. Thus reagents that were intended as new 'drugs,' with a five- to ten-year product-development cycle, can now be used in the context of a medical device with much greater margins of safety, enhanced effectiveness, and much shorter product cycles. For the manufacturer of the biological, this single 'concept' is appealing and translates into an opportunity they cannot 'afford' to miss."

Can concept brokering help Alpha's CEO resolve his dilemma? Okarma thinks that Alpha could have realized a dollar value in the concepts it already owns, then placated its board by coming up with a plan to commercialize those concepts. "Even if nothing immediately marketable has come out of the research, they must have concepts that can be linked to developments at other companies. Perhaps they could strike up a licensing agreement with a company that has been unsuccessful at developing a new product or device but lacks a critical piece. Maybe some obscure technology developed in Alpha's lab could bring someone else's technology to market. In any case, the scientist-manager should know the general field well enough to pull off some creative concept brokering."

What other qualifications should the scientist-manager bring to the job? Three things, according to Okarma. "First, he must have an experiential base understanding of the science itself. That's fundamentally important. Second, he's got to have an experiential base understanding of the user marketplace. In my own case, that takes the form of being a practicing clinician who knows what doctors and patients need, as well as someone who has been trained in molecular biology. Finally, he's got to have good business sense and an understanding of how to make his research structures work."

Okarma also maintains that the scientist-manager advocates on behalf of the scientific staff and mediates their complaints. But be careful, he warns. On the one hand, scientists tend only to trust other scientists. On the other hand, scientists-turned-managers sometimes ignite the suspicion of their fellow researchers. "There's a saying among scientists," Okarma says with a laugh. " 'Those who can do, do; those who don't, teach and manage.' The degree to which a scientist-manager is successful depends on what he did when he was a scientist. Did he really produce, or did he go into management because he was a failure in science? If the guy is respected for his scientific talents as well as his managerial skill, he'll be accepted and can work very effectively on behalf of the whole company."

In addition to mediating between research and management, the scientist-manager, Okarma believes, must also play the role of teacher: "One of the most critical functions of the scientist-manager, usually in the position of chief technical officer, is to make sure that the CEO and top management have more than a cursory knowledge of the technology. At Applied Immunesciences I hold private meetings with the CEO, and we have a program in which the scientists present data to the business types in the company. We also conduct weekly staff meetings in which the heads of all divisions bring everyone else up-to-date on what's going on."

Alpha's CEO might have lacked such a forum, Okarma suggests, or he may have received insufficient or misleading information about the details of the research. "Scientists who don't understand managers tend to oversimplify the process and leave managers with the idea that the fruits of the research goals are closer than they really are. On the other side, managers tend to think they know more about the science than they actually do. It makes managers feel better about themselves. If management can go around talking with investors and board members in a quasi-technical way, it makes them appear 'in control.' A well-rounded scientist-manager gives his board a balanced perspective of the technical truth in layman's terms.

## Revealing the Hidden Agenda

Applied ImmuneSciences' president and CEO, Jim Gregg, also faults Alpha's management for not properly preparing either the stockholders or the scientists for the full implications of the OMEGA program. "It doesn't matter how good Alpha's scientists may be," Gregg says. "If they haven't been enlightened that their work has to have some tangible results at some point, then they're going to be ineffective. The stockholders should also have been enlightened with a barrage of PR about the potential benefits of the program."

Gregg agrees with Tom Okarma, his senior vice president of development, that scientists can and should become more bottom-line-oriented. "The key is to find the right kind of scientist," he says. "In the hiring process you have to be up-front about identifying the difference between the academic and business environments, and to tell people what to expect. The very words of the Alpha scientist, 'Virtually unlimited funds. No pressure to produce,' are indicative of a dangerous attitude that should have been corrected from day one."

Gregg believes that the Alpha scientist's attitude comes from a misunderstanding of the term "open-ended research." He observes, "It's not a question of whether or not companies can afford to be doing pure research. Obviously the company has to have a marketable product if it's going to survive. But open-ended research also has a place in determining where marketable products will go."

To shape that direction he believes you should educate senior scientists about management, so they understand what running a business involves, why they need to accept certain real-world objectives, and why they must be accountable for results. "This doesn't mean having a class every day at three o'clock," he continues. "It's more of an informal get-together of management and senior scientists to talk about what they're doing and what the business is doing. Alpha certainly could have profited from this kind of interaction."

Wouldn't academic scientists resist such reeducation and remain in the protective cover of the ivy nest? "The business environment has several main attractions," answers Gregg. "First, in your scenario, there's a certain sense of wonderment about an environment like ours. There's generally more money to get things done, better equipment, and better support resources. There are also terrific opportunities to communicate with other scientists in the field. Sure, there are trade secrets, and things that you can't talk about, but it's not really any more restrictive than an academic setting where people guard their work in progress."

Gregg shares Okarma's belief that a key solution at Alpha is to get the scientists more involved with the running of the business, by elevating one or more to management positions. "A scientist can manage your resources so you can get results without taking away freedom," he maintains. "Once the freedom is gone, so is the creativity and the will to discover."

Even though turning scientists into managers will help, Gregg believes that the culture of science and the culture of management will inevitably clash. But foreknowledge of the conflict will short-circuit a lot of problems, he concludes. "If I just assumed that research and management people were peacefully coexisting, we'd be in trouble. It's working because *we're* working on it."

## Spinning Off the Brainpower

Jim Stanchfield, a biochemist and CEO of Betagen, Inc., a start-up company involved with developing automated gene-splicing equipment, does not share the view that Alpha should give scientists managerial roles. "When upper management suddenly starts turning scientists into managers, it will cause ripples of distrust through the rest of the scientific staff," he cautions. "That kind of maneuver indicates upper management wants to get a firmer grasp on controlling the research program. And such control runs against the scientist's basic need to feel that he's charting his own research course.

"Besides, scientists-turned-managers tend to be distrusted and ostracized from their peers. After all, they aren't working in the lab every day—they're pushing papers and wearing three-piece suits. I'm not saying it's impossible for a scientist to become a manager eventually, but you can't do it overnight, and certainly not as a response to a crisis."

Although Stanchfield shares with the other players a fundamental belief about the natural conflict between the two cultures, he also challenges it. "It's not inevitable. The two can peacefully coexist as long as management sets *consistent* goals. The real problem at Alpha is that the goals have changed midcourse. Alpha advertised an open environment and got top people who were seeking that kind of setting. So if you have two or three Nobel laureates who came there for the working conditions, you're just going to get a blank stare when you tell them that all of a sudden they have to come up with a marketable product in eight months. If you push it, they'll just pack up and go."

That's precisely what happened at Biogen Inc., the Geneva- and Cambridge-based biotech firm started by Nobel laureate and former Harvard Professor Walter Gilbert. Soon after the company laid off thirteen percent of its staff in late 1984, Gilbert himself resigned. Industry watchers speculated that Biogen's upper management wanted to develop near-term, marketable products, while Gilbert felt drawn to long-term research that could bring big payoffs, such as anticancer drugs. As one analyst put it, Gilbert viewed the company's capital as "a different version of a research grant."

If, as the Biogen experience shows, key brainpower will walk out the door rather than compromise its ideals, what can Alpha's CEO do but fire the lot and start over again with a fresh research crew? "Spin off a nonprofit research institute and staff it with the whole OMEGA crew," Stanchfield suggests. "The institute would receive funds from the company as well as other sources. The company's contributions would keep its hand in long-term research, and it could then recruit other scientists to focus their attention on shorter-term, more profit-oriented products. As a result, Alpha's CEO just might be able to have his cake and eat it too."

## Linking Scientists and Managers

Business professor Joe Raelin, an expert on managing salaried professionals and the author of two books on the subject, believes that Alpha's managers and CEO have failed to devise a way to convince the scientific staff of the product-oriented, rather than development-oriented, mission of the company.

"The CEO must send an explicit message to his professionals that they're in the business of turning a profit," Raelin advises.

"Look at Genentech—aside from being a financial success, it's a real symbol of the right way to merge science and management. When Robert Swanson built the facility, he had the research lab put right next to the executive offices. That leaves no question about what the company stands for."

But you don't have to move your headquarters into the research trenches to make your intentions known. Raelin points to a number of "linkage devices" that he believes could breach the gulf between management and scientific staff. "The linkage device promotes egalitarianism by erasing or moderating the social distance between the manager and the scientist. Linkage might be formal, such as periodic seminars where some of the scientists explain their work to management, or informal, like the 'ho-hos' at Genentech, where everyone relaxes and enjoys each other's company over beer and refreshments."

In addition to creating linkage mechanisms, Raelin stresses the importance of mentorship as a means of absorbing scientists into the business culture. "In the case of scientists," he says, "the role of the mentor is not so much to provide technical information but to teach protégés the ropes—how to advance in a way that promotes the interests of the company as well. This is also a way to inculcate a certain amount of loyalty to the company."

Given the typical goals and orientation of the salaried professional, Raelin understands the need for overriding commitment. "There are many things that distinguish professionals and managers," Raelin explains. "Managers are primarily involved with their own careers and will play the internal chess game. Professionals, on the other hand, thirst for autonomy and pretty much want to establish their own agenda. As a result, the manager tends to extend loyalty to the organization, while the professional extends loyalty to his or her profession. The organization just comes second."

One way to deal with this problem is to develop a "dual-career" ladder. "Beyond a certain level, you can have two separate career tracks, one for the traditional manager, with the normal ascension of jobs leading to the top, with corresponding recognition and salary. The other is a 'professional ladder' that allows scientists, engineers, and other salaried professionals the benefits of prestige and salary while staying within the confines of the craft. For example, instead of becoming vice president of marketing, you might become a 'principal engineering fellow' or 'principal engineering associate.' "

Such an approach does not preclude a scientist or other professional from advancing along a conventional career track, provided you prepare yourself for possible pitfalls. "The difficulty I've observed," warns Raelin, "is that scientists tend to forget where they came from once they change hats and tend to boss their peers around in ways that they themselves would have found insulting. As a result, they may be perceived as renegades. But my research does show that if they're really interested in the job and have been adequately trained for it, they are much more successful in dealing with professionals than the average business manager. But you have to think about a reasonable transition period; you can't just wave a wand and turn a professional into a manager."

## Scientists Know Best

Physicist-turned-corporate executive Michael P. Schulhof, Director and Chairman of Strategic Planning for Sony Corporation of America, takes a radically different stance when he defines the problem our scenario raises, not in terms of how Alpha's CEO should manage his scientists but in terms of why *non*-scientists were allowed to manage the company in the first place. "You can't ask a financial person to commit major resources of a large corporation over a long period of time— three to five years—before ever seeing the first dollar of returns unless he also understands what he's investing in. That's one of the fundamental flaws of many high-tech companies in America. They get started by an entrepreneur who has a scientific background, but ultimately the management gets turned over to professionals who typically have come out of business schools and have no basic understanding of the technology that drives the business they're managing. As a result, they're less inclined to get involved with 'risky' technology ventures that might keep them on the forefront."

Sony provides a unique example. Started by people with backgrounds in physics or engineering, Sony still reserves half of the seats on its board of directors for physicists or people with training in physics. According to Schulhof, "Sony benefits from the fact that the company has always been managed by people who share the premise that if you believe in your technology, you can build a market around it."

Schulhof cites the development of Sony's compact disc to illustrate his view that scientists know better than anyone else which products or technologies the organization should pursue. In the late 1970s Sony began developing error-correction codes for optical media and later joined Philips, also managed primarily by technologists, in working out the specifications for digital audio that would eventually lead to an impressive consumer product.

Explains Schulhof, "Before we could put CD players on the market, we had to develop the ability to press the digital discs. And we had to have the confidence that we could do it in a relatively inexpensive way. Sony's top management believed that this was clearly going to be the replacement for the LP record, and by the time the first CD was sold, Sony was willing to invest in excess of $100 million and to spend more than eight years developing the technology. Never, however, did we commission a market-research study, go to an outside consultant, or ask anyone else's opinion except our own. It was totally the conviction of top management, which is basically science-oriented, that this was an idea whose time had come." The moral of the CD story? "No financial manager, unless he's just relying on his staff, could gamble that way unless he understood the technology."

Should Alpha then convert some of its scientists into managers, as other players have suggested? From Schulhof's point of view it's too late for such medicine, because most technology-intensive companies that aren't initially managed by scientist-executives have dismal track records. "It is my belief that the decline in productivity in the United States over the past twenty years and the rise in the role of the financial M.B.A. in American management is not coincidental. Major corporations have typically approached the problem of scientists in a compensatory way. American management at most high-tech companies believes that if you create a dual-ladder system to compensate and motivate the technical manager so that he feels he's the equivalent of the business manager, that you've somehow solved the problem. But, in fact, that's myopic—all it does is soothe some egos. It doesn't come to grips with the problem of who's making the fundamental decisions about where the company is headed and what resources will be committed."

What if Alpha Biomedical's boardroom had included scientists from day one? Could they have done a better job of convincing the stockholders of the value of the OMEGA project? Again Schulhof draws on his experience at Sony: "It is important that the shareholders agree that the company's growth and strategy is correct. At Sony we try to take the time to explain to investors and securities analysts what we're doing because we think it's important that they understand it. We invite securities analysts to our factories in the U.S. and Japan and show them what we're doing. But at the same time, we've never focused our attention on quarterly earnings. We never used our shares as an acquisition vehicle and are therefore less worried that short-term fluctuations in the stock price will damage our ability to conduct business."

## Spreading the Talent Around

"This problem at Alpha sounds all too familiar," says Pierre Dersin, president of Transimatics, which makes diagnostic devices for automated manufacturing lines. Dersin, who holds a Ph.D. in electrical engineering from MIT, also studied management at the Sloan School. "Since the shareholders want a quick return on their investment," he points out, "you must come up with a quick answer to placate them. Bring in a consultant to do a market study that shows a near-term product somewhere in the OMEGA project. Give that product a deadline, and the irate shareholders should be appeased. But be sure you get someone whom the shareholders can trust."

Dersin doesn't believe that putting a scientist in charge would necessarily ameliorate the situation. "In the noblest sense, pure academics are looking for breakthroughs that will advance the knowledge of mankind. In the most selfish sense, they are looking for recognition. So, a priori, there's no reason that they should be linked to money-making activities."

While Dersin does not oppose turning a scientist into a manager, he believes a successful transformation depends on the person. "There are brilliant scientists who can't tie their shoes," he jokes. "But even when it works, I don't think transplanting individuals from the lab is the whole answer. You have to have access to external resources."

The university makes an excellent resource, and Dersin suggests that you can harness it to act as a buffer between basic scientists and the corporate world. After all, no one gets upset about universities doing basic research—that's their job. Dersin cites the relationship between his own company and an academic institution as an example of a symbiotic relationship with an educational institution. The parent company of Transimatics, located in Europe, draws on research from the University of Brussels, which also owns stock in the company. Since the university receives royalties from the sales of the product, it, too, desires practical results. "But this kind of arrangement will not work if you depend on the university for developing the product," he cautions. "There's still a problem with deadlines. Let them do basic research, and let your company bring the product to market."

Dersin believes that scientists may also do more productive basic research in a university setting because they don't feel constrained by working for one particular company. "Scientists employed by a company may be bound to secrecy and not allowed to publish. I know several talented people who had to stop publishing when they joined a company. That conflicts with the basic goals of the scientist."

He also points out that from a company's perspective, while it wants to lock up scientific talent and keep it at its own disposal, this might actually be detrimental if the corporate direction shifts. "As the company changes its policies it should have access to very different kinds of expertise. Today a biotechnology company might be interested in monoclonal antibodies. Perhaps a few years later it might find that the best investment is in biochips. That requires a different blend of knowledge and talent."

Dersin raises the fascinating possibility that scientists might best serve the corporate world by not accepting ties to just one company. Such fanciful thinking has actually been realized at the Microelectronics & Computer Technology Corporation, a joint venture started in 1983 to make the U.S. more competitive against the Japanese computer manufacturers. MCC, whose founding members (many of them arch-rivals) include Boeing, 3M, NCR, Honeywell, Sperry, Eastman Kodak, and other giants, set as its primary goal the generation of breakthrough knowledge that the individual corporate owners could then translate into actual products. Does it work? William C. Norris, chairman of Control Data Corp., who initially proposed MCC, told *The Wall Street Journal* that his firm's $13 million investment in MCC during the first three years garnered a handsome $120 million worth of research results. Some critics claim that MCC has misdirected its long-term research by aiming it too far into the future and that solving short-term problems will eventually win the technology race. Whatever the outcome, the concept represents an innovative approach to bridging the gap between the worlds of business and science.

Perhaps Alpha Biomedical could convert its OMEGA program into an MCC prototype, Dersin suggests. That way Alpha could concentrate on product development with tangible returns on investment, thereby appeasing its board members. However you tackle the issue, though, Dersin worries that boards like Alpha's can easily drive scientists into hiding behind the university wall. "The entire expansion of the West ever since the Renaissance," he muses, "has resulted from the linkage of the risk-takers, the money-makers, with the knowledge-holders, the scientists. We must keep those links between the scientists and the businesspeople. Otherwise we will return to the situation in which the scientists were estranged from the rest of the world and the artisan was the only one doing useful work. I don't think we can afford to be in that position again."

## Soaring With the Eagles

"You speak of this 'culture' of science. I'd rather talk about scientists as people who happened to be emotionally glued to their work in a unique way," says Dr. Nicolaos Arvanitidis, CEO of Liposome Technology, one of the pioneers of a revolutionary new drug-delivery system. Arvanitidis, who holds a Ph.D. in engineering and economics, jokes that his areas of expertise don't entitle him to be called a scientist. But they have given him insight into managing the special needs of scientists.

"I believe there are three types of scientists," he says, "eagles, solid scientists, and middle-of-the-road scientists. Eagles are the most talented and innovative. They are solo creatures who don't soar with the flock. The goal of the eagle is to promote certain ideas that he feels are most important. He might have a healthy ego, but he doesn't believe in small progress made in a small way. He also tends to follow instincts more than a pragmatic approach."

Arvanitidis says that when you land an eagle, you want to make sure he stays in your corporate nest. But if you try to shackle him with traditional management objectives, you will surely scare him away. "You can't try to get him to digest a five-year strategy or put up with quarterly or intermediate reports. That's a guaranteed fight. After all, he's looking for 'megajumps,' and great leaps in technology cannot be planned in advance.

"The right way to manage an eagle is by gently defining the boundaries in which he can freely roam," continues Arvanitidis. "If he says, 'Nick, I want to do this and I need twenty people and two years to come up with the product,' I respond by imposing a resource boundary. I say, 'Fine, do it. But you can only have ten people and one year.' So we negotiate until the terrain feels right. They are likely to stretch the bounds, but ultimately they're very reasonable people, and they aren't out to break the bank."

The next category, the solid scientists, are dependable researchers who understand both the science and the business. They're organizational people primarily interested in making a contribution to the company. "You can put them in various roles and they'll be glad to do it," says Arvanitidis. "While they're interested in solving problems, they also want to advance up the ladder. But they don't have the wild, free spirit of the eagle."

Nevertheless, you can't manage solid scientists with traditional techniques, either. "Although they're motivated by promoting the organization, they're also intrigued by solving problems. You don't want to discourage them by boxing them in with excessive reporting requirements. You give them latitude, as you do with the eagles, but not quite as much. Let's say you have a problem in stabilizing a peptide. You might say to your researcher, 'This is critical to the company. Here's the goal, here are the resources, here's when we need it. Now go and solve it.' What you've done is taken a broad problem and made it into a specific goal. You specified the ends but haven't bound the means."

Arvanitidis's last category, middle-of-the-road scientists, punch the nine-to-five clock, despite their Ph.D.'s and master's degrees. They have given very high priority to outside family commitments and are essentially there to earn an honest living. "These are the bulk of your scientists," Arvanitidis says. "They do good work but won't put in twelve or fourteen hours a day, as your eagles and solid scientists will. They really need to be led, and you can do that by traditional means."

Recognizing the distinctions among the three types of scientists would help Alpha's beleaguered CEO. First, he should isolate his eagles and leave them unfettered in the OMEGA environment. "There probably wouldn't be more than ten percent eagles," estimates Arvanitidis, "so you'd strip this overblown project down to a reasonable size."

Alpha's CEO should then put the remaining solid scientists and middle-of-the-road scientists on more near-term projects. "Come up with a different name for the new project," Arvanitidis advises; "you have to use the right words. Words have a way of upsetting people. Present the new project to the stockholders in a way that shows its more limited scope. Say that you are still doing things for the future but that you've drastically cut down on the money and people allocated for that aspect and that you've shifted a substantial portion of our resources to more goal-oriented work."

Arvanitidis believes this approach will give you the best of both worlds. "You can still do your long-term research with your select group, your eagles, while the other scientists will be shifted to shorter-term projects. You don't have to worry about your middle-of-the-road and solid scientists. They really won't care if the goal of the project shifts. It's your eagles who will fly when the goals are changed."

As evidence of the eagle's tendency toward flight, look what happened at Bell Labs when profitability entered the picture. The same antitrust decree that brought up the Phone Wars has allowed Bell Labs to make money in businesses that earlier decrees had put off-limits, and it has prompted the company to place greater emphasis on hiring scientists of the applied, rather than the theoretical, persuasion. As a result, some Bell scientists, feeling pressure to engage in practical and marketable research, along with tighter restraints on what they can publish or disclose to their colleagues, have begun migrating to other companies and the safe havens of university campuses.

Organizations like Bell Labs would do well to take a look at the way firms in other industries manage their eagles. Interior-design firms, for example, while they don't manage scientists, do depend on an even more volatile group of creative people: artists. Conant Associates in Salt Lake City, one of the top ten interior-design firms in the country, keeps its eagles by allowing them to test their wings on projects without close supervision

and rewarding them handsomely whenever they achieve spectacular results. As long as they pay close attention to Conant's
business interests, they can exercise their full creativity. Some
who work for the firm say the sky is virtually the limit. But then,
how else can it be for an eagle?

## Lessons from the Game

1. Accept the fact that scientists and other creative spirits are
   difficult to manage. Recognizing the difficulties will position
   you to solve inevitable problems as they arise.

2. Don't assume that scientists and other professionals understand the goals of the company. Offer them explicit education about the company's mission and what it takes to keep
   the labs open.

3. Look for ways to get scientists more committed to the goals
   of the company. Remember, salaried scientists, like other
   professionals, give first loyalty to their field. A dual-ladder
   system, in which the scientist ascends to high status positions, may be one mechanism.

4. Be sure that the people who sign off on research projects
   firmly understand the technology. Otherwise they are less
   likely to consider taking calculated risks.

5. When selecting a scientist who will be elevated to a managerial position, look for someone who is trusted and well
   respected by both the research staff and the upper management. Scientists can be suspicious of a colleague who "de-
   fects" to the other side. A trusted peer who has done good
   research will minimize those feelings.

6. When turning a scientist into a manager, be patient. Let him
   learn the ropes. If you push too fast, you may have someone
   who is neither scientist nor manager.

7. Look for ways to create an environment in which scientists
   and other salaried professionals can thrive. Professionals
   need peer recognition and the opportunity to communicate

with their colleagues. Provide that, and you've won half the battle in keeping them happy.

8. Give your most rarefied talent freedom to soar. Suggest boundaries that enable these people to flex their wings yet bring you the returns you are seeking.

CHAPTER 6

# The 24-Karat Mousetrap:
## *Introducing the Perfect Product*

## Opening Moves

Shoe designer Richard West loves to run. Every day he and his colleague, Sally Stanton, jog six miles during their lunch hour, and on the weekends they push themselves to ten or fifteen miles, enabling them to compete in marathons around the country.

One fine spring day Richard stops halfway along the route to complain bitterly. "Look at the sole of this shoe! I've only had this pair a month and already it's shot." He angrily shakes his foot so Sally can see the loose sole flapping against the mid-sole.

Sally examines her own treads. "You think *you've* got problems," she says with a sigh. "After about five hundred miles these shoes look as smooth as a baby's bottom."

"Jeez," mutters Richard as they begin the long trudge back to the office, "we can put a man on the moon, make radial tires that last more than forty thousand miles, but we can't make a running shoe that'll survive one full season."

Sally points to an old refrigerator lying in the weeds alongside the road. "You don't see many of those in the trash," she says. "How many refrigerators will you buy in your life? Why can't shoes last as long?"

What if companies *could* make products that would last a lifetime? Would they and their competitors grind to a standstill? This question brings to mind the 1952 film, *The Man in the White Suit,* in which Alec Guinness played an inventor who created a miracle fabric that never wore out or soiled, sending shock waves throughout British textile mills. The mill owners tried to bribe Guinness into destroying his formula, while the mill workers, fearing that the new fabric would spell economic doom for the entire industry, tried to bully him into forgetting the secret.

To see what real executives would do with a nearly perfect product, we asked our players to cast the fate of the ultimate running shoe.

## The Game: When the Shoe Fits

You've been running the Trident Athletic Shoe Company for twelve years and have always managed to keep your products near the front of the pack. Although recent winners of the Boston and New York marathons wear and have endorsed your professional model, the TX, you have been longing to introduce a shoe that would leave your competitors in your dust. So, when the head of your research lab, Richard West, volunteered his nights and weekends to develop "a shoe that would last a full season," you offered to pay a $10,000 bonus if he succeeded.

Nearly a year has elapsed, and you have all but forgotten about the top-secret SX project, when a bleary-eyed but obviously ecstatic West bursts into your office and runs you down to the lab, where your chief financial officer, old Dave "Razor" Wilcox, and your marketing director, Sally Stanton, have already gathered to witness Richard's unveiling of a breakthrough that, as he puts it, "will change the future of the foot." As all eyes fix on the silver chafing dish gleaming on the lab bench, West lifts the lid with a flourish. "Ta da!"

"Looks like somebody ran over a hair ball with a steamroller," hisses Wilcox, squinting his eyes.

"Close," West says proudly. "I've tried everything from macromolecular celluloid derivatives to the fibrous roots of the Haitian yam. I won't bore you with the details, but I've woven and compressed strands of a new miracle fiber to produce a running-shoe sole that will last at least 8,000 miles before showing any signs of wear. And it won't cost us a cent more to produce."

Wilcox whistles softly.

"Richard!" exclaims Sally Stanton. "This will put us light-years ahead of the competition. And what a weapon against offshore manufacturing!"

Wilcox shakes his head. "Yeah, and it will put *us* out of business too. What about our existing lines?"

West, Stanton, and Wilcox all begin shouting at once, and for the next two hours you listen to a raging debate about Trident's responsibility to offer the public its amazing breakthrough versus the company's need and right to protect its existing interests. Finally, you ask for bottom-line suggestions from your department heads: Marketing insists that the company immediately put SX on *all* of Trident's running shoes, from the lowliest tennis sneakers to the professional competition models. Sure, customers will buy new shoes less often, but according to Stanton's calculations, Trident could increase its market share by thirty to fifty percent.

Adamantly opposed to such an all-out program, "Razor" Wilcox suggests putting SX on a special line of professional running shoes and pricing each pair at $600. If other producers close the gap with similar long-life materials, Trident could gradually reduce the price and extend the invention to a wider range of products. West just sits in a corner, grinning like a monkey.

As the president of Trident, you must decide whether to introduce a remarkable new product that could change the standards of your industry—or to keep it under wraps.

## Strategies and Tactics

### Respecting the "Newness Threshold"

For Paul Fireman, president and CEO of Reebok International Ltd., the commotion at Trident Running Shoe boils down to a tempest in a teapot. "Look," he says with confidence, "you can't force a business into obsolescence. There's not a product, invention, or idea that can't be transformed into another product, invention, or idea. So I really wouldn't worry about the super sole ruining my other lines. The guy who wants to bury it or give it an outlandish price is just being foolish."

Fireman raises an interesting point when he proposes the idea of transforming products and ideas into new business lines. After all, transferring concepts and technologies from one industry or product to another has become a tradition. Look at U-Haul, the brainchild of Samuel Shoen (Doctor Sam), who spun $3000 in start-up capital into a $300 million empire. When the do-it-yourself moving market that he created began to lose its magic due to excessive head-to-head competition, Doctor Sam extended the U-Haul concept to a broader rental market, making available bikes, motor homes, VCRs, garden equipment, cameras, and just about everything else imaginable. Why let a great idea wither with changes in the times? As Shoen proves, if you've got a good idea, you can always put it to work somewhere else.

As for the issue of hiding potentially lucrative technologies to save existing lines, companies that adopt such measures usually lose out to smarter, less paranoid competitors. Nothing illustrates this better than the way American tire manufacturers, in what one business reporter described as a "classic abuse of market power," postponed the introduction of radial tires as long as they could. Although radial technology existed long before they began employing it, American manufacturers continued to sell nonradial tires, which last a fraction of the time, until Michelin rolled into the U.S. market. As a result of their attitude, American manufacturers had a tough catch-up game with their European competitors.

In the case of our scenario, Fireman believes that the issue of sitting on superior technology may be moot, because he doubts that the public would accept an 8000-mile sole. "Everyone wants to feel that they own something special, something unique," he says. "And a product that doesn't wear out tends to diminish that feeling. Consumer items are also very different from utilitarian products such as refrigerators. When you buy footwear or other fashion items, there's a certain 'romantic pleasure,' and I think it would be clouded when you start talking about utilitarian issues."

Fireman also observes that like many consumer products, running shoes have a "newness threshold." It might be 500 miles or it might be 1000 miles, but when that point is reached, people rush to the shopping mall for a change. Faced with a shoe that suppresses the newness threshold eightfold, customers might well start finding deficiencies, real or imagined, in the miracle shoes. Suggests Fireman, "Consumers might say something like, 'This lasts a long time, but it's just not as cushiony as brand *X, Y,* or *Z*.' Reality lies in the mind, not in the foot, of the running-shoe buyer."

What would Fireman do, then, with the Trident super sole? "Don't put it on every shoe," he recommends, "but do make it available to a narrow specialty audience that would purchase a shoe primarily on a technical basis. Sell the product at a higher margin, then use the profits to develop new ideas and keep the fire burning."

Regardless of which shoes you put it on, Fireman believes you should introduce the super sole in the most dramatic way possible. That means using the discovery to create advertising allure and excitement that reaffirms your position as an industry innovator and leader. "In fact," concludes Fireman, "such recognition could well be the company's most valuable reward for developing the super sole."

## Redefining Home Base

Like Paul Fireman, marketing consultant and former advertising executive Art Tauder dismisses the notion of withholding the SX from the marketplace. "No consumer product is so unidimensional that you can solve all of its problems with one development. So the fact that we have solved the wear-out problem of the shoe and have now leapt ahead of competition in that area means that we can focus on other dimensions of the product."

Tauder would immediately charge his market-research director with the task of determining the leader in shoe fit. "Maybe the combination of the fit and the wear will give us a second dimension to work with," he muses. "Perhaps there's a small company that has approached perfect fit, who we could team up with. Then we might wind up the leader in two dimensions: fit and wearability."

The history of business offers some stunning examples of companies that joined together to take advantage of combined marketing and distribution resources. For example, Para Research, a small publisher of psychic books and materials ranging from how to read Tarot cards to hypnotic past-life regression, decided to move into more mainstream general books by publishing *How to Get a Job in Sixty Seconds* and *How to Get a Raise in Sixty Seconds.* Although Para had mastered the art of selling to highly targeted audiences interested in paranormal subjects, it lacked the ability to reach traditional bookstores. The answer? Team up with one of the masters of paperback marketing, Bantam Books, to whom Para sold the rights to its two potential best-sellers for a handsome sum.

Even if Trident were to strike up such an arrangement with another firm, what about the possibility of the SX ruining the company's existing lines? "It's all in the packaging," Tauder says. "A lot really depends on how you advertise it. You *can* unwittingly damage your own sales. Not by introducing a superior product but by failing to encourage consumers to keep on consuming." He cites Arm & Hammer's bicarbonate of soda as an example of a product that a company must remind customers to discard and repurchase. When Arm & Hammer proposed hazardous odor zones, such as refrigerators, they showed people opening boxes of the white powder and sticking them on the back shelves. But the image implied that you could leave the stuff there forever. After initially advertising the product for odor reduction, the company added a new "feature" to the packaging: a reminder chart that tells the consumer when the product reaches saturation and should be replaced.

While odor might also signal the time to buy a new pair of SX running shoes ("Maybe we should get into the foot-deodorant business while we're at it," Tauder jokes), changes in fashion would sound the shoe's death knell. "When I talk about consumer marketing, I always point out that the communications and sales are all made to one person at a time," Tauder says. "You don't sell to a 'market,' you sell to individuals. There's got to be a segment of the population who might feel guilty about buying a new pair of shoes because the old ones are still in good shape. It might cause some inner tension. But, on the other hand, most consumers make a conscious decision about buying shoes when the colors or styles change. 'These shoes don't have mesh or stripes or reflectors or whatever everyone else is wearing. To hell with them.' "

Tauder recommends that Trident should consider opening a separate subsidiary that does nothing but manufacture soles, or perhaps just licenses out the technology. That's similar to the path W. L. Gore chose after it developed Gore-Tex, one of the most successful waterproof fabrics ever created. Rather than producing clothing and other products themselves, the creators of Gore-Tex chose to be a fabric-supplier resource to companies such as Orvis, the Mercedes of fishing and camping gear, and hundreds of other companies that manufacture sportswear and camping gear.

Dolby labs chose the same course. Rather than going into the stereo-equipment manufacturing business, which would have just created an army of competitors, Dolby licensed out its technology to equipment and recording studios throughout the world. The result? Like W. L. Gore, Dolby achieved success in far more markets than it could have possibly penetrated on its own.

Perhaps creative licensing of the SX technology would whisk Trident into a whole new business. "We have an innovation that should enable us to redefine our business," Tauder advises. "Perhaps we should shift our whole focus. We should say, 'Look at what we have been able to create in this shoe,' and use this opportunity to take stock of our talents, make sure they're being applied in the right way.' Perhaps we should be making car or bicycle tires with our amazing innovation. Who knows?"

If Trident winds up shifting industries as Tauder suggests, it wouldn't be the first company to do so. Take the case of Wilkinson Sword Ltd., a two-hundred-year-old British sword manufacturing company that tried to move into high-end gardening tools. This was a seemingly sensible strategy, because it would exploit Wilkinson's skill at putting a lastingly sharp edge on stainless steel. In the early sixties the company tried to cut a swath in the U.S. garden-tool market and, in an effort to promote its tools, sent dealers stainless-steel razor blades to demonstrate its company's technological prowess. Oh, the tools worked fine, but it was the razor blades that impressed the daylights out of everyone. Dealers couldn't get enough of them to give away or sell. For a while a customer hankering for a close shave could only buy the blades at a gardening store, but Wilkinson picked up on the sensation it had inadvertently created and soon began injecting its blades into drugstores around the globe. Stainless-steel blades, which American manufacturers had to adopt themselves, now account for seventy-five percent of the company's profits.

Tauder wraps up his advice by noting that, above all, Trident should make sure it doesn't allow the SX discovery to make the company smug. "Let's take advantage of the fact that we *can* make such discoveries, and see if we can push ourselves to do it again," he insists.

How? "Give that West guy a $20,000 bonus and see if he can create a 16,000-mile sole next time."

## *Pulling Your Athlete's Foot out of Your Mouth*

Alex Randall, Ph.D., anthropologist, entrepreneur, and founder of The Boston Computer Exchange, agrees that Trident should seize this opportunity to revolutionize its business, and he recommends a two-prong approach. Before you start blasting SX products out the door, he says, you should find out if anyone really *wants* the 8000-mile sole. "Maybe it's not such a big deal, but assuming that some segment of the running population did want it, the key thing is to follow a principle, rather than react from the gut. And the principle I'd follow is to put your money where it will do some real good—go and find some way to get an objective endorsement for the product."

Since celebrity endorsements by sports people (Larry Bird and Converse shoes, Mary Lou Retton and Wheaties, Jim McMahon and Honda scooters) are so prevalent, Randall suggests a bolder maneuver, perhaps prodding the federal government to set up a commission that rates the quality and wearability of sports products, putting a sort of Underwriters Laboratory stamp or Good Housekeeping Seal of Approval on everything from basketball shoes to billiard balls.

If bureaucratic red tape snarls up that approach, consider starting some kind of institute that would develop wear-rating standards for shoes and other sports items. Perhaps the national orthopedic association would endorse the shoe if you proved that it also saved wear and tear on feet and knees. And, of course, if the shoe really lives up to its promise, consumer product reviews might hail it as a great footwear breakthrough. Whatever way you manage to obtain your seal of approval, it would give your promotional campaign much-needed credibility.

"Think about buying an air conditioner or a refrigerator," Randall says. "Even without looking at any other features, you're going to gravitate to the one that has the highest efficiency rating. Same with the shoes. The idea is that the public will know that they're buying ten out of ten on the rating scale. Even if they don't ultimately care about wear, they're still going to be impressed by the fact that they're purchasing something that's been highly rated by someone else. You're talking Crest toothpaste. Endorsed by the American Dental Association. You're talking A-1 Steak Sauce—look at A-1's label. It says that it was proclaimed 'A-1' at international expositions in 1862, 1867, 1878, 1880, 1889, and 1900. Did it ever win anything since then? Who knows and who cares—it has an 'objective' endorsement. The 'fact' that A-1 is a prizewinner is all people need to know."

Randall's claim is well supported. Research studies have shown that putting a seal of approval, the results of product testing, or an approval rating on a product is highly effective in making it sell. At the same time the studies also reveal that the source of the endorsement doesn't make much difference; the Good Housekeeping Seal of Approval may carry no more weight than "Kitchen Tested by Fred's Rating Service."

Randall wouldn't be the first executive to create an outside organization to help him achieve his marketing goals. The American Tobacco Institute serves its supporting sponsors admirably well when they need to find scientific evidence that smoking may not be as dangerous to your health as scientists claim.

Other industry groups serve similar functions for their constituents. When Americans began to shed their cotton garments in favor of polyester products, the Cotton Institute launched a campaign to get the country back into cotton clothing, and when diet-conscious people began eating fewer T-bone steaks, the American Cattleman's Association promoted the merits of beef. Just about every industry boasts its own objective campaign.

Assuming that Trident garners the endorsements it needs, on what kind of shoes should it use the breakthrough technology? "Put it on a variety of shoes and maybe add a ten-dollar premium," Randall urges. "You might also want to do a limited 'gold' edition for the high-end runner. Like a limited edition art print. You could advertise it as 'the ultimate running experience.' "

But don't stop there, Randall advises, because figuring out how to exploit SX in your existing business takes little imagination. "SX might be a great opportunity to create a whole new line of products, like 'Executive Adidas.' I've always wondered why no one ever made a high-quality running shoe that looks like a wing tip. You could run from the boardroom to your BMW, or play O. J. Simpson and run down the concourse to knock on the door of the plane as it's pulling away from the gate. Why bill SX as just a super running sole? Use it to create excitement and innovation throughout the whole industry."

Randall would also encourage Trident to catapult itself into new businesses. "But first," he says, "I'd have to get my people to stop thinking solely in terms of shoes. Assemble everyone in the boardroom and say, 'Look, we have our athletes' feet in our mouths . . . we're trapped by our shoehorns.' Then I'd say to West, 'Go back to the lab. I want a Ping-Pong ball made out of SX stuff by four o'clock this afternoon.' It just takes one example of a different use for the SX to open a floodgate of thinking. Bounce the SX Ping-Pong ball around the room and say, 'A thousand-dollar bill goes to the person who comes up with the most outrageous and impractical list of applications for the SX.' "

To get people's minds working the right way, Randall stresses that they must think of general principles rather than specific applications. Ask: "Where's the wear? What product wears out that shouldn't? What else can we do with a material that doesn't wear out?" There must be five hundred uses, he maintains. "Maybe it's the ultimate new material for a floppy disk or phonograph record. Maybe it's the cover material for a running track or tennis court. I'd tell Stanton and Frabbitz and Quimby from marketing to go study every market in which wear is a major problem."

Looking at the flip side of the general principle can also be a rich source of ideas, Randall says. "What can't afford to break?" he asks. "Lots of things—condoms, diaphragms, and heart valves to name a few. Imagine using SX to prevent the unexpected beginning and end of life!"

Such freewheeling thinking has lead to many applications of "generically" useful materials. For instance, DuPont's super-tough fiber, Kevlar, can be found in products as diverse as combat helmets, flak jackets, circuit boards, belting for auto tires, and ropes used to hoist oil-rig mooring anchors. None of these uses would have come about without an environment that stimulates creative thinking. This raises an interesting question: Can an executive really get his or her people thinking more creatively? "Absolutely," insists Randall. "There are only a handful of ways to change a product: 'minify,' magnify, stretch, contract, etc. People just need to be shown how to open their minds and start thinking in those terms."

Equally important, though, Randall points out that there are 147 statements for killing a good idea. What's the number-one statement? " 'That's not our line.' How crazy," Randall criticizes. "Never dump a good idea just because it doesn't fit in with what you're doing today. That thinking also suggests an underlying kind of self-referential stupidity: We can't do it because we don't do it."

## Skimming the Profits

Rob Settle, Professor of Marketing at San Diego State University and co-author of *Why They Buy: American Consumers Inside and Out,* takes a more pragmatic approach to the SX situation. "Introduce the product at a high price—skimming first—at $150 or $175 a pair, offering a top-of-the-line model," he recommends. "Then you put a little of this fiber in with the regular stuff and extend your line, so you wind up with different blends of the regular and long-lasting sole materials. But, in any event, let the $175 model sell the other shoes."

The idea of boosting your whole product line by associating it with a top-of-the-line model has benefited many businesses, according to Settle. Ford and Chevrolet, he says, used the Thunderbird and Corvette to lend a little prestige to their basic models. Some Ford ads in the 1950s actually superimposed an image of the sleek Thunderbird over the standard Ford sedan, noting the similarity in lines and claiming the car was "Thunderbird-inspired." Chevrolet initiated similar advertising with Corvette, but instead of using imagery, the company described how the lessons they had learned in developing this awesome sport car were applied to other models.

"When you do this kind of prestige association, you've got to be careful that you're not jeopardizing your higher-priced product by diminishing its worth," Settle continues. "This is called 'trading down.' If the prestige in a product is largely psychological, like it is in a Cross pen, trading down could hurt you. People buy Cross pens because they want a distinctive pen, so it isn't likely Cross would trade down to cheaper lines. In the case of the running shoe, the prestige is functionally based, so you really don't have much risk of stripping away the superior image of the top model."

Just as important as pricing decisions are considerations of the timing and the manner in which you introduce the SX. "If you bring in a radically new technology too early, no one will buy it, and your competitors will have time to develop their own versions while the public is warming up to the idea," Settle notes. He cites the development of color TV as a prime example of what can happen when a company moves too far ahead of its consuming public. In the 1950s, RCA, Westinghouse, and Bell Labs competed for the FCC to adopt their respective standards for producing color TV images. RCA won and, as a result, was forced to commit vast resources to developing and manufacturing actual products. But it took the public a number of years to accept color TV, during which time RCA's competitors waited in the wings and developed their own products. By the time color TV became a rage, RCA had lost its initial advantage and shared the market with many other consumer electronics manufacturers.

The same thing could happen with the SX running shoe if it appears to be too radical, too far beyond the range of believability, Settle maintains. The solution? "Keep the shoe looking like other 'normal' running shoes and market the sole, not as a revolutionary new item but as a superior form of what everyone is accustomed to seeing and wearing."

In addition to avoiding "techno-shock," Settle argues that Trident should pay great attention to all the other qualities of its shoes. Sometimes a breakthrough in one area can cause you to overemphasize that area at the expense of others. "A tremendously long-lasting sole might actually be perceived as a negative factor unless you find a way to improve the durability of the tops as well. People might figure that the tops are going to go, so what's the point of having soles that last forever? I think you've got to keep a careful balance between the durability of the uppers and the durability of the sole. So you'd better send the guy who sat there grinning like a monkey back to the lab and tell him to make a super top." As an alternate strategy, if you can't make a totally durable upper, Settle suggests adding an ingredient to the sole that would at least give it the "appearance" of slight wear, so the whole shoe looks used at some point.

Assuming you could improve the complete shoe, however, could the success of the SX damage Trident's other lines? "You could conceivably develop yourself right out of the business, just like the dentists have," Settle says. "For years they talked prevention, and now that they've succeeded, their profession is in trouble. Since they're unable to fill cavities—their old stock-in-trade—they're now concentrating on cleaning and cosmetic enhancements."

What equivalent spin-offs could Trident pursue? A shoe-cleaning service that makes soiled but undamaged SXs look good as new? Long-lasting shoelaces? Velcro-attached style additives? To avoid racking your brains for follow-up services, Settle recommends finding other uses for the amazing SX material. "I really don't approve of mindless diversification, like when a steel company absorbs a fast-food chain. But this is a hell of a technical innovation, and the company should back off and think of other uses for it. And not just in terms of running shoes—that's myopic. You have to ask yourself, what are some other situations where you need friction, but friction causes wear. Tires, brake-lining material, and clutches are obvious choices. I don't think the company should start making these kinds of items, but they should at least be developing some lucrative licensing agreements with people who are in those businesses."

Even if Trident does not choose to exploit its superior technology, Settle believes the last thing it should do is sit on it. "As long as the public is ready to accept it, you're crazy not to develop it," he maintains, "because eventually someone else will stumble on it. And they'll be the ones to reap the rewards."

## Blending for Profits

Chemist and entrepreneur Sanford Schwartzman, president and CEO of American Carbonyl, Inc., a specialty chemical manufacturer, dislikes all the options presented in the scenario. "All of the alternatives in your story are flawed," he says. "It's a waste to just ignore the discovery—there's a handsome profit to be made of it. But I also wouldn't put it on every shoe I make—we don't know how people will respond to it. And I really wouldn't recommend starting off with a sky-high price and then gradually reducing it as competitors join the fray. All we'd be doing is inviting the competition to pursue the lower end of the market. In doing so, they'll wind up making the whole market unprofitable for everyone, especially us."

So, what other options would Schwartzman pursue? "I'm much more inclined to blend the new fiber material with the old sole material. And I'd do it in ratios that allow me to predetermine the useful life or the wear life of the sole," he responds. "I'd put out a 6-month or 500-mile shoe, a 12-month or 1200-mile shoe, and a 24-month or a 2400-mile shoe. If possible, I'd even try to develop a lifetime, or 100,000-mile edition.

"By being able to predetermine the average life and wearability, we could then offer a shoe in each category, from the lowest tennis shoe to the most expensive professional running shoe. That way the purchaser has the option of paying for whatever durability he can afford. I'd also want to extend the concept to walking shoes too."

The idea of offering wearability options, of course, has never occurred to footwear manufacturers. But why not? We live in a world of standard- and premium-grade beers, coach and first class airline seats, standard and "luxury" sedans. Sears even organizes its entire merchandise mix according to "good," "better," and "best." As the automakers learned long ago, up to a point, the more choice you provide the consumers, the more they feel empowered to make intelligent buying decisions.

Still, you must go beyond just creating choices for your customers, Schwartzman insists. In the case of the SX soles, you must convince consumers that each of your shoes outdistances comparably priced shoes from your competitors. "Trident must make shoes in its least expensive category more durable than those of the competitor at the same price. This should even be verified through some kind of objective wear test. My end goal would be to have an option available in each of my present lines from short life to long life, and shoes that are in every case better than my competitor's. Once I've achieved that, I could go ahead with a PR campaign and then advertise the hell out of my products."

Could the SX sole be too successful? Schwartzman believes that SX could eventually put Trident out of the shoe business, which supports his recommendation that you refrain from putting a 100 percent SX sole on every shoe. "No question about it," he concludes, "If you stuck it on everything, you'd increase your market share, but I think you'd eventually diminish your overall market to the point where you had served it so well that you were no longer really in the business. Remember, nothing is as comfortable as an old shoe."

## Expanding the Marketplace

"The company that stops innovating is the company that dies," observes Michael Schulhof of Sony Corporation of America. He thinks that Trident would be foolish to hide the new SX material because of the potential threat to its other shoe lines. Comparing the situation with new products at Sony, he says, "We've never tried to suppress an idea because we thought it would financially damage other products. The danger of having that kind of an attitude is that you immediately start to stifle creative talent and start to plant seeds of doubt in your own managers about the philosophy of the company they're working in. It's a very unhealthy approach to business."

Burying the SX treasure would not only derail the company's morale, according to Schulhof, it would mean denying consumers a remarkable new product. "If a product is good, the use spreads. It proliferates. People generally buy a new Walkman, not because the devices have gotten smaller but because they have one for the house and want one for the office or one for the kids to take down to the beach. They just find new places where they'd like to have one handy."

What if the SX decreases the overall shoe market? Schulhof smiles. "No problem. Develop a full line of products around the SX, and then find other uses for the material. If the market for shoes suddenly drops off because everyone has one pair of running shoes and doesn't need anything more, then we'll look for other parts of the sportswear business to get into. At Sony, the attitude would be, 'What a terrific product. Now we can really try to expand the number of joggers.' "

Schulhof views obsolescence as a natural by-product of innovation. "It's not something to be feared and can rarely be planned for, because one never knows when a brilliant new idea will result in the replacement of an existing product." He goes on to say that a company can and should create an environment characterized by a healthy mix of standby products, as well as new products that emerge from a spirit of innovation.

"At Sony," he explains, "we spend as much time trying to build products that are durable and will not break down as we do innovating, because product reliability and durability are important to us. If a customer decides to replace a product, it should be because new technology has provided opportunities for us to do things that weren't possible before, not because the products have broken down."

Whether you make running shoes or consumer electronic goods, Schulhof maintains that your product must properly fulfill a function. If people buy a product because of an image you've created, but it doesn't fulfill their expectations, you're going to lose that customer next time around. "You can't force-feed a product to people. Advertising might be able to shape an image in the short term, but in the long run the reality catches on, and if the public perceives a discrepancy between the ad and how the product really performs, you've lost it all."

## Selling by Increment

Christina Darwall, president of New Venture Services, Inc., and a member of the board of Bell Bicycle, which makes bicycling and sports gear, sees the introduction of the "Marathoner SX," as she nicknames it, as an excellent opportunity for Trident. If the SX causes a decline in sales of Trident's other lines, she believes that the corresponding increase in market share stolen from competitors, together with an increase in dollar volume, will balance the equation. In any case, Darwall wouldn't dream of sitting on the product, because although such a protectionist stance may benefit the firm in the short run, "the net present value of your business will be at its highest if you move as rapidly as possible to give the customer what he wants, right now."

While Darwall believes that Trident can't lose with the SX, she cautions the company to address all aspects of the product, not just its durability, and that it market the product to the right runners. Consider what happened with an actual long-life product, the light bulb that never burns out. Well, almost never. Kevin Keating, founder of Diolight Technology, Inc., coin-vented a light bulb that could shine more than six years if burned continuously. How easy it would be, Keating thought, to sell such a creation. Not so easy, it turned out. At first he couldn't find anyone to produce it for him, because as soon as he told prospective light-bulb manufacturers about the life of the product, they responded by saying they were in the bulb *replacement* business.

When Diolight finally did find a manufacturer, wholesalers flinched at a bulb that retailed for $4.99 to $5.99. Even though Diolight's bulbs might save consumers money in the long run, they knew that people were used to paying pocket change for light bulbs and would resist shelling out five times more for something that offered no immediate benefits. Eventually Diolight did find its niche: hard-to-reach places such as exit signs or high chandeliers, where the cost of labor needed to "relamp" is high. As the makers of Diolight learned, the law of the jungle is "find your niche or die."

To avoid Diolight's problems, how would Darwall introduce the SX? Her answer is to do it incrementally. Assuming that the running-shoe market contains five or six segments, she would test-market the shoe in one segment before moving on to others. "I'm not sure that all of them really want these shoes. We need to determine what shoes various kinds of runners really want, instead of feeling obliged to give them all the same technology. The different market segments probably have very distinct characteristics."

At the bottom of the market, Darwall identifies the yuppie secretaries in New York who wear jogging shoes to work but don't actually run. "If their walk-to-work shoes lasted five years, they'd still probably throw them out after one year because styles change." Next she identifies the style-conscious teenagers and the fashion-conscious people who never go jogging but who wear their jogging suits to the supermarkets; followed by the "techie" runners who jog but, like many campers and fishermen, seek the very latest equipment. She then points to the serious joggers, and lastly, the marathoners, the people who make a living destroying shoes.

Since only people in the last segment would likely be sure bets for buying the long-lasting, SX sole, Darwall would restrict marketing the Marathoner to them. If other segments began purchasing the product, then Trident could cascade the sole down to lower-end models.

Suggests Darwall, "Even though the SX shoes cost us the same amount of money to manufacture, we have to charge slightly more. First of all, it is value added to the consumer; no one else has the technology, and we spent a year funding Richard West, so we need the return on our investment in his time."

If SX takes the high-end segments by storm, wouldn't you still need to build in obsolescence? "Not at all," she insists. "Planned obsolescence is a thing of the past in certain product lines. In general, you will always have a winner if you consistently look out for the consumer. Those who have the best market research and who give the customers what they want, as fast as they discover it, will win.

"When a market does reach maturity, as the refrigerator market has, the producers must look for innovations that create new variations on the old theme. In the case of the refrigerator market, you have to say, 'What can I vary?' Shelf space, for one thing." She mentions the new "subzero refrigerators," which have shorter shelves to make more food visible, as the hottest subsegment in the refrigerator market. "Innovations can be made in any market, even in the most mature one," she says. "At some point I believe a radical new technology will ultimately emerge in the refrigerator industry."

For the time being, Darwall keeps stocking her five-year-old refrigerator. How about her running shoes? Would she want a pair that lasts 8000 miles? "Oh, no," she says with a laugh, "I'd prefer to get a new pair of shoes every year than a pair that lasts me three years. But then again, I'm not a marathoner."

## Flaunting Your Technology

Unlike the other players, Gary Kreissman, corporate vice president of VAL-PAK, a national coupon broker, has no problem with the idea of a $600 SX-soled shoe. "Don't sell it, though," he says. "It's essentially a showcase item that highlights your brilliant technological prowess and superior capabilities. Auto manufacturers do this all the time with racing machines that they don't plan to sell. It's a terrific image builder." Kreissman also points out that beyond a show of force, the $600 SX running shoe could generate great PR, especially if Trident sponsored an ultra-athletic event and shod all contestants with complimentary shoes.

Would he do anything else besides flaunting the SX technology? "Absolutely!" he says. "Vigorous line extension. Take a cue from the polyester mavens and improve your product by using just a *bit* of SX. Primarily, you sell improvement by changing perceptions. Even though the soles might increase the wear eightfold, you only want to charge 50 percent more. The idea is not to be selling a radically new technology but to promote an extension of your present offering."

Such "line extension" also enables you to snare more shelf space in stores, which in turn will help you sell your old brands. "Your other models take on an image of being 'standards,' " he explains. "It's a truism that whenever you introduce a line extension, regardless of whether it's a superior or inferior product, you'll improve your overall sales just because of its presence."

The concept of introducing line extensions "for their own sake" influences almost every mass marketer, especially in the fashion, consumer electronics, and food industries. Kreissman points to flavored spring water and wine coolers as prime examples of how to proliferate a line and buy more shelf space with just a slight change in the original or standard product.

The key to a successful line extension with the SX, according to Kreissman, is to avoid "blowing the whole technology by failing to upcharge." Remember, "you're banking on a combination of your existing technology and the new technology to set your entire offering apart in the marketplace, and to expand your present product mix. The new technology won't have perceived value unless it costs more."

Blue smoke and mirrors? "That depends on whether you're dealing with function or fashion," Kreissman responds. "Where personal taste is the driving force, function really becomes irrelevant. Look at polyester suits. From a practical point of view they're superior to wool. They last forever and hold a crease. Yet aesthetics and tradition dictate that wool is the material of CEOs and bankers."

Kreissman also points out that buyers traditionally view running shoes as disposable products, and that in general, "it is not a great idea to take a product made to be thrown away and make it more durable. People have a fixed idea of what kinds of products are meant to be kept forever and what kinds are meant to hit the trash cans at expected intervals. It's a way of organizing the world of goods, and you don't want to disrupt it." Kreissman cites the failure of the everlasting light bulb to capture the market as an example of how a challenge to the consumer's worldview can be a dangerous maneuver.

Okay, but doesn't that mean that the SX is doomed because it alters the rules of consumption? "I don't think you want to push the SX as something that will last forever," Kreissman answers. "What you want to stress is that the shoe is constructed of a superior material. Period. End. Let the consumer read into that what he or she wants. You just have to put the seeds in their minds."

You can accomplish that goal, he thinks, by giving the shoe a name that implies stamina for both the shoe and the wearer. Maybe you call it "Endurance." Then put a guarantee on it—3000 miles/12 months, or whatever seems reasonable. And when you go to advertise it, find a confidence-inspiring figure to hawk it. "I can see it now," Kreissman says with a chuckle, "Lee Iacocca looks you in the eye and holds up the shoe, saying, 'Endurance. If you can find a better-built shoe, buy it.' "

## Creating an Abundance of Dollars from a Scarcity of Shoes

How would a professional runner and the owner of a national chain of athletic shoe stores handle the SX? "By first distinguishing two groups of serious shoe buyers," answers Sally Edwards, triathlete and president of Fleet Feet, Inc. "On the one hand, you've got technical runners, who need a lot of cushion and support and can even feel slight differences in the mid-sole [the material between the outer sole and the upper part of the shoe]. Technical runners might be interested in this product, but what they really want is a *mid-sole* that will last forever. I throw my shoes out after a few hundred miles because the mid-soles are shot. But I think you could probably interest technical runners in the long-lasting outer soles and maybe add $10 a pair. Solve the mid-sole problem and you could probably sell the SX shoes for $100 to $150 until there was some competition.

"On the other side, you have a group of serious joggers. They won't be as sensitive to the mid-sole issue, but their shoes tend to last 1000 miles or more. So they might be mildly interested in the super sole for a small premium price."

Edwards brings a unique viewpoint to the scenario. In addition to being a triathlon star (when we interviewed her, she was relaxing after winning the 1986 Bud Light U.S. Triathlon for her age division), she holds an M.B.A. and sells shoes to the high end of the athletic shoe market. Although she sells serious running shoes, Edwards sadly acknowledges that aside from a small segment of the running-shoe market, manufacturers wage an ongoing "war" between fashion and function. "In the past," she explains, "the athletic business catered to people who used shoes for function. Today most manufacturers are catering to the fashion market. But there are some players who are trying to drive consumers back to function. Nike and Adidas, for example, have coined the term 'authentic athletics,' which separates functional shoes from leisure wear and 'athleisure' shoes [a combination of the athletic and recreational shoe]. But even 'authentic athletics' have a fashion touch to them.

"One way or another," she continues, "all footwear is fashionwear. This makes it especially difficult for the specialty merchant. It's hard to talk about fashion, which has to do with personal taste—color choices and styling choices. There's not much you can really sell, because the customers already have it fixed in their minds what they're looking for. They know that colors change each year, and if they had bought red, white, and blue last year, and the popular colors are pink, lavender, and green this year, they won't touch the 'outdated' models."

While you can't easily predict or control fashion, Edwards says you can use the technology to your benefit. "This SX sole, while it doesn't address the mid-sole problem, is revolutionary enough that it *can* be sold if you do it right." To push the SX out the door she would reinvent the Cabbage Patch doll phenomenon. "Create a scarcity, promoting and advertising your SX shoes as hard to find. And market them through the specialty shops that feature top quality. Avoid mass marketing or distributing them through sporting-good chains or department stores until they become popular. Remember, creating the desire first will drive customers through the door."

Once the SX caught on, Edwards might extend the soles to different levels of shoes. This technique of filtering the technology down from top-of-the-line models has become something of a tradition in other product areas. Motorcycle manufacturers, for example, have done it with direct drive shafts. Drive shafts vastly outperform drive chains, which cause vibrations and can snap at dangerous times, such as when you're zooming down the expressway. Initially drive shafts appeared on only the largest and most expensive models, with engines of 1000 cc and higher. Now drive shafts are available on some bikes in the 500-cc range.

But motorcycle drive shafts are here today, and the 8000

mile SX running-shoe sole is just a product of our imagination. Or is it? Could Edwards ever envision herself having to sell a product as perfect as the SX? "This whole scenario is not that farfetched," she admits. "I recently visited a major running-shoe manufacturer who told me that they had created a virtually indestructible sole. They also said they had no plans to bring the product to market!"

## Lessons from the Game

1. Never sit on an innovation that fulfills or creates a need. Today's innovative and competitive business environment demands that you exploit every avenue at your disposal.

2. Beware the tendency toward tunnel vision when assessing the possibilities for a new product. If you limit your gaze to what you do now, you may miss even more lucrative opportunities for the future.

3. Maintain an atmosphere where people feel free to conjure up outlandish uses for new products. Although only one out of a hundred potential uses may make real-world sense, genuine innovation only occurs in a setting that supports free thinking.

4. Avoid creating "techno-shock" by introducing a radical new technology before the public can appreciate it. Sometimes it is better to promote a breakthrough product in terms of its superior qualities rather than announcing it as a revolutionary mousetrap.

5. Know your market. Every innovation appeals more to one segment than to another. Test the product on that segment before adapting it or selling it to your entire customer universe.

CHAPTER 7

# Growing Pains and Hormone Shots:
## *Surviving Hypergrowth*

## Opening Moves

Skip and Sally Weston couldn't wait for their "baby" to utter its first words. They had uncrated their JEEVES personal robot the moment it had arrived from Robot Shack, a mail-order catalog company that offered a veritable menagerie of electronic gadgets for the home, from programmable guard dogs to purring-cat alarm clocks.

Sally claps her hands with delight. "Gee, Skip, he looks better than the picture in the catalog. Look at his cute bow tie. How do we get him to talk?"

"Easy," murmurs Skip, thumbing through a 240-page user's manual. "All you have to do is program the remote-controlled voice synthesizer. Says here he has a built-in 2000-word vocabulary."

A few hours later the Westons are sitting in their living room waiting for JEEVES to bring them the *L.A. Times* and two gently stirred martinis. When the little bubble-shaped robot glides into the living room on its "silent butler" acrylic wheels, Skip presses three buttons on the remote-control panel.

"Hi! I'm a rowboat," announces JEEVES. "Hi! I'm a rowboat. Hi! I'm a rowboat. Hi! I'm a rowboat."

"Oh, no!" exclaims Sally, "we paid $995 for a robot that thinks he's a dinghy!"

Ah, well, at least JEEVES didn't mangle the paper, and his perfect martinis are . . . well, perfect. Not until a few weeks later, when they meet neighbor Jones's robot butler, do they regret their purchase.

"Yup," boasts Carl Jones as his machine, designed to greet guests, recites the Gettysburg Address in tones that would turn Demosthenes green with envy. "You guys should've waited for this new model from the Silicon Showcase Catalog. Puts 'ol JEEVES in the shade. And he only costs $695."

The Westons excuse themselves. "C'mon, Sally," mutters Skip, "let's take 'old rowboat' for a dip in the lake."

Why didn't Sally and Skip simply call Robot Shack when "old rowboat" garbled his speech? Actually they did, but the company was wrestling with such an enormous financial crisis, it could not offer the technical support it had promised. How could the premier robot catalog company in the country get itself into such dire straits? After all, its meteoric rise had rewritten the corporate record books.

An old expression advises that nothing kills like success, and in the business world those words can ring painfully true. Every executive sets his sights on stellar growth, but uncontrolled growth can destabilize and ultimately topple even the most thriving concern. Such "hypergrowth" can also blind management to the need to keep pace with increased competition, diversify, become more efficient, lower costs, and increase profit margins, all of which can spell the difference between failure and success. Finally, like money, hypergrowth generates a need to sustain itself, creating a pressured environment quite often characterized by nearsighted or hasty decisions. When we invited our players to solve Robot Shack's hypergrowth problem, they showed us some intriguing ways to put the brakes on a company rocketing swiftly toward oblivion.

## The Game: Lost in the Mail

When Roger Hopewell's brother, Bill, came to him with a plan that would persuade a group of investors to ante up $1 million for a new direct-mail catalog venture, Roger immediately ran the numbers through his computer and manipulated them with his Kharma 3-4-5 spread sheet. "Looks like gold to me, Billy Boy. Every doctor, lawyer, and tinkerer in these here United States will want one of these robots." Since Bill Hopewell had won accolades from *Corporate Weekly* magazine as America's "Catalog King," Roger's investors eagerly kicked into the project not one, but *two* million dollars. Together Bill and Roger would buy fifty-one percent of the company with sweat equity.

Soon Robot Shack mailed its first catalog to five million well-to-do upwardly mobile young professionals who had cut their teeth on microchips and Cuisinarts. From Robot Shack these upscale consumers could order JEEVES, a talking personal valet, as well as K9KOP, a mechanical dog trained to bark at and even bite burglars; refrigerators with programmable inventory control; and a whole host of cutting-edge electronic household gadgets priced at $450 and up. As a special introductory offer, the first one hundred buyers would receive a pair of computerized Trident running shoes that announce mileage, time, and blood pressure every sixty seconds.

The whopping three percent response to the initial mailings put the scheme firmly in the black, and within three years the catalog business was generating $60 million in sales with earnings of $10 million. Robot Shack had grown overnight from a shabby basement operation to a four-building complex housing three hundred employees. As mail-order king Bill Hopewell's enterprise ballooned in sales and size, business manager Roger and the cartel of investors grew increasingly concerned about Bill's ability to manage such a sprawling organization. But whenever Roger hinted that perhaps they should bring in seasoned management to help run the show, Bill lashed out angrily. "Hey, I got us this far, didn't I? Stick with me, Roger ol' buddy, and this gold is going platinum."

Sure enough, Bill got so enmeshed in the details of Robot Shack that he failed to notice a growing contingent of competitors following in his successful footsteps with "me-too" catalogs, some offering the same items at a lower price, others offering cheaper knockoffs manufactured in Guatemala. Although customers still perceived Robot Shack as the Mercedes of the industry, the company's financials were beginning to bleed red ink. The direct-mail response rate, which had hit nearly five percent, quickly declined to two percent with clear signs of continuing to sag.

Despite the changing market, Robot Shack had built such an enormous and costly infrastructure based on the illusion of continued hypergrowth that it began choking in its own fat, with losses approaching a hefty $1 million a month. The Hopewells finally hire your consulting firm to guide them through their current mess, and a study by your staff reveals the core problem: Bill Hopewell's initial assumptions were grossly incorrect, and the market for robots simply became saturated far sooner than he had anticipated.

What advice would you give the Hopewells to keep their top-heavy organization from sinking under the weight of its own success?

## Strategies and Tactics

### *Starting the Real Game*

"The obvious business approach is to assess your resources and leap to firm ground," comments Alex Randall, founder of The Boston Computer Exchange. "But we need to do something more here, because there's a perceived problem with market saturation."

A *perceived* problem? "Right," says Randall. "These guys haven't even started to do business yet. They might have tapped the general population, but there are millions of other consumers waiting to be satisfied with a different product. There's no such thing as market saturation. There's only saturation of the imagination."

Randall would push the Hopewells to think more creatively about their products. "When you label your business, it can be no more than that label. If I say, 'I'm in the used computer business,' then I sell hardware. But if I say, 'I'm in the information business,' my perspective opens up and I can create a global enterprise that trades information about computers. That's how we expanded The Boston Computer Exchange. It's the old Whorfian hypothesis. You know, Benjamin Lee Whorf proposed that language shapes thought. Since the Eskimos have names for eight different kinds of snow, their thought patterns about snow are different from the rest of the world. It's the same here. Once 'We make robots' gets articulated, that puts a lock on people's imaginations and perceptions. These guys need to go up a level of abstraction. Instead of thinking, 'We make robots,' they should be thinking, 'We make chips that walk . . . we make mobile intelligence . . . we bring intelligence services to the user.' That opens up a whole new world of possibilities."

Randall maintains that if the Hopewells stay locked in a restrictive mind-set, they'll find themselves in the same predicament as the railroads, which should have said, "We're in the transportation business" rather than, "We're in the boxcar business." Randall thinks that "once they break out of their mental vice, they should use their technology to create new products designed for specialty niches. For example, create a line of robots that make reservations and sell plane tickets. Maybe even open a travel agency staffed by 'bots. Call it 'Bots Abroad.' Perhaps create a line of bank-teller 'bots, ticket selling/taking 'bots, or Federal Express 'bots."

The Hopewells could make smaller versions of their product, too, Randall says. "They've been working with 'bots that walk around and function as surrogate humans or animals, 'bots that are programmed with a large number of functions. There would probably be a huge market for small 'bots dedicated to performing a single intelligent function."

Randall asks us to imagine a robot that senses when you've gone to sleep. It might turn down the thermostat or switch off your stereo or might even be programmed to sense your sleep cycles and wake you when you finish dreaming so you can remember all the color and detail. Maybe it wakes you up in the morning and tells you that you're a nice person. Or fancy a coffee-maker robot that measures your caffeine intake according to the time of day. How about a robot that uses infrared beams or lasers to measure your girth and remind you about your diet, suggesting menus for the stove robot to cook? "Going in this direction might mean redefining what a 'bot is—it might be more of a sensor or black box than a thing on wheels or feet. But it doesn't matter, as long as it fills or creates a niche for a different market using the basic robot technology."

And if all these fail? "Only one thing to do," says Randall with a grin. "Start an amusement park totally staffed by 'bots. Then get into the entertainment business."

## Keeping One Step Ahead

Pamela Alreck, marketing expert and executive director of Associated Business Consultants, believes that the Hopewells face two dilemmas: Not only have their markets become saturated, but they're peddling flawed products. "If this thing doesn't even know it's a robot," she says, "how can you expect it to do its butler chores? Besides, it sounds like the company isn't providing very good customer service."

Before doing anything else, Alreck would clean up the company's technical problems. "Whatever you do, you've got to regain the public's confidence in your product. You can't afford to have a reputation for faulty products, or else everything you do will be in vain. So you'd better fix the bugs and shift a lot of people to technical support."

Assuming that you iron out the technical wrinkles, Alreck proposes several strategies. Like Randall, she would shift emphasis toward a different market. "With a saturated market, one of the first things to explore is other applications. The Hopewells might want to look at the commercial and industrial market. In the commercial areas, for example, there might be a way to use robots in fast-food chains, dentists' offices, or doctors' offices. Also look at the international market; they might be able to do well with overseas sales."

On the other hand, she would consider staying in the same market but with an altered product. "It may well be that everyone who's going to buy a robot butler or burglar chaser has already done so. But are there untapped uses within this market? For example, maybe you could develop robots to do things that people find particularly obnoxious, like changing the cat-litter box, cleaning drains, or cleaning portable outhouses after public events.

"They could also trade down to cheaper versions of the butler and the basic models, undercutting the rest of the market and riding it out until the market shakes out. This would be difficult, though, given the Hopewells' credibility problem. A cheaper model of something that doesn't work well isn't going to win new customers. They also have an inventory problem they have to solve, so they might have to wait till a later time before they can think about putting out a low-end version. More important, though, they have the image of being the premier robot company, and I'd hate to see them lose it."

According to Alreck, maintaining their image bears on the way the Hopewells address their internal problems. "They'll obviously have to do some major cutbacks in terms of overhead and inventory. But it must be done in a way that doesn't make it look like the company is falling apart."

To accomplish this trick Alreck recommends bringing on three types of people. "First," she says, "you've got to hire a cost cutter, someone who can really get those costs under control. You really want to have someone who can do it creatively and effectively." Apple did it when they brought in Alice Devries. She was so good that they used her in the *In Search of Excellence* videotape. Osborne tried to do it too, but it was obviously too late.

"Next," Alreck continues, "you need someone who's a real motivator type, like Buck Rogers at IBM. Finally you need a shrewd personnel manager who can reduce personnel costs without inducing massive layoffs. While employee overhead must come down, the Hopewells don't want to scare people that the company's on shaky ground. The press loves to pick up on companies in trouble."

One solution Alreck suggests for the personnel problem is the Hewlett-Packard approach, whereby you put as many people as you can on short work weeks, adopting long weekends and flexible hours. "The basic idea is: When they aren't doing something useful, let them go home. Maybe you could also give them each a robot to take home during their idle hours. They could do product reviews and feel like they're personally involved and doing something worthwhile. The information would certainly be useful to you in creating a better product. In any event, keep as much of your staff as possible. Later on, when you need them to work fourteen-hour days, they'll gladly do it."

What about the genius who lacked the ability to manage a mushrooming operation, old "Billy Boy"? "Get him working on new products that he can market," Alreck advises. "He's obviously got a great flair for launching direct-response ventures, and the company should use him where his talents are strongest."

Given Bill Hopewell's particular expertise, Alreck believes the company should harness his marketing creativity to as many new types of products as possible. "I think that today people value their time more than they did ten years ago," she observes, "so being able to use 800 numbers and buy things with credit cards will become an even more popular way of shopping. People are looking for things to be more convenient, which is why prepared food sales are skyrocketing. Places like Pizza Hut have even gotten into home delivery to cater to this growing trend. So I think if Bill's direct-mail expertise can be tapped into, the Hopewells are likely to succeed."

Suppose success does return. How can the company avoid making the same mistakes in the future? "They should always anticipate the fact that whenever Bill has a brainstorm, he's going to create competition. That means they've got to set an overall strategy and a pricing policy for the products they introduce, and the best way is to go according to the life cycle of the product. That means being flexible, especially if the life cycle is short. With a short life cycle they've got to keep inventory small and overhead especially low. Get temporary help, lease the facilities and equipment. Especially if they've got fad products like hula hoops. Who wants a warehouse with ten million plastic hoops when the fad dies?"

But in all likelihood, entrepreneurs like the Hopewells won't reinvent the hula hoop, start a chain of fingernail boutiques, or christen a chain of gourmet popcorn shops. Their products are more likely to have longer life cycles. "In that case," Alreck concludes, "we go back to that quality and image factor we talked about earlier. Whatever they do, they've got to make their product stand head and shoulders above the crowd. That's the most powerful ammunition anyone can have against their competitors."

## Calling in the Cavalry

"This is a double-whammy situation," observes Jonathan Pond, president of Investment Management Information, Inc. "First you have very rapid growth, which in and of itself can be a harbinger of disaster because of the strains on working capital. You have to increase inventory and receivables as your sales increase, so expenses skyrocket and you have an enormous amount of money tied up. That could bring the company down if the market changes—which is the second problem here; this company has the overhead and the inventory but no customers."

Pond would chide the Hopewells for naïveté in not anticipating the fierce competition their success would surely invite. "As soon as the word gets out that you've got a three percent response and huge gross margins, everybody from Hong Kong to the Silicon Valley will start making and marketing these things. Success breeds knockoffs."

For an example, just thumb through all the clones that the Sharper Image catalog has spawned over the past five years. Though Sharper Image still commands respect as the Mercedes of executive toys, subscribers to business magazines have recently found their mailboxes crammed full of knockoff catalogs offering the same, or similar, items. According to studies by the Direct Mail Marketing Association, more than 7000 catalogers are vying for the contents of American pocketbooks. While a typical household receives more than eighty catalogs a year, as many as seventy percent of them go straight from the mailbox to the garbage can.

But Sharper Image's wily founder, Richard Thalheimer, is attempting to overcome those statistics by opening retail stores where customers can actually test-drive the electronic gizmos and high-tech gadgets.

Could Robot Shack steal a page from Thalheimer's story? "Possibly," Pond says, "but I'm not sure how wise it is. And I don't know how well Sharper Image will fare with it, either, in the long run. Going from mail order to retail isn't necessarily a prescription for disaster, but you have to recognize that it's a different business altogether. With mail order you're not dealing directly with the public, so you don't necessarily need to be charismatic. Retail requires a different skill set, and if you don't have it, you can easily alienate and drive away your customers. Also, you need a lot of cash to set up the right environment and have inventory on hand, which of course requires a whole different management mind-set."

Given these dangers, Pond would stress several precautions. "Having set up some stores for a boutique company that we're involved with, I'd recommend that the two brothers maintain an extraordinarily high level of control over the layout and the stocking of the stores. I'd also suggest a very extensive training program for key employees, teaching them how to generate the kind of image the Hopewells need to sell their products. They might train a general manager in advance, then have him or her work with the branch stores in terms of setting up the stores and monitoring the way goods are displayed. It really comes down to setting up a tight internal control system that includes regular inventories and the daily reporting of financial information."

What if the Hopewells veto the retail approach? "Study the

competition very quickly," advises Pond. "They need to find out who's got what on the market, what is coming out, what the prices are, etc. They also need to do a study of their own costs. In all probability they're going to have to bite the bullet and get rid of some people. The quickest way to save money is to cut heads. Besides, with this kind of growth they've inevitably built up enough fat so that there's plenty of opportunity to trim. Unfortunately this is the last thing a typical entrepreneur wants to hear; there's always the possibility that some great stroke of luck might happen tomorrow."

Such deafness afflicted Capri Beachwear, Inc., a once thriving family-owned company with $20 million in sales. The problems began when Capri, at one time the largest manufacturer of swimsuits in the country, won an exclusive license to manufacture Jane Fonda's line of workout clothes. Following a sales show extravaganza at New York's Shubert Theatre, orders for the new line hit $7 million in the first week alone, and Capri saw visions of a mega-million-dollar line. Unfortunately making workout wear turned out to be more difficult than making swimwear, and the orders began to back up. At the same time retail stores ran into unexpected customer resistance to the expensive sweat suits and began returning them to Capri for credit. Despite the impending disaster, Capri continued to take orders. Nine months after the gala show at the Shubert, Capri limped into bankruptcy court with a crippling $10 million debt.

Will Robot Shack meet such an unfortunate end? "Look at it this way," Pond muses. "I can stand in front of my business class and say to my students that the two brothers have created this horrible mess, and they need to step aside so professional managers can be brought in to clean it up. Well, the fact is that there wouldn't *be* a Robot Shack in the first place if a professional manager had started the organization. It takes one set of skills to grow a business, particularly a technologically advanced one, and it takes another set of skills to continue it successfully. So I can't really fault the Hopewells. Suffice it to say that it's time to bring in some reinforcements."

## Controlling Your Ambition

"The most common problem with companies in trouble, like the one in your scenario, is that they lost sight of what business they're in," concludes Myron Blumenfeld, marketing consultant

and business professor. "That's pretty common with hypergrowth. You get so caught up in the psychology of success that
you think everything will turn to gold. This Hopewell character
thought he was in the business of selling robots through catalogs. In fact, he was selling consumer items via direct mail to a
limited audience."

According to Blumenfeld, Hopewell should redefine his business in one of three ways. First, he might decide that he's in the
direct-mail business. "If he chooses to stay in his present business," says Blumenfeld, "he'll have to improve the way he runs
the operation. It's a matter of taking what he has now and doing
it vastly better. When he was king of the market, he didn't have
to worry about being efficient. Now he does, which means he'll
have to cut overhead drastically and find the lowest price suppliers he can.

"He's also got to decide about the level of product he's going
to offer. Does he want to be on the leading edge? If so, he must
search out new products and spend a lot of time thinking about
what new applications there might be. Maybe he wants to go
mass market, like his competitors. In that case, he's got to find
a way to undersell them. But since he started off as the king of
this market, it might make the most sense for his to be the
catalog that offers breakthrough technologies. Besides, the advantage of being on the leading edge is that it's not price-sensi-
tive, and his margins will be much better."

Regardless of whether the Hopewells take the high road or
the low road, Blumenfeld recommends that Hopewell consider
starting a retail operation. "Retail can support their catalog activities and vice versa. There's a synergistic relationship. By
opening a retail outlet, he'll get new names to put on his mailing
list, names that he wouldn't have gotten before. At the same
time his lists can become more productive; whenever he does
a mailing, he should announce happenings at various stores.
Brookstone started off as a catalog and went retail, and has
opened numerous stores around the country, with plans for
additional openings in the future."

But what about the high costs associated with going retail?
"No question," Blumenfeld concedes, "it's an expensive measure, requiring a lot of capital for bricks and mortar and inventory. But if Hopewell doesn't have the capital, I think that he
could paint a convincing picture to venture capitalists and the

banks, especially since he was successful with his first company. He might have to demonstrate that he'll bring in additional management that knows the business and can handle a large company. But that's not a major stumbling block, either."

And if Hopewell decided that he wasn't interested in retailing robots? Option two: Drop the robots and look at other product lines that he might get into, advises Blumenfeld. "By starting off in robots, he can take a natural side step into high-tech. He's already got a proven mailing list—his own. Maybe it's things like portable compact disks. He could wind up with a whole product mix using his ability to do direct mail. He could also do a retail version if his more general direct-mail efforts paid off."

Perhaps the Hopewells should study L. L. Bean, which started off selling boots to hunters. L. L. Bean later expanded into clothes for the fashion-conscious, and now it offers one of the most complete lines of casual wear in the country. Lillian Vernon and Spencer Gifts evolved in a similar way, starting off with inexpensive items such as mugs and mailing labels; now both catalogs sell an extensive mix of gifts and items for all occasions.

Should Bill Hopewell decide that he doesn't want to expand his offerings in the direct-mail business, he might choose option three, in which he becomes a purveyor of robots. In that case, he simply would turn away from the glutted consumer market and look toward alternative markets, perhaps in the business world. "Look for any new applications for robots," urges Blumenfeld. "Maybe you have office-filing robots, mail-delivering robots, typing robots, or security-guard robots. Market them by mail order or go wholesale with a sales force."

A number of major corporations have built empires on the horizontal strategy. Take Monsanto, for example. Started in 1901, the company originally manufactured only saccharin. But within four years it was churning out caffeine and vanillin, and by World War I it was producing a variety of chemicals that the U.S. had previously imported from Germany and other European nations. Today, of course, Monsanto flies under the banner "Without Chemicals, Life Itself Would be Impossible." Monsanto's founders thought of themselves as being in the chemical-processing business, not the sweetening or flavor-enhancing business, a horizontal vision that enabled the company to become a major industrial force.

Regardless of whether the Hopewells pursue a horizontal or vertical course, Blumenfeld would caution them to be wary of making the same mistakes twice. "This guy has got to stop playing superman; he can't do everything. Instead he's got to surround himself with qualified people who can take a look at the business and ask, 'What does it need to grow profitably?' If it's a catalog, he needs people who can price the product, process the orders, and use overhead most efficiently. In short, he needs to have people who can make sure that the product gets distributed at the lowest cost to the greatest number of people."

To illustrate his point, Blumenfeld describes a former client who narrowly escaped disaster brought on by his own success. From a humble storefront in a depressed part of town, this company grew into a statewide chain of auto parts centers. "The guy who started it got in just at the right time. There really wasn't a lot of good competition out there. He went public in the late seventies, and at the age of twenty-six was a millionaire. That was the beginning of the end, though. He lost all rational perspective and started to change the business around, getting into all kinds of product lines that were unrelated to his main business. He then lost all his controls and started opening stores wherever he wanted, without doing any kind of analysis. Because of the rapid increase in stores, he went on a hiring spree that netted him people who didn't know what they were doing. The rest is typical supergrowth lore: inventory skyrocketed and profits slid. It was only by selling off the inventory and real estate that he saved his skin."

Blumenfeld believes that like most businesses suffering from the hypergrowth syndrome, his former client lost his head over success. "We're bred to think that success is the ultimate achievement, the end of the line," he says. "But a company is always growing, changing, and evolving in some way. And its needs will change too. If you stop catering to those needs, the business dies. Then where's your success?"

## Getting Back to Basics

Katherine August, executive vice president of First Republic Bancorp, Inc. and a former McKinsey consultant, agrees that getting the right people into Robot Shack will make all the difference in the world. "The person who started this company should become the chairman," she says. "He shouldn't be involved with the day-to-day management of the company. The company also needs to hire an experienced CEO, a very strong financial person, a savvy marketing person, and a good quality-control person."

Once these people join the team, August would chop overhead to bare minimum and put all her chips on one product. "They've got to resurrect their image as the premier company. Given their situation, it's unlikely that they could bring back their original quality in one fell swoop. So they should start with their best product and gradually revitalize the whole line once they've regained control."

According to August, quality, more than anything else, can rescue you from the adverse affects of a saturated market. "Oh, you could try to undercut everyone else," she says, "but I suspect there are a lot of people who wouldn't buy one of these robots because they're afraid the things will break down or be hard to understand. If the company could rebuild its superior product image and bring its customer service department back up to its original high level, they could probably open up whole new segments of the market. I think when you say this market is saturated, you really mean that all the people who are willing to take a risk on a new product have done so. Now the Hopewells should go after the rest of the world by offering an irresistible guarantee. Maybe they should even be willing to come to your house and pick up the little monsters if they act up."

Chrysler performed a similar maneuver after Lee Iacocca pulled it out of the grave with his government loan maneuver. In addition to offering new lines of fuel-efficient cars, Chrysler attacked its image problem head-on by astounding Detroit with the country's first 5-year/50,000-mile warranty. What better way to build public confidence than to offer customers such an unheard-of guarantee?

But even if the Hopewells aggressively attack the quality issue with an unbeatable guarantee, they must still clean up the management mess. In August's view, the financial officer should take the initiative, provided you give him the power to develop an ironclad budget. The two brothers must support him no matter how grim the cost-cutting measures. "Fixing a company's finances are really the same as fixing personal finances," she explains. "Let's say personally you're out of control and you owe much more money than you make. How do you fix it? You go back to basics, you live very simply. You figure out what your problem is, how you're going to solve it, what revenues you can bring in, and what your borrowing capacity is. It really has to be back to basics."

One venture that probably should have gone back to basics is the Osborne Computer Company, manufacturer of the first portable computer, whose sales skyrocketed from $5.8 million in 1981 (its first full year of business) to $68.8 million in 1982. In February of the following year Osborne's sales soared to 10,000 units a month, but by April its sales had plummeted to a mere 100 units a month, and by September Osborne had stopped production altogether.

What happened to Osborne? Some analysts cite the lack of financial controls. Others point to the fact that while the founders were brilliant entrepreneurs, only experienced managers could guide the company when it started to achieve record growth. Still others faulted the strategic blunder of prematurely announcing a new computer that would address the shortcomings of its earlier model. Dealers stopped ordering the earlier machine, the Osborne I, but the new computer, the Executive, was not ready for delivery, a situation that dried up Osborne's cash flow.

August thinks that situations like those at Osborne can be avoided if you have someone keeping tight control over the money. She believes that "idea-driven organizations" often fail to provide finance people with sufficient clout, in which case they might as well not be there. "This is particularly problematic with high-tech companies," she says. "They somehow believe that the finance side is not important. In reality they need a very hard-nosed business person to make sure they're not selling to a market that doesn't exist or a market that has dramatically changed. Oftentimes, the idea generators can't understand that. They may want to keep on trying to sell even if no one is buying. But that's symptomatic of an overall lack of balance in the management structure. Well-run companies, in contrast, tend also to be well-balanced in terms of finance, production, product development, and marketing."

Balanced management certainly paid off at Compaq Computer, which, like Osborne, entered the computer world with a portable PC. But while Osborne looked to Chapter Eleven for protection, Compaq began setting growth records, becoming the first company in history to hit $111 million in its first production year. Unlike Osborne, Compaq managed its growth gracefully and has since become the leading manufacturer of IBM-compatible machines.

How did Compaq survive the stress of its success? For one thing, its managers brought strong experience to bear in the key areas necessary to run the business. And one of the venture capitalists behind it, Benjamin Rosen, who became Compaq's chairman, had helped bankroll the spectacularly successful Lotus Development Corp., as well as several other impressive start-ups. Compaq also took extreme pains to monitor its dealers' credit, selling rates, and inventory levels, thereby eliminating cash-flow drains. And when the company introduced new models to compete with IBM desktop units, it did so in a way that did not jeopardize sales of its initial products.

Will the right mix of managers at Robot Shack guarantee survival of hypergrowth? "There are no guarantees in business," she responds. "Sometimes a product just doesn't sell. But if that's the case, your greatest danger is not recognizing the situation. You can't afford to believe your own press."

## Harvesting at the Right Time

"This company tried to pluck the fruit before it was ripe," observes management consultant Jim Koehlinger. "During a product's introduction and early success stages the company must reinvest its proceeds to enhance its line and develop technological changes that allow it to manufacture the product for less. During the next stage the company should take its larger profits and reinvest them in new products and, in general, should be prepared to meet competition through price reductions as the needs and enhancements of the market dictate."

People like the Hopewells call Koehlinger out of desperation. They've usually squandered their profits on overhead and internal expansion and failed to meet customers' needs. At that point Koehlinger can do little but recommend that the founders locate outside investors. But who wants to risk their money on a company in as dire straits as Robot Shack? Koehlinger answers that they must hammer together a sound plan that give people a reason to invest. That plan, he says, should have a one-two punch.

During Phase One you salvage and enhance what you have. "If the market is saturated, there's no point in reviving the company from the grave," says Koehlinger. "There has to be some reason for its continued existence. And while they shouldn't go spinning off into major product lines now, the founders should demonstrate that they can offer accessories and new functions for existing models and can supply the public with desirable goods that the competition can't offer. Maybe they could supply a line of manual and electric brooms for the housecleaning robot; perhaps they could change his programming so that he can do things like refill the toilet paper holder or clean the fish tank. That's the general idea—show that they're in some way adding value to the product."

Phase Two would involve an aggressive cost-cutting program that would keep the company afloat in the short run while it works to overcome market competition. "This would include closing its manufacturing plants and purchasing products offshore, maybe moving the plant to a less expensive part of the country. There's nothing necessarily creative in cost cutting here, but the important point is to show potential investors that you're dead serious and will do what needs to be done to breathe life into the company."

Koehlinger believes that a consultant or other outside individual would be essential for getting Robot Shack up and rolling again. "The Hopewells would have no objectivity or credibility as far as the outside world is concerned," he says. "After preparing the plan and bringing in the investors, the brothers would of course have to lose most or all of their percentage of the company and would be reduced in their management responsibilities. In general it's like taking a broom and sweeping the place clean."

Even with the new game plan in place, Koehlinger warns that Robot Shack won't enjoy the same freewheeling latitude the second time around. "The company has scars, and caution is the rule. The investors are going to get panicky if they see any spending behavior that's not part of the plan. The good news, though, is that the name can be built upon, so the company's got a fighting chance."

But even if the company does receive a cash infusion, how will that solve the problem of playing in a saturated market? "I'm not convinced there is a saturated market," says Koehlinger, "I think *hotly competitive* might be the right words. It's hard to believe that there would be more robots than people would want. Besides, I'm not sure if there even is such a thing as a saturated market. Look at the television market. Heavily penetrated? Yes. But people still keep on buying and replacing them. In most cases saturated market means, 'I can't beat the competition.' That, I believe, comes down to having higher overhead. I know I've said this several times, but the whole name of the game is, reinvest your profits and look out for tomorrow. Fat city generally won't come for three to five years. While you're waiting, set up shop in your garage and sweat it out."

## Gazing Toward the Future

"Where's the vision?" asks Craig Hickman, management consultant and coauthor of *Creating Excellence.* "This seems like a case of shortsighted vision in the sense that everyone assumes there's not an ongoing company that can be perpetuated here. The first step is to envision a reapplication of all the Hopewells' work—a new thrust, a new market, a new product, service, or some new approach that will take advantage of what they've done the first time around. If these people grew their company so rapidly, they clearly have some great skills and abilities that can be tapped."

If so, Hickman sees two choices. First, the Hopewells should consider defending their ground and dominating the market they've already carved out. "It may already be too late for them to do that unless they're able to acquire some of the companies that are building smaller, cheaper units. They've got to change this saturated market by bringing about some consolidation in the industry through acquisition, much like the airlines have done in recent months. At that point the Hopewells may be able to underprice the remaining competitors and regain their position of dominance."

The second choice involves staying ahead of the game through high-tech development. "What's the next generation of robots? What will the next generation of robots be used for? These are the kinds of questions they should be asking," says Hickman. "If what they're really good at is staying on the leading edge, they should have the vision to create the next wave in the industry."

At the same time they can't succumb to the urge simultaneously to stay on the cutting edge while developing low-end
models to scoop the competition. "They really can't cater to
both markets at the same time. The skills that they need to
dominate the high end are very different from those needed
to stabilize the low end. The strain would probably bring the
whole company down. Companies that have mixed images
about themselves tend to be in for a struggle. It will be interesting to watch Sears and Penny's as they try to maintain their
affordable family image while trying to bring in upscale customers with designer clothes and other more expensive items. I
think they have a grand scheme and vision, but they may still
face difficulties if they fail to present a coherent image to the
public."

In the Robot Shack case, given a choice between being on
the leading edge or stabilizing and defending the low end, Hickman himself would opt for the prospector/innovator mode.
"Not that there aren't problems with being in that position," he
admits. "Often it doesn't generate a lot of money, because you
generally have to stay small if you're really going to be effective.
Also, the company that develops a new product doesn't really
get the value out of that product until it starts cranking out
thousands and thousands of them every day. Still, these people
seem to be good at breakthrough products, so they should
focus their resources on their strengths. I think that to stay on
the leading edge they'll have to come out with maybe two or
three versions of whatever they develop and capitalize on the
product. But they shouldn't plan on defending the market forever. Move on in five years. By the time the competition is
flocking in and undercutting them, they'll already be making
inroads elsewhere."

To train themselves for this kind of fancy footwork the Hopewells might subcontract much of their manufacturing and create a variety of joint-venture deals around the world. "The point
is," Hickman insists, "they've got to maintain the maximum
amount of flexibility in terms of their overhead and their capital
investment. They have to be able to be lean and move fast, so
flexibility is really the vital factor in their success."

Hickman speaks from experience. He and his coauthor, Michael Silva, guided a once prosperous holding company, Bennett Enterprises in Salt Lake City, out of financial trouble and

into a highly profitable future by adhering to the principle of flexibility. Almost overnight they diversified Bennett from its vulnerable paint and glass business to one that included financial services, computer sales and services, advertising, specialty retailing, interior design, and management consulting. Eventually Bennett went from a relatively unknown regional operation to an international enterprise with joint ventures throughout the Pacific basin.

"It's funny," Hickman concludes; "even innovators like the Hopewells fear or resist change. But if we welcome or even create it, we can roll with the economic and environmental punches that business always throws our way."

## Segmenting the Organization

Michael Silva, CEO of Bennett Enterprises, Inc., now a highly successful holding company, extends Hickman's line of thinking. "Organizations have life cycles," he says, "just like people go from birth to toddler to preteen and so on. The various stages require different approaches. In this case the problem is classic: the owners of the robot company are assuming that one person is able to run the organization through all of its life cycle. This doesn't mean that every time it goes through a stage it has to get rid of its executives. But it does mean that the way they operate has to change."

According to Silva, when an organization comes out with a new product, it automatically enters the "crisis stage." It must be sales-oriented, constantly pushing for growth. During the next stage it must control that growth, an endeavor that requires totally different skills of the firm, which must shift from a freewheeling marketing organization to a more orderly manufacturing one. The two demand very different types of leadership.

Explains Silva, "The kinds of people drawn toward marketing and manufacturing are very different, and so are the types of controls that are needed. In manufacturing you use words like *power*. In marketing you use words like *empower*. In manufacturing you want to be single-minded; in marketing you want to be as diverse as possible. These are some of the basic differences, and you can see that very different personalities would be needed to run the two kinds of groups."

Silva believes history teaches us that no individual can successfully manage all the stages of organizational development. "Unfortunately," he says, "the transition often leads to friction and bitter feelings from shattered egos. Apple is a great example of this type of evolutionary problem. The kind of culture, skills, and mentality that takes it from nothing to competing against IBM is very different from that needed to maintain market share and continue to compete. Steven Jobs wasn't able to do that, and so we see the transition to Scully. Ungraceful but inevitable. It would have been far smarter for Jobs to have hired Scully independently, giving him ninety percent of a free hand and having him report on a quarterly basis. If Jobs had done this, he would have still maintained order and authority, but he would have delegated the things he couldn't do well."

Could Bill Hopewell find himself in Steven Jobs's shoes? "Yes," says Silva, "unless he immediately segments the organization. That means drawing clear-cut lines among the different groups that have different functions. Now, this goes against the grain of every CEO today; they want to integrate so that manufacturing and marketing see eye to eye. With segmentation the CEO should be a buffer or coordinator between the two groups but should still run them according to very different rules."

Although he bucks the trend toward greater integration of organizations, he understands why most executives prefer it to segmentation. Silva suggests two reasons. "First," he says, "we came out of the seventies from post-Vietnam to an 'I'm okay, you're okay, we can work it out' mentality, saying, 'Let's head out to the mountains and see eye to eye.' That's fine, except that it presumes you *want* people to see eye to eye. As I've said, that's not necessarily the best approach when you're trying to get the maximum performance out of two different organizations within a larger organization. Don't worry about fragmenting the culture. All organizations operate in an environment of complexity, and the best-managed allow for paradox and diversity rather than trying to mold everything into a lock-step uniformity. A great leader commands trust from all the factions."

Another explanation for the push toward integration, Silva says, comes from the fact that executives think it's easier. "People like to take shortcuts. And the easiest shortcut is for the CEO to run with what he knows best. If he is a sales guy, he goes with sales. That narrow vision can be very counterproductive, as in your scenario. One of the most telling lines is the

CEO's saying, 'Stick with me,' suggesting that he believes he can get through all stages of development. Since he's a marketing person, he's probably ignoring manufacturing. That's a real mistake, because there are probably significant cost savings to be had in the manufacturing end. Also, because of his marketing orientation, he probably operates under the idea, 'When in trouble, double'—increase the sales volume. This just shifts attention even further from the manufacturing problem."

Assuming the Hopewells begin resolving the manufacturing issues, in what direction would Silva take Robot Shack? "This company has the reputation for being the first with significant technology," says Silva. "Then everyone else came in and started taking away market share. Most case studies would say, 'Hunker down and beat the competition.' But that would mean exploiting their own weakness, because at present they don't have the ability to carry out good quality control, as evidenced by the problem with the talking robot. Instead I'd want them to exploit their strengths, working on new products and then getting the quality of the old ones up. The idea is to rely on their strength as innovators. Their niche is leading the competitors. But in crisis they'll probably move from their position of strength to their position of weakness."

## Lessons from the Game

1. Discard labels that crimp your creativity. When you think that your market has been saturated or growth has plateaued, revitalize your imagination, backing off from specifics and moving to a higher level of abstraction.

2. Never lose sight of your identity. If you don't know why you're in business and what made you successful, you're likely to overextend your reach.

3. Beware the "Superman Syndrome." No one can single-handedly manage all domains of a company, and those who try usually keep the company from performing to its fullest or cause it to fail outright.

4. Maintain strong financial controls. Many companies in the fast lane to success ignore the need for good financial controls.

Strong finance must go hand in hand with strong marketing and production.

5. Never double when in trouble. It's better to cut back to halves or quarters. There is no magic to cost cutting other than the simple phrase, "Get back to basics."

6. Reinvest profit. If you harvest profit too early, you might lose the seed for the future.

7. Limber your corporate muscles. Flexibility is one of the most important survival qualities. Those who can adapt to changing market and economic conditions will survive into the next century; those who can't will become tomorrow's dinosaurs.

CHAPTER 8

# The Platinum Lawsuit:
## *Recovering from a Product Liability Crisis*

## Opening Moves

The two lovers passionately embrace, sinking deeper into the plush green pillows. "I love you," she whispers. He takes her lovely head in his hands. "And I love you. I love your hair, your nose, your lips, your eyes ... your *eyes*!" Recoiling as if strung by a wasp, he leaps from the couch.

"Cut!" screams the director. "Jackson, you've ruined this scene. At this rate we're gonna be here all day."

"But Linda's *eyes,* they're weird!"

While the astonished film crew looks on, the young actress bolts for her dressing room, where she peers in the mirror and shrieks: Linda McGuire, queen of daytime television, with her lush auburn hair, cute upturned nose, sensuous pouting lips, and fiery green eyes. No, make that one purple and one orange eye.

The following day Linda's lawyers file a $50-million suit against MaxLite Optical, manufacturers of Ultra Extended (UX) Wear contact lenses, claiming that the actress's new pair of UXs have discolored her irises and ruined her career.

ACTRESS DISFIGURED BY CONTACT LENSES, shouts the headline in *Variety,* and MaxLite suddenly finds itself avalanched by lawsuits and a raging fury of bad press.

MaxLite's executives must now confront one of the most dreaded issues in the business world: product liability. Defective and dangerous products can turn a thriving company into a mere statistic in the annals of bankruptcy, as demonstrated by Johns Mansville, which collapsed under the weight of multimillion-dollar lawsuits over its asbestos products, and by the folding of Bon Vivant, whose botulism-contaminated soups killed twenty-three people. Even when a company can survive the financial damage, a tarnished image can erode consumer confidence and sales.

What measures could MaxLite take to avoid being branded as a menace to society? Our panelists, who played the role of MaxLite's CEO, gave us an interesting blend of whimsical and pragmatic solutions.

## The Game: Here's Lookin' at You, Kid

In recent days the boardroom of MaxLite Optical has taken on the big-tent atmosphere of the Ringling Brothers and Barnum & Bailey Circus, with the controller juggling figures in his IBM AT, the marketing vice president looking as though he's just swallowed a sword, and the harried president watching the medical staff dance like clowns with their pants on fire. Along one wall sit cages of chickens, rabbits, cats, and dogs—some with purple and orange eyes.

As MaxLite's CEO, you have helped write one of the greatest success stories in business history, pushing sales from $20 million to $200 million in less than two years on the strength of MaxLite's revolutionary new product, Ultra Extended (UX) contact lenses, which can be worn indefinitely, provided the user administers a special eye drop once a day. Priced below conventional lenses, UX has captured forty percent of the market, with more market share expected to be won once MaxLite overcomes customer loyalty to other brands and convinces a few recalcitrant ophthalmologists to accept the new product.

One of the holdouts has been the renowned eye researcher Dr. David Arkle, who began noting a strange discoloration in the eyes of his lab animals during his own tests of UX. Arkle, who could not explain the effect, duly published a cautionary article in the *Journal of the American Medical Association.* Within months the news of the first human eye discoloration arrived in the form of the story in *Variety*, bemoaning the fact that daytime television star Linda McGuire's comically mismatched eyes could shatter her career.

MaxLite's switchboard lit up like a Christmas tree with calls from worried UX users; TV and newspaper reporters accosted MaxLite executives in the parking lot; lawsuits began piling up, including several from prominent public figures; and MaxLite's formerly reeling competitors launched vicious attacks on the faulty lenses.

Initially MaxLite's medical staff was baffled by the discoloration phenomenon. They had tested UX on animals and human volunteers for more than 200,000 hours before approving the release of the product. No discoloration or other side effects had ever occurred. After persuading Dr. Arkle to give your medical staff his data, and after scrutinizing the medical histories and daily habits of the people who have suffered discoloration, you eventually identify the culprit, which turns out not to be UX, but the eye drops supplied with the lenses.

Normally the eye drops reacted with natural tears to form a compound that kept the lenses soft and clean, but for reasons not yet clearly understood, some people who took more than the Recommended Daily Allowance of vitamin A along with the drops could suffer iris discoloration. Arkle's animals, it turned out, suffered discoloration because a lab assistant had accidentally mixed a vitamin A preparation in with their feed. Fortunately for the human users, discontinuation of either the vitamin A or the special drops would result in a return to normal eye coloration within four to six weeks.

Despite your relief over proof that UX is, after all, everything it promised to be, the circus continues. Your own medical staff worries about introducing your next product, a lens that will speed the natural processes whereby aging frequently corrects nearsightedness; the press that was so eager to break the discoloration story now seems bored by your exoneration. And previously satisfied customers are still returning carloads of lenses under your "lifetime guarantee." Can you somehow create order out of this chaos?

## Strategies and Tactics

### *Switching from High Octane to Regular*

Chemist Sanford Schwartzman believes that although MaxLite must honor refund requests, it must also continue to sell its UX lens. "There's nothing wrong with the lens," says Schwartzman, "it's the super drops that you want to pull off the shelf. Why bankrupt yourself over a product that works perfectly well? Temporarily issue some kind of regular drops that use an already approved mixture of ingredients. Then tell people to take the lens out every two days or two weeks or whatever period of time is safe with the regular formula."

To minimize the inconvenience and to maintain brand loyalty, Schwartzman suggests that Maxlite give a free six-month or year's supply of the regular drops to all UX lens owners. To receive their complimentary supply, users merely need to send the company a photocopy of the purchase receipt.

Such voluntary product actions not only avert potentially disastrous lawsuits, they win the company vital public trust. Consider a voluntary recall undertaken by Corning Glass Works in 1976 after it discovered that the handles on one of its coffee percolators could fall off. Corning made an all-out effort to alert owners to the defective product, urging them to swap their percolators for free replacements. In all, the commendable maneuver cost the company an estimated $17 million, but it bought trust from an ever-wary consuming public.

MaxLite, too, could recover far more than the cost of a similar action. Schwartzman maintains that even after shifting to the regular drops, the company would not suffer irreparable financial losses. "The UX lenses are already priced below the competition. So they should continue to sell, especially with the free solution and the fact that at worst they're equal to, possibly even better than, conventional lenses. All you will lose is the claim for the ultra-long wearability. In the meantime you've bought goodwill and at least a year to overcome the problem of vitamin A incompatibility. Ideally you will develop a long-life eye solution that is not vitamin-A-sensitive. And when you do release it, you'll have a comprehensive PR and advertising campaign to herald the new development. Again you'll offer money-back guarantees to show people that you stand behind your product."

Beyond the immediate crisis, Schwartzman would look for ways to turn adversity into prosperity. "There are two ways to look at it," he says. "One is, 'We have a defective product that has a side effect we don't want.' The flip side of the coin is, 'We now have the ability to change eye color. If we can stabilize the color mismatch, we can offer all kinds of color-coordinated lenses. We might even go into color-coordinated accessories, earrings, bracelets, barrettes, etc.' "

Schwartzman's key concept involves making a fashion statement out of a potential problem. You might even increase the market share to include people who don't actually need corrective lenses but desire the cosmetic benefits.

Schwartzman also believes that the problem with the vitamin A drops might hold exciting possibilities for MaxLite. "The discovery of the discoloration could reveal all kinds of vitamin-A sensitivities and cross-reactivities that we didn't know about before. Whatever solution MaxLite finds to the problem might have general applicability in the pharmaceutical world. Who knows? MaxLite might even find this an opportunity to enter a very lucrative new business."

## Taking the Heat

Marketing consultant and professor Mike Blumenfeld believes that MaxLite can reap opportunities from the situation, provided it restores public confidence. "Your first order of business is to completely acknowledge the fact that your product has a problem," Blumenfeld says. "And even though the effects are only temporary, some people are just going to feel uncomfortable about the lenses. Don't fight them. Give them a swift refund."

Indeed, don't fight them. While the economic fate of a company grappling with a major product-liability problem will depend on the outcome of complex legal wrangling, part of the battle will be fought on the front pages of the nation's newspapers. One would think that in this post—Watergate era no company would attempt to resolve a product-liability dilemma by stonewalling or denying any wrongdoing. But it still happens, and those who duck responsibility usually pay a heavy price. For example, when the French company Kleber refused to recall potentially defective tires, it lost an estimated $6 million in sales from consumer boycotts. In the U.S., Firestone Tire and Rubber invoked sharp criticism for denying that its tires caused any fatal accidents despite a recall that cost it $180 million dollars. And A. H. Robins earned the scorn of consumer groups and the media as it steadfastly denied that its Dalkon Shield had caused infections and/or infertility.

Clearly, if MaxLite stonewalls the situation, it will embark on a road leading to disaster. That's why Blumenfeld insists that the company must go beyond what most people would consider adequate and honorable steps. "As an added show of good faith, they should keep track of all returned lenses and hold them in storage for the people who sent them in. You're banking on the fact that this is a short-term problem that will be corrected soon," he says. "By storing the lenses for people, you can offer them back at a discount price and save them the time and costs of getting fitted. I think this would also help build public confidence. In effect, you're saying, 'I'm so sure that this is a harmless situation and that you'll want your lenses back that I'm going to the expense and trouble of warehousing and keeping track of them.' Of course, you'd make a big deal of that to the media and in the literature you send to registered customers."

Blumenfeld believes that the fears resulting from the UX lens problem stem from two sources. First, the discoloration came as a total surprise. With no hints of a problem or an impending crisis, the situation just burst into the news. More importantly, people are very sensitive about their eyes, and the idea of blindness scares them out of their wits.

"Taken together," Blumenfeld concludes, "these two factors create the potential for hysteria; people are more likely to just throw the lenses into an envelope and say, 'I'm not taking any risks with these things, I want my money back!' That's why MaxLite has got to be completely aboveboard. Invite the press in to show them what the research has revealed."

Such honesty and openness about product flaws has won the day time and again. Look at how well Johnson & Johnson recovered from the Tylenol tragedy. Immediately after the Tylenol poisonings in Chicago, the leaders of Johnson & Johnson convened emergency strategy sessions twice a day, opening the company's doors to the press. Though J&J had fallen innocent victim to a madman's whim, it realized that the massive loss of consumer confidence could permanently mar its name. Its prompt national recall of Tylenol cost the company $100 million, but contrary to the predications of doomsayers, within a month and a half Tylenol made its way back to the shelves, this time in protective wrapping, ushered in with a strong PR and advertising campaign followed by positive media coverage. Within a year Tylenol had regained a substantial portion of its market share.

In a similar move, Hygrade Food Products addressed with equal deftness the charge that razor blades and other foreign objects contaminated its Ball Park Franks. Coming on the heels of the Tylenol incident, the Ball Park Franks adulteration attracted widespread attention that could have destroyed the company. But Hygrade recalled tons of hot dogs and ordered plant employees to work overtime inspecting their product with metal detectors. No blades or other objects came to light, and a police investigation later exposed all claims as false. When the dust settled, the media, which Hygrade had kept closely informed with a well-coordinated PR effort, began writing sympathetic stories about the company.

MaxLite could reap the same positive press and media attention and public trust if it stands up and takes the heat. To bolster the company's claims, Blumenfeld would offer incontrovertible proof that the discoloration causes no harm and will soon disappear. "Get the CEO and his wife to gulp down vitamin A and use the drops, then show their 'recovery' on television over the three weeks or whatever it takes for the discoloration to go away. In fact, get all of upper management to discolor their eyes and recover. Show how the company goes about functioning normally while its employees' eyes are discolored and as they return to normal. An adman could come up with some wonderful headlines and copy."

After such measures have soothed public hysteria and restored a modicum of confidence, Blumenfeld would look for a silver lining in this seemingly black cloud. "I would think that MaxLite has stumbled onto something very positive and would begin applications for this brand-new technology. I'd announce that we are working on ways to control the color-changing process—not *dis*coloration, mind you—and get just the colors we want, and to regulate how long the effects last. We'd say our goal would be to get the color change down from weeks to days, hours, or even minutes. Think of how important this could be for fashion, mood, or matching a mate."

But since it could take years to field an actual product and get FDA sanction, what do you do in the meantime? Blumenfeld claims that simply announcing that you're working on this remarkable technology will create immediate psychological benefits. "The idea is to shift people from a crisis mode to a mode of awe and wonderment. The message is that there can be a positive element to surprises like this. You might even remind them of all kinds of serendipitous discoveries that have benefited us, such as penicillin. But there's another way to take advantage of the situation while you're developing new products: Get your marketing people to approach rock stars like Madonna or Boy George. I bet they'd love to walk around with one purple and one orange eye."

## Foraging Safely in the Marketplace

"I don't see this thing as a disaster for MaxLite," says Philip Kemp, president of J. E. Morgan Knitting Mills, "because they have a superior product. It's fundamentally better than the competitors', so they should not be blown out of the water by a liability problem. There's every reason to fight this one through."

Kemp, like the other players in this chapter, believes that total honesty forms the only policy in such cases. He sees the MaxLite situation as not just a PR crisis, but as a practical problem of making eye drops that don't react with vitamin A and proving to everyone's satisfaction that you have eliminated the side effects.

"Go to Linda McGuire and convince her to drop the suit and take some stock in the company," says Kemp. "Offer her the chance to make millions by a stock issue. Since she was the first to bring it to the public's attention, she'd be the ideal spokesperson for saying, 'The problem is solved!' "

Kemp acknowledges that MaxLite must somehow turn the tide while developing the new eye drops. "Perhaps you could make different-colored eyes chic. Maybe sell tinted lenses and start a fad. Make a big deal out of King Alfred the Great, who drove the Danes out of Britain in the ninth century. Legend has it that when he was finally caught by the enemy, it was because he had two different-colored eyes. You could turn him into kind of a cult hero and maybe find some other interesting historical figures who also had two different-colored eyes and start fads around them too."

Fun and fads aside, even after correcting a product flaw, a company like MaxLite must exercise extreme care. Citing the recent case in which Gerber sued the federal government for prematurely causing stores to pull its product from the shelves, he comments that many companies still suffer an unfair rap. "I think there comes a point where the truth has to come out and you say, 'There's nothing wrong with our product.' Whether or not you can get away with that obviously depends on whether there *was* a real problem. And if you do have a problem, you have a moral, ethical, and legal obligation to the public to fix it. In the case of Gerber, the reports of glass in the product were false, and the company could have suffered horribly for it. I empathize, because I used to sell soap, and one of the great problems with soap is that you can get pieces of metal dropping off machinery into the bars, or worse, sabotage. But people used to send us soap bars in which there would be a quarter inch of a nail or a pin sticking out and they'd say, 'Look what's happened—we found this in our soap.' After a while you get tired of being a victim to such insanity."

While Kemp believes MaxLite should stand its ground after fixing its product, he chides companies that fail to anticipate product-liability problems. "It's a matter of not recognizing what is critical to the company's life at the time," he says. "Let's say you invent chocolate-chip cookies and you start off in your kitchen and build a booming business. If someone said, 'Justify your existence,' you could probably do it in thirty seconds: 'I invented chocolate-chip cookies and they're the best in the world,' or something like that. When you have a product-liability crisis, though, you don't have to justify your product, you justify your credibility, which is not only more difficult, but it becomes the key issue in the company's life. If you take a secretive approach and keep focusing on your product, then you're likely to come unstuck."

Another problem with product-liability cases arises from the fact that few companies, especially large ones, receive a single summons to court. "Big complex companies are always being challenged," says Kemp. "How many lawsuits does GM have pending against it at any one time? Probably many. One of those could be critical to their long-term survival, while the others aren't. If people get lax, they may not distinguish the trivial ones from the critical one and get taken down the drain."

Kemp therefore suggests that product manufacturers operate in an anticipatory mode. "It's impossible to predict everything that can happen to your product. You can test for certain things, but it is impossible to predict every way that a product might get you involved in a liability suit. And what makes things more difficult is that the rules are constantly changing. Life-styles are changing all the time, and people's perceptions of what you're responsible for, and what they're responsible for, change too. It used to be that parents were expected to keep children away from drugs and hazardous substances. Now manufacturers are expected to provide childproof caps. That change is for the good, but you have to be aware of shifts in the mood of the country and the people who make the laws. I think that above having a product that you feel is safe, your only protection is to be as aware as possible of trends and events that might cast ill winds toward you."

How, precisely, can manufacturers do this? Answers Kemp, "It's what I call 'peck and search.' Have you ever watched a bird eating in the wild? It takes a peck, and then it looks around and sees if anything will jump on its back. That's the same with your product. You have to keep looking to see what's happening to your competitors who make similar products. Are they being stalked? If so, eventually you will be too."

Kemp says that the current controversy over drug capsules demonstrates the value of a peck-and-search view of the world. "The problem started with Tylenol," he observes, "but, of course, it affects all drug manufacturers. At the first instance, all of them should have realized that the end of the capsule was near. Only Johnson & Johnson gave up and went into caplets. Then Anacin and Excedrin got hit. They'll have little choice but to go into caplets too."

Why the lag? "In part it's inertia," Kemp answers. "You've got all this equipment set up to do capsules. What will you do with it? There are lots of rational reasons why they shouldn't make the switch, such as the fact that it will wreak havoc with the balance sheet. But in this day and age when the stakes are so high, I can't imagine anyone who can afford to operate with such a short-term view of the world. Can you?"

## Switching Into Nonlinear Thinking

Michael Silva, CEO of Bennett Enterprises, believes that in the end, long-range vision is the only guarantee of success in today's competitive and often hostile business environment. "Look at Delta Airlines," he says. "They were down in the first five years of the eighties, and their earnings put them in the middle to the end of the pack. But they've come to the top of the pack. The reason is that they refused to lay off employees or cut costs like other airlines during downturns. Delta looks terrible during those downturns, but over the long run, committed employees will give them an edge to be a winning company."

Silva insists that MaxLite should adopt a similar long-range perspective, one that comes from shifting into a "nonlinear mode of thinking." According to Silva, regular or linear thinking limits your vision. "With linear thinking, you can look one point back and one point ahead and see where you've been and where you're going. It's based on precedence. In contrast, non-linear thinking makes radical departures into the unknown, which often makes it look wild or irrational."

Nonlinear thinking can lead you to unexpected and often rewarding insights, Silva himself being a case in point. When the thirty-three-year-old Silva took the helm of the faltering Bennett Enterprises, everyone in Salt Lake City expected the brash young executive to act precipitously. Sensing those expectations, Silva went to Hawaii for a month and did the unexpected: nothing. Then, when he returned after a long and relaxing vacation, he quickly short-circuited local uneasiness about Bennett's financial position by making another surprise move: He bought a bank.

Silva suggests taking similarly surprising action with soap-opera actress Linda McGuire. "I'd never have let the actress sue me," Silva says. "If she makes $400,000 a year, once her eyes returned to normal I'd pay her $1 million to promote the product. Sure, your settlement, if you had to make one, would be less than a million. The linear approach would dictate fighting the suit and paying the consequences. A nonlinear approach says that there's no price tag on what you're buying in the actress—any amount of money will be paid back over the long haul in terms of goodwill and rebuilt public confidence."

Silva analyzes the Johnson & Johnson case from a fresh perspective. "The crisis simultaneously presented a danger and an opportunity. They have this sabotage problem, and it costs them their capsule business. Linear thinkers at the time would ask: 'How can we save our capsule business?' as their minds traveled the course from liability to lawsuit to loss of revenues. A nonlinear thinker would jump ahead to the broader issue of forecasting regulations for developing safe drugs, which is exactly what Johnson & Johnson did. Now, who's ahead with caplets? Johnson & Johnson. As a result, they were able to take a crisis and turn it into a significant opportunity, gaining a tremendous lead in developing and selling caplets."

Silva also finds the J&J case instructive in that the company realized that its strength was what's inside the capsules, not the capsules themselves. As a result of this understanding, they spent a lot of money revamping the mode of delivery. Likewise, MaxLite's strength is its contact lenses—not the moistening drops. "This is important for MaxLite's management to remember," Silva says, "because there would be a tremendous temptation for linear thinkers to say, 'Let's cut our losses and get out of this business!' But that's really irrational; why toss out their strength? A nonlinear thinker would say, 'Take a short-term beating and spend the money on developing an alternative mode of enabling long-term wear.' I think this would have the added benefit of giving MaxLite an important opportunity to tell the public that they not only have a good product, but that they have the ability to solve problems."

According to Silva, the history of business successes and failures is directly correlated to the ability or inability of people to think in nonlinear terms. He cites NCR, once the giant of cash registers, as a case in point. "What killed NCR and the cash-register industry is that people refused to make the jump from mechanical to electronic tabulations. There was no precedence for it. The linear jump from mechanical tabulations would have been more refined mechanics."

At the other extreme, Silva goes on to praise IBM for making a nonlinear jump several years ago when it decided that it was not just in the computer business. Deciding that it was in the communications business, it went out and bought MCI and

Rolm. "Those weren't linear decisions," observes Silva. "The linear view would have been to make a bigger or faster computer. The same with the railroad industry—if they had made a nonlinear jump, they'd have wound up owning all airlines and auto companies today."

Nonlinear thinking doesn't just take place in the business world; it occurs in many other domains of human activity, such as politics and war. Silva uses General Douglas MacArthur's "island hopping" approach to illustrate his point. "After the Japanese had taken over more than ninety-nine percent of the Pacific islands, the U.S. high command decided to take the islands one at a time. You can't get much more linear than that! But MacArthur opted for taking one out of every ten or twelve, and starving the ones in between. By determining the strategically important islands and cutting off supplies to those in between, MacArthur was able to win all the islands with an expenditure of much less energy and fewer casualties to his own forces."

Silva believes that generalists, not specialists, are best at managing a crisis. "That's why most CEO's are lousy crisis managers, and why they need consultants to help them out of messes. A person who has been in an industry for thirty years tends not to focus on approaches outside the proven way. In effect, he's become a specialist. For nonlinear thinkers, general preparation is more important than the planning. In a linear approach, a limited number of options will be available. But in a nonlinear approach, there are infinite options, and it takes a generalist to appreciate them and bring them into play."

By Silva's definition, planners try to see into the future and then apply a variable to control it before it happens, while preparers simply arm themselves to deal with whatever the future throws their way. "It's like Noah's Ark," he says. "Noah had no idea of when the flood was coming, but he was ready to deal with it."

Companies like MaxLite must operate from a basis of preparedness, Silva maintains, or else they'll likely be washed over by the times. "Our litigious culture has radically changed industry over the past ten years," Silva concludes. "As a result, a lot of staid industries will have to become freewheeling, flexible, and nonlinear. This may seem overly dramatic, but what we're going to be seeing is the death of the linear manager in an era so fraught with change."

## *Letting It All Hang Out*

Media consultant Marc Bender offers a nuts-and-bolts approach to the scenario, basing it on a key point that all of the players have touched upon: the truth. "In many PR crises you've got to worry abut what *not* to expose. In this case it appears there's nothing to hide; the side effects of the product are both harmless and reversible. So the truth will be your biggest ally."

According to Bender, MaxLite's recovery campaign should include eight overlapping steps that, when orchestrated properly, will minimize losses and rehabilitate MaxLite's image as an industry leader. Step one entails tackling the goodwill issue. "Goodwill is so basic to the survival of any company that MaxLite must protect it at all costs," Bender insists. "It's a form of corporate life insurance. The company should immediately offer at least full credit for returns of the lenses and eye drops. 'Double your money back' would be twice as good. And invite people to take advantage of the refund offer through 'no-nonsense' TV, radio, and newspaper ads. If there are additional guarantees that make sense, like free opthalmological testing or consultations and pledges to reimburse consumers for any product-related costs and inconveniences—carfare, baby-sitters, etc.—they should be offered as well. The point is, MaxLite must go far beyond the call of duty to demonstrate that it assumes appropriate responsibility for its products."

Bender also suggests two other goodwill-generating tactics: First, create a research grant to search for ways to develop a system that can address any "truly serious mishaps" of this kind in the future, a gesture that "coincidentally" confirms the "lucky" nature of this innocuous problem. Second, endow a fellowship for medical journalists to help them hone their "investigative reporting skills, so well demonstrated in their coverage of the MaxLite affair," to keep the public informed of potential health hazards of all sorts. "They might even name the grant or the fellowship after the afflicted actress," says Bender with a grin. "But that obviously depends on the outcome of her lawsuit and the innate wisdom of her agent."

Step two in Bender's overall scheme involves conquering consumer fear of the product, which he thinks will do more than anything else to insure future marketing success. "This is where MaxLite really has to spend its money. And fast. This incident can set off rampant, irrational, inconsolable, irreversible panic that can brand the company as a 'corporate leper,' so speed is critical. Any delayed reaction on MaxLite's part will encourage suspicions that will quickly erode people's confidence in the company."

How would Bender put people's minds at ease? "Well, definitely set up an 800 hot line—that's pretty basic. They've also got to develop a multimedia campaign quickly, which can be combined with the goodwill messages already discussed, to direct inquiries about the lenses and MaxLite's reassurances to a company-operated information center. They should blanket TV and radio networks, as well as major daily newspapers. And don't forget the professional journals; you want to convince the eye doctors of America that this is a false alarm and arm them with all information that will enable them to direct their patients to the proper MaxLite channels. Again, the company's got nothing to hide, so the worst thing the company could do is scurry for cover."

Bender also recommends immediately soliciting objective professional advice from physicians about the safety of the product, and using their testimonials in the media campaign. These "objective voices" not directly associated with the company will reinforce the perception that MaxLite has hidden no skeletons in the corporate closet. "One option for this 'medical media' might be time-lapse photography to document how the effects reverse themselves. You've got medical truth on your side, so let it all hang out."

The preceding actions tie into step three, which is to focus on public safety as a generic social concern. According to Bender, MaxLite must appear to be a responsible "corporate citizen" by withdrawing and/or recalling the product from all vendors, pending some kind of blue-ribbon review. "MaxLite doesn't want anybody but itself to suffer a loss because of this problem. They also must demonstrate that they're confident the problem will not be ongoing, or one that might spur others. This is critical, because any perceived lack of confidence on MaxLite's part will infect the public's confidence. What could be more assuring than the company's willingness to take every measure, even one that could label its product 'unsafe' and thereby threaten its very existence? Of course, it's not much of a gamble, because MaxLite knows that a full review will give them a clean bill of health. But they score big points for appearing to put concerns for public safety above their own profits and future."

Step four of the plan resolves the legal hassles by not only settling existing ones but preempting future ones. "MaxLite should not reinvent the wheel here. They aren't the first and won't be the last to have a product-liability problem. MaxLite's CEO should not hesitate to turn to colleagues for help. He ought to hop on the phone and seek advice from his counterparts at other companies that have been through this kind of thing. Maybe Johnson & Johnson would lend him its 'liability SWAT team.' In any case, I think outside, noncompeting companies would be flattered by the request for advice and would let MaxLite tap their legal and PR folks for know-how and tips."

Step five, addressing the stockholders and the investment community, entails boosting confidence in MaxLite as a company. Says Bender, "While you don't want to be a social activist, you also don't want to appear defensive to Wall Street—that's like bleeding in front of a shark. It will only attract attack."

How do you restore investor confidence? "Form a credible advisory committee that can look into the problem. MaxLite should allow government and consumer watchdogs to name people to the committee, and it should promise a thorough, warts-and-all report as soon as possible. I wouldn't have a six-month delay between the start of research and the airing of findings. That will destroy MaxLite's credibility and unnecessarily prolong corporate agony, paralysis, and losses."

Bender believes that MaxLite must also carefully determine the attitudes of people not directly affected by the problem and that the firm probably has the wherewithal to do it. Any company MaxLite's size could conduct a telephone survey overnight, he suggests, and while the results might not be as precise as sophisticated long-range testing, they would provide a useful benchmark. Besides, they will help the company assess its potential revenue loss, which leads us to step six.

"Obviously there's going to be revenue losses from product returns, an unexpected emergency media blitz, and a plunge in sales," Bender concludes. "And while there's nothing MaxLite can do to prevent the hemorrhaging, top management has to minimize the effect on the company. Now's the time to pull out the 'Product Liability Contingency File' that MaxLite's prescient corporate attorneys and accountants prepared months ago. Otherwise, one way to get an idea of what this thing will cost is to have someone thoroughly research other product-liability cases. Look for examples of safe products that had inadvertent side effects, with both favorable and unfavorable outcomes. There probably won't be a one-to-one comparison, but MaxLite should look for parallels that will suggest what kind of ride the company is in for. This research is critical, because it will help determine how everything else in the overall campaign is structured."

While all the preceding steps focus on the public and the outside world, step seven looks inward, at maintaining internal corporate confidence. "MaxLite's management must realize how devastating a crisis like this can be on employees," says Bender. "They must take all measures necessary to make their employees feel as informed as possible. And while they're offering explanations and assurances, they might consider 'leaking' internal 'morale-boosting and public-spirited crisis-management discussions' to the press. That's a great way of indirectly demonstrating MaxLite's concern for the public.

"Just remember there's a fine line between being confident as a corporate entity and being smug. MaxLite's PR blitz can say how confident they are in their product, but nothing will demonstrate that confidence like putting their corporate future on the line. MaxLite must make it clear it's willing to back its 'reversibility' claim and must do so in impressive ways. Maybe offer $50 million to anyone whose eyes are permanently changed by the UX drops. Or try to feature the soap-opera actress in its ads. They could argue, 'We're so confident this is a temporary problem, in six weeks you can see for yourselves, when we put her on the air. We'll show close-ups of her eyes.' "

The eighth and final step involves girding against government action. The last thing MaxLite wants to do is wait until the FDA knocks on its front door, Bender says. Instead it should preempt government action by collaborating with government officials and stealing their thunder. "Look at Johnson & Johnson. Rather than waiting until the government mandated a single- or double-safety-seal system, J&J voluntarily developed a triple-seal system on its own and lost millions throwing out products already on the shelves. That was smart for two reasons. First, it carried enormous weight with the public. Second, J&J demonstrated the old maxim that 'the best defense is a good offense.' It's even wise to assert yourself when you have little to assert, rather than react to other people. A reactive position is always less favorable—it leaves the impression that you're defensive, somehow guilty."

At the minimum, Bender says, MaxLite should invite the government to scrutinize the product and independently corroborate the company's findings. "There are all kinds of creative things MaxLite can do, too, such as proposing and financing the emergency information system I mentioned that would facilitate government-industry efforts to alert the public about future liability problems."

Once you've put out the basic brushfires, Bender would also encourage you to find ways of turning the company's liabilities into assets. To do this, he suggests looking into hidden benefits. "There's got to be all kinds of intriguing medical applications here. Maybe MaxLite's stumbled onto a new way to monitor vitamin intake and levels. If so, talk about them in articles and on the radio. Make the public feel as if MaxLite's on the cutting edge of a positive medical breakthrough. At the very least this will augment your efforts at restoring confidence within and without. It may even inspire a new, highly profitable R&D agenda."

## Priming the Company Spokesman

Adding to Marc Bender's eight-step media strategy, David Simon, president of Simon/McGarry Public Relations, Inc., the nation's first PR firm devoted exclusively to high tech, tells us how the company should deal with the press.

Simon stresses that while a basic purpose of public relations is to communicate information and shape perceptions, even the best PR can't make up for irresponsible or inept management decisions. The company has to do what's in the best interests of the various publics they deal with, including customers and prospects, employees and shareholders.

To handle the communications aspect of the crisis, MaxLite should begin by restricting the employees who interact with the media and designate a list of authorized spokespeople. The company's top PR executive should play a role in determining when and how to release certain information but does not necessarily need to serve as the only spokesperson. Perhaps the company's CEO, top scientists, or the chief of marketing would fit the bill, depending on each one's ability to deal gracefully with probing reporters. But regardless of which people get the job, Simon urges that they observe six basic rules.

"One wrong statement or response can put the company in a very bad light," says Simon. "For example, reporters very often ask difficult, negative-sounding questions. An executive who's not used to dealing with a reporter will very often repeat the question. Unfortunately, when the news is aired or printed, the negative aspect may be the focus. A wrong answer to 'Why are your lenses causing eye problems?' would start, 'Our lenses are causing eye problems because . . .' A better answer might start, 'The real issue is what our company is doing to address the unusual situation,' and continue by describing the steps being taken. That way, even if the statement is taken out of context, it won't cause a negative image. So rule number one is: Don't repeat the question."

Simon's second rule dictates that you never say, "No comment." That immediately suggests to reporters that you're hiding something, and any suspicions of a cover-up will only lead to more aggressive questioning. "Sometimes people will say, 'No comment' because they get stumped by a question. But it's better to answer a slightly different question than to say, 'No comment.' You should never feel you have to answer the question as is. That's rule number three. For example, the question might be put, 'Have you solved the problem yet?' He could answer by noting that the researchers are making progress (if that's accurate) and saying, "As soon as we've confirmed a fix, we'll announce it right away." That's why you have to be very careful about putting scientists in front of a camera. Their explanations can be overly convoluted and difficult to follow in their attempt to be precise."

Rule number four: Keep it brief. "When you're on the TV cameras, you'll only be on for twenty to forty seconds, even though the filming might have lasted two to three minutes," Simon explains. "Since you don't have much time, confine your answer to about the length of time you'll likely be on the air. If you have a long-winded answer, what you're saying might get taken out of context. So be concise and make sure everything you say is either self-explanatory or won't lead to a confusing or negative image if it had to stand on its own."

A given reporter's style will strongly influence the tone and direction of the interview, and Simon's fifth rule involves fully preparing the spokesperson not only on technical background issues but on the nuances of the publication or station that will be running or airing the piece. "The more you know about the reporter and the publication or station he works for, the better prepared you'll be. If *Fortune* magazine is coming in to do a question-and-answer session, it's important to have someone grill the spokesman in *Fortune* style. This will help him focus on what kind of information *he* wants to communicate. Remember rule three: You don't have to answer the question as it is asked."

Simon's last rule: Never speak "off the record." According to Simon, that phrase never gains you anything, and you often wind up regretting it. "Some publications have a rule that anything they are told is usable, no matter what restrictions have been attempted; they simply don't honor 'off the record.' There's also the danger that the 'off-the-record' material isn't marked sufficiently well in the reporter's notes, and he uses the information inadvertently. The safest route is simply not to say anything that you wouldn't want to see in print."

Is the ability to remember these rules the chief criterion for becoming the company spokesperson? Answers Simon, "Feeling comfortable with the points I just discussed is very important. But they're also looking for someone who will keep in mind that specific information must be conveyed to project the desired image. That person also has to be able to put up with hostile reporters—temper can be a real problem, and again, one outburst can undermine their whole effort."

When an article appears or the segment is aired, Simon counsels, "Read or hear it as an outsider would. A lot of executives see a minor point that got garbled and start screaming that they were misquoted. But as long as the overall message was conveyed, that's all that counts. Few will notice, and no one will remember the minor points."

Simon believes that in the first few days after the incident, MaxLite must openly respond to all press queries, but after the initial flurry of excitement, the company should adopt a proactive stance. "Establish a list of the key media and go after them. MaxLite has to tell the world how they're going about solving the problem and the significance of their research. In short, they need to aggressively show that they're doing the right things for the right reasons."

Will a well-trained company spokesman save MaxLite from its liability problem? "Oh, there's no guarantee that their PR efforts will save them from disaster," says Simon. "The idea of the PR campaign is to get the right information to the right people at the right time. If they can do that, they've bought some time to work out the problems. In the end, though, what they're doing to correct the problem and reintroduce a safe product will determine their fate."

## Lessons from the Game

1. Give the media unlimited access to your company to show you have nothing to hide; the truth is your best ally.

2. Never deny or stonewall. History shows that you're guaranteed to lose.

3. Keep abreast of constantly changing life-styles and laws that relate to your industry. Even the safest product can be dangerously used in ways for which it was not intended; who's responsible depends on the judicial sentiments of the times.

4. Study your competitors and related industries to see how they're faring with product-liability suits. Extrapolate the situation to your own product.

5. Be prepared. Design a contingency plan for any disaster that might befall your company.

6. Go beyond the call of duty when making good in a product-liability crisis. Not only will you solve the problem faster, you'll impress the media, your customers, and your stockholders.

7. Try nonlinear thinking. Prepare yourself generally, and consider surprising and unexpected moves.

8. Preempt whenever you can. If you steal the thunder of a potential detractor or regulating body, you will come out

looking like a hero; if you wait to be hit or regulated, you'll look like you're on the defensive.

9. Choose your spokespeople carefully. They need both the right information and the right temperament to manage the media.

CHAPTER 9

# Unruly Stepchildren:
## *Turning Around a Troubled Acquisition*

## Opening Moves

Molly and Paul Saunders sit in their disabled vintage Citroën on a lonely highway halfway between Portland and Seattle. "I *told* you we should have taken the '57 Chevy," complains Molly. "You have enough experience with auto parts to know it'll take weeks to get a rebuilt water pump for this jalopy."

True, Paul has managed a wholesale auto-parts store for years, and he could take apart and reassemble even the most exotic car in a few hours. But Molly is right—it could take weeks to get that pump. "You're the puzzle solver," he mutters. "Why don't you figure out a way to deliver parts from Paris to Skookumchuck overnight?"

A silly idea? To someone who doesn't love tinkering with old cars, maybe, but for Molly and Paul Saunders it marked the beginning of M&P Systems, a computerized wholesale parts warehouse in Portland that could guarantee same-day delivery of even the rarest fuel injector to any retail outlet within 500 miles. By hiring only people who shared their passion for the business, they were able to turn a frustrating breakdown in the boondocks into a turbocharged million-dollar-a-year enterprise.

What happens when entrepreneurial companies like M&P Systems, fuel-injected with personal commitment and passion, grow to the point where they attract takeover attention by a conglomerate? Sometimes the adoption goes smoothly, with parents and stepchild alike benefiting from the relationship. But more often than not, the larger company finds itself with an unruly brat on its hands.

In the following scenario we see how M&P Systems becomes a troubled acquisition when it gets swallowed by a muscle-bound corporation. We asked our *Executive Chess* players to recommend a strategic course of action for salvaging the situation.

## The Game: Breakdown in the Fast Lane

When Molly and Paul Saunders took their business plan and five-year profit-and-loss projections to Bob Clayborn at First Commercial Bank, begging for a loan to start M&P Systems, a computerized auto-parts delivery company styled on the Japanese just-in-time inventory method, they could tell by the skeptical look on Bob's face that their pitch was falling on deaf ears. "Your business plan does look solid," mused the bank president, "but I can't approve a $150,000 loan for a business in a stagnant industry like auto parts."

On their way home Paul fumed while Molly set her jaw in determination. "Our idea *will* work," she muttered. "When we make our first million, we'll buy that blasted bank, and the first thing we'll do is replace Bob Clayborn with someone who has a little imagination."

For the next two and a half years the Saunders moonlighted, lived like paupers, and scraped together enough capital to start M&P systems, and three years later their business reached pre-tax revenues of $7 million. The determined entrepreneurs didn't buy the bank, but Bob Clayborn, who went on to become CEO of Belico Industries, ended up buying *them* for a cool $14 million. Having never forgotten the gleam in the Saunders' eyes, he had watched them build their business until it was ripe for acquisition. After all, if a naïve young couple could push sales to $7 million a year, Belico's sophisticated management and marketing teams ought to be able to accelerate it to three or four times that figure quickly, and within five years the nationally franchised M&P parts-delivery system should have the potential to ring up annual sales of $100 million.

Unfortunately for Belico, the race to riches stalled halfway around the track. Once the Saunders had accepted Belico's terms, Belico immediately fired all the veteran M&P managers and further computerized and robotized much of the operation, reducing the line staff by seventy percent. Oddly enough, despite Belico's high-tech approach and army of finely tuned M.B.A.s, M&P began to *lose* money. Same-day shipments arrived two days late, retailers often received the wrong parts, and M&P's inventory sometimes lacked seldom-ordered parts. Although sales have doubled over the past two years, profits have gone so far into reverse that M&P has become an embarrassing drain on Belico's own balance sheet.

Bob Clayborn still believes in M&P's potential, but few of his colleagues care enough about auto parts to give him time to turn the situation around. And even if they did, Belico would face the prospect of the Saunders themselves getting back into the business because the non-competition agreement they signed will expire next year. Paul and Molly, bored with restoring antique Rolls-Royces and Victorian mansions, long to follow their hearts back into the parts business. And if their new venture enjoys the same success as the old one, the competition could put the coffin nails in Belico's investment.

Belico's chief financial officer, figuring the company ought to cut its losses while it can, suggests that Bob sell M&P back to the Saunders. He believes that the problem isn't Belico's management of M&P, but outside factors, such as the proliferation of Japanese imports requiring dealer service. Why did the Saunders succeed? "A fluke," he snorts.

The senior vice president directly responsible for M&P argues, however, that the Saunders and their people made the company successful because they held a deep and abiding passion for its mission, a passion Belico's managers will never share. "We're just used to looking at it from our own narrow viewpoint," he insists. "We're overlooking the basics. I'd like a chance to put M&P in the black."

If Bob Clayborn hired you as a consultant and asked you for your advice, what would you say?

# Strategies and Tactics

## *Governing with a Soft Touch*

The easiest and most obvious solution, according to Arnold Goldstein—attorney, author, and small-business turnaround expert—would involve dumping the poorly performing acquisition. "Some enlightened soul in the company could then hold up a copy of *In Search of Excellence* and say, 'See, we didn't stick to the knitting. That's why we blew it. We gotta stick to the knitting, guys.'"

End of story? Possibly, but Goldstein proposes an alternative, what he calls the "IBM approach." He explains: "IBM has a broad and diversified portfolio of subsidiaries, and they work not only because they're related in some way, but because they have a very careful balance of centralized and decentralized management. They've allowed their acquisitions to remain largely autonomous."

Take IBM and Rolm. The marriage of stuffy Big Blue and Silicon Valley–slick Rolm, with their strikingly different styles, could have courted disaster, but IBM has kept its pin-striped hands out of Rolm's hair, allowing Rolm instead to maintain the kind of environment and perks that its elite engineering corps has come to expect. The result has surprised many observers who predicted that IBM would force Rolm into its own mold, thus squashing the latter's creative energies. Instead the two companies work harmoniously, sharing technological expertise and engineering inventiveness.

Although hands-off arrangements seem to work best, most acquiring companies immediately eliminate redundant administrative and management structures, a move that Goldstein says can make sense. But, at the same time, he believes that such a tactic often leads the parent company to smother its acquisition. In our scenario he thinks Belico not only made the mistake of journeying into unknown waters, but took a successful little company and killed it by applying a big-company corporate mentality to it. He asserts, "Belico shouldn't have been anything more than a moneylender. In fact, a parent company should be nothing more than a bank and a temporary management consultant. It should see itself as an umbilical cord that provides temporary nourishment. Ultimately the relationship should almost develop into one of franchiser and franchisee."

Nothing better demonstrates how a parent company can crush an acquisition than the W. R. Grace/Mr. Gasket fiasco. The saga of the Mr. Gasket Company began humbly in 1957 in the basement of drag racing enthusiast Joseph Hrudka. Frustrated with losing races because a simple engine gasket would disintegrate under high heat, Hrudka began fiddling with a material that could withstand the rigors of racing. His heat-resistant gasket worked so beautifully that he eventually set up Mr. Gasket in his home, hoping to make at least $10,000 a year. Two years later, with a whopping $600,000 in sales, he knew he had hit on a winner, and two years after that, a public offering took in $2.7 million.

Success continued for Mr. Gasket to the point when W. R. Grace & Company bought it for $17 million. Ten years later the forty-five-year-old Hrudka came out of retirement and was back on the scene. Mr. Gasket had languished under Grace's management, and the large conglomerate jumped at the chance to sell the slumping auto-parts company back to Hrudka for $4 million.

Hrudka immediately brought back impassioned employees, fired eighty-two people, and began running the company with his old verve and entrepreneurial cunning. Within four years after regaining control, he pushed sales to $120 million. The company, a recognized leader in the field, now manufactures 6000 different auto parts.

The difference? As one analyst noted, decisions that Hrudka and his close-knit group could make in less than a minute took more than a month of committee processing at Grace. And the demands of auto-parts consumers were changing too rapidly for decisions to be mired in layers of bureaucracy. Also, the original sales force hung out at the racetrack where they lived and breathed their products, making them an integral part of their lives.

A large bureaucracy and a lack of personal commitment probably stalled M&P Systems too. As Goldstein says, "Belico must pull back and return control to a separate management crew that has its own mandate. Preferably get the guys who started it back in. Offer them your resources and support. Tie their incentives into *long-term* profits so they don't just wait out the noncompetition clause. But most important," he says, "Belico must keep its grubby hands off. It's not their ball of yarn."

## Swallowing the Whale

Dr. Max Tesler, CEO of PharmaControl, Inc, agrees that Belico's smothering of M&P is a perfect example of how a big corporate mentality can ruin a small company. "What you've got here is the typical kind of situation that occurs in a large company," declares Tesler. "We see it all the time in the pharmaceutical industry. I think a lot of giant companies actually make money in spite of themselves. Every once in a while I go to a meeting in one of these places and I'm amazed at the rows upon rows of drones sitting in cubbyholes, little corrals with all sorts of reference books, and I turn to my financial vice president, and out of the side of my mouth I say, 'Tom, what the hell are all these people doing?' I just don't understand it—we run corporate headquarters with seven people."

"What happens in these large companies is that they become buried in layer upon layer of bureaucratic nonsense, so that decisions are made by committee. As a result, it becomes a matter of administration based on "cover your backside"; people don't make a decision because it's the right one but because it's the decision that protects them so they can pass the buck or move the responsibility laterally in the kind of scenario you gave here."

From Tesler's perspective, entrepreneurial people can't survive bureaucratic conventions. "Everyone in my company puts out whatever it takes. We don't work by the time clock. At these major companies, though, come five o'clock the switchboard closes and you can't find anybody. At our company people know that the best time to get us is literally from seven-thirty in the morning until nine o'clock at night."

When a large company takes over a small, entrepreneurial one, it seldom appreciates that kind of heartfelt dedication. "These guys who head the management of the parent company —most of them punch out at five. The fact is, they just don't care about the company like we do, and that's the problem. They have a job and a job description. Simple as that."

Beyond the lack of passion, Tesler also decries the fact that many parent companies treat their acquisitions like uneducated foundlings, installing managers who seldom understand the business and may not be the most competent to operate it. "They may not run the company with as keen an eye toward material movement, cost of goods, acquisition of goods, and other key factors," contends Tesler. "And in many businesses, tiny increments in price can have a tremendous effect on profitability. I suspect, though, that since the parent company often makes its money at the retail end, they really don't care what the costs are. That might be the case in the story here, so of course, when you look at the company by itself, it's going nowhere, it's a loser."

The shift to a large corporate environment also carries with it a dangerous attitude, according to Tesler. "An entrepreneurial company has to run lean and hard, or else it's out of business. The big companies tend to run fat and slow—if you don't achieve your goals, you slough it off. You say, 'What the hell, Big Brother's going to pick up the difference.' So there's no sense of ownership, accountability, or responsibility, and a winning company like the auto-parts distributor becomes a losing company real fast."

Can't a small company ever benefit from its parent? "Oh, I don't say it's impossible," qualifies Tesler. "I've been talking about worst-case situations, which unfortunately are the norm, rather than the exception. I think that a small business *can* potentially benefit from the resources of the large company, *if* the parent is smart enough to leave the subsidiary alone. And by that I mean leaving the people in place, especially the middle-management people who've made it a success, and by not trying to put in an elephantine system that is needed at corporate headquarters. Let it have its own accounting, bookkeeping, inventory control, etc. The small company can benefit from the parent's health plan or the pension plan, their marketing expertise, and, of course, cash infusions to help it grow and expand."

One company that enjoys a happy relationship with its adoptive parent is Häagen-Dazs, built from the ground up by veteran "old-world" ice-cream maker Ruben Mattus. When Pillsbury Co. bought Häagen-Dazs from Mattus in 1983, the upstart commanded twenty to twenty-five percent of the "super-premium" ice-cream market, with annual sales of $115 million and a growth rate of twenty-five to thirty percent a year. At the time of the acquisition, William H. Spoor, chairman and chief executive officer of Pillsbury, told *The Wall Street Journal,* "We think we can grow [Häagen-Dazs] faster." Three years later, Häagen-Dazs surpassed Spoor's predictions, sporting sales of $183 million, an annual growth rate of thirty-two percent, and more than two hundred new retail stores, of which Pillsbury owns two thirds.

Tesler introduces a tantilizing reversal of the M&P scenario when he digresses to the question of how small companies can swallow larger ones without suffering indigestion. At the time of this writing, Tesler's own drug company has actually begun acquiring a drug distributor many times its own size. "This is really a situation where the minnow is swallowing the whale," Tesler comments laughingly. "We do $2.5 to $3 million in sales, and this company does $25 million, with the potential to go to more than $150 million. Funny, but it's being spun off from its parent company for the exact reasons given in your scenario."

How will he avoid the mistakes that Belico made with M&P? Dr. Tesler thinks he has a sound prescription: "Most important, we're not going to treat it like a stepchild. We want to make sure it gets the first-class attention we put into our own company. That means we'll carefully look at all costs all the way down the line so the new company is as profitable as possible. We also aren't going to milk it or make it pay 'country club dues,' all kinds of charge backs that can hamper its ability to operate well. In addition, we plan on paying close attention to our material movement and make sure that its production is as efficient as possible. Then there's the issue of its product lines. They currently make 1300 products, and there's no way you can make 1300 products and still be profitable. They have no idea of the cost accounting for a given product; they don't even know if they make money, lose money, or break even. They just know that the parent buys a drug from them, so they make it. We're going to educate them about what makes money and what loses money and cut out the nonprofitable items. In short, we're going to revitalize it and let it operate like a fire-breathing start-up."

## Preserving Your Best Assets

Jonathan Pond, president of Investment Management Information, Inc., sees the Belico/M&P situation as a classic example of the ineffective operating style of many American companies. "What Belico has done," Pond maintains, "represents the typical corporate mentality surrounding an acquisition in terms of the need for the new parent company to establish who's in charge. And that's usually done by making heads roll and lives miserable. If you look at the situation fundamentally, though— and we can't expect most American managers in large corporations to step back and look at things fundamentally—you have to ask yourself, 'What made that business I'm buying successful?' The answer is: people. So, by getting rid of the existing management, you throw out the real strength of your acquisition and cancel any intelligent reason for buying the company in the first place. That's a crazy way to do business."

Is there an alternative path? Yes, and Pond has driven down it himself. Explains Pond, "I'm affiliated with a privately held, Zurich-based holding company that has businesses all over the world and has a unique criterion for acquisition: they will not entertain a purchase if the owner, entrepreneur, or whoever, does not commit himself to long-term involvement in the business. They have one acquisition that they made when the owner was sixty. Now he's seventy-eight, and they're quite worried about what will happen with the company.

"The last thing the [parent] company wants to do is phase out management. They truly believe that people are the backbone of any successful enterprise, and what they're really buying is expertise. As they see it, their role is simply to help you when you need it and give you the wherewithal to grow. Many who have been acquired by them say it's no different a day after, a year after, or two years after they were acquired than it was before. You just send your financials to a different location."

Pond says that this philosophy allows his parent company to acquire enterprises quite different from itself and operate in fields as diverse as pharmaceuticals and travel agencies. "It's always the same formula," says Pond. "Buy a company where you're comfortable with the management and then say, 'Go back and run it as you have been.' I suspect that they're not unique among foreign companies in this regard. The idea of buying companies and firing the people seems to be more of an American idea about how to do business."

Pond also points out that in addition to firing key people, traditional wisdom dictates that you foist your own culture upon the survivors, which can wreak havoc. Resisting this temptation takes great confidence, but doing so can spell the difference between success and failure in the merger and acquisition game. Bank of America, for example, exercised admirable restraint when it bought Charles Schwab, the discount brokerage. When Schwab himself had run his company, he routinely rewarded high performers with expensive foreign cars. At Bank of America, executives drove American sedans, not BMWs, Jaguars, and Mercedes. Originally the acquiring management thought it should terminate Schwab's policy, but they wisely realized that they were dealing with two very distinct cultures, each with its own reward system. Destroy the reward system and you might destroy a lot of incentive to achieve peak performance.

Pond suggests that had Belico paid more attention to cultural difficulties, it would not have imposed its impersonal style on M&P. But what can you do now? He proposes that you get the Saunders back in the game. "But they're dealing from a position of power," he cautions, "so you're going to have to make it extremely attractive. Even more important, you've got to give them nearly complete autonomy."

Are the Saunders the only ones who can save M&P? "Oh, not necessarily," Pond answers. "They would certainly be a logical choice, but the fact is, as the executive search people say, 'Not only is there an ideal fit somewhere out there, but that person *will* join the company.' There's someone out there who can do it. That person would be the one that would come in and say, 'You know, you really messed this thing up, and this is the way it can be made to work again.' "

What key characteristic would that person possess? Says Pond with confidence, "He'd be an impassioned entrepreneur. What made this thing work in the first place was the fire in the bellies of the two entrepreneurs. And that's what you need to spark its revival."

## Remembering Your Heritage

Alan Lustig, president of Fabrics International, believes the situation with M&P may have deteriorated to the point of no return. "It's not because Belico lacks the ability," advises Lustig, "but because of their mentality. They have no deep understanding of the product or why customers want it. The Saunders' success really came from their ability to serve their accounts.

Since the Saunders and all their lieutenants are gone, I don't think the present ownership has a chance of saving the business."

Like Pond, Lustig believes that acquiring companies make a big mistake when they get rid of the people who made the adopted enterprise work in the first place. "Sometimes the parent company makes changes for its own sake," he says, "but often it's done because the parent actually believes that their own people have a better feel for achieving the desired goals. When you're talking about making changes in general management, or maybe a controller, that's one thing. But when you change the people in areas where the manufacture or sale of the product is clearly affected, you're asking for trouble. It's only by knowing the details of the product and having some insights into why people buy it that we can expect to respond to the marketplace and remain competitive."

Therefore, Lustig believes, the way to save M&P is to bring the Saunders back, while at the same time striving to make sure that M&P's line managers listen closely to what that market wants. He'd also do some detective work to determine where things went wrong. "I'd immediately go and find out why there are complaints in terms of late deliveries, nondeliveries, and stock outs, which apparently didn't happen when the Saunders ran the business."

The answer, Lustig projects, will probably come down to the people factor. "When you see that their sales have been increasing, yet the net effect of increased sales isn't resulting in the type of return to the corporation that they expected, the only conclusion is that bad decisions are being made in other parts of the company."

Lustig, whose company supplies fabric for many kinds of products, offers a graphic example of how such poor decisions can affect a seemingly unshakable money-making machine. "I had a customer, a family business, that had a genius for making money in the personal-comfort products business. The beginning of the end came when they sold out to a large conglomerate, just like in your scenario. Several of the family members were retained to help out operationally, but ultimately they left direct supervision to become part of the conglomerate's board, where most of their responsibilities revolved around looking for new acquisitions. Within four years the company lost most of its market share, so the conglomerate sold it. But the story goes on. The old president and sales manager bought it back, and in two years they almost regained all their segment of the market."

What happened under the conglomerate? "Several things," Lustig answers. "One—and this happens to lots of acquired companies—was that by the time they made their dollar contribution to the parent company to pay for their share of administrative functions, their profits were badly eaten into. They also suffered from a loss of good personnel, because the conglomerate assigned new middle-management people who saw no future for themselves in this 'dying company.' These people just stopped caring, which made the situation even worse.

"Perhaps most deadly, though, they eventually couldn't sell through discount outlets anymore, so they lost a huge chunk of their market. There were two reasons for that. First, to compensate for the dollar contributions to the parent, they had to raise the price above a level where they could sell to discounters. Second, their manufacturing costs skyrocketed. They used to buy fabrics from me when they could get the best price, even if they weren't going to use them for a few months. The costs of warehousing the materials were minimal, compared to the savings they were getting. Yet under the conglomerate's reign they couldn't do that; the conglomerate's computer would look at an order and say, 'These goods won't be sold until May, so there will be no authorized buy orders for the fabric materials in September.' In April, the costs of the fabrics might have been three times higher."

Despite the disaster with his former customer's company, Lustig still believes that a large company can acquire a smaller, entrepreneurial one if they bring to it the right motivation and management approach. "I think that an acquisition done to gain exposure in another market, or expansion in one's own market on a vertical basis, makes sense, provided that the smaller company is left intact and isn't subject to the kind of bureaucratic systems that force it to do things that aren't beneficial, like missing good deals on raw materials. Maybe a big company isn't set up to store large inventories of raw materials, but a small company can't afford to pass up substantial savings on them. The parent company must also be sensitive about bleeding the smaller company with charge backs. It should be the other way around; they should provide an infusion of cash for enhancing inventory, developing new products, upgrading capital equipment, and beefing up sales and marketing budgets."

As evidence that a large company can overcome the typical myopia of large conglomerates, Lustig, who was the chief industrial engineer for a division of Honeywell, cites the policy of his former employer. "At Honeywell," he says, "there was a policy that said one division was not compelled to buy parts from another division if the prices and services weren't competitive with the outside world. For example, if you're in the industrial-products division and you require some electronics parts that are manufactured by a smaller division of Honeywell, you are primarily obligated to request a quotation from that division, but they must sell their goods competitively, or you may buy outside of Honeywell. So each division has its own profit point and profit center. A stockholder can look and say, 'Honeywell is Honeywell,' but each division really has its own responsibility for generating profits and remaining competitive."

Lustig believes that the Honeywell example demonstrates that a big company can think in terms that are suitable for running smaller operations, but he adds, "How quickly they forget. At one time every big company was just a small company, run by the seat of someone's pants. I think they need to remember their roots."

## Buying at the Right Time

"This is a ridiculous marriage, but it's what we've come to expect these days," offers venture capitalist Fred Nazem, who has started more than sixty successful companies. From Nazem's point of view, acquisitions motivated by financial considerations alone generally fail. These "transaction companies," as he refers to so many of today's big holding companies and conglomerates, lack a central core, existing as a series of modules strung together with only one goal: making money. "Transaction companies, the Belicos of the world, do things purely for the sake of fiscal 'progress,' to show stockholders how brilliant they are at maneuvering," Nazem comments. "But it's the stockholders who lose. Oftentimes these companies clean out their gardens and keep the weeds. I see this happen time and again."

In contrast, Nazem says, "operating companies," like IBM and Hewlett-Packard, do contain a central core to which they can logically append subsidiaries that fit together like pieces of a puzzle. "Operating companies are in a much stronger position to deal with acquisitions," he insists, "as long as they buy companies that fit within their operating environment. If something goes wrong, they can still run the business, because they understand its fundamentals. Alternately they can strip it down and incorporate it into their own structure. If they buy a company purely on a transaction basis, give it to a division and expect it to work, they're asking for trouble. If it goes sour, they have no idea of how to run it and have no rationale for incorporating it. The only option is to get rid of it. This is the sad case in your story."

Nevertheless, Nazem believes that a transaction company can positively influence an acquisition's future. "Perhaps the parent can hold some notes or some stock in the acquisition," he says encouragingly. "Treat the acquisition as a real P&L center all by itself. Let it have nothing to do with the organizational and administrative morass of the parent. The parent should look at it like an equity investment, just like it would invest in a venture-capital situation."

Beyond selecting a potential acquisition on the basis of whether it fits into your operating environment, Nazem thinks you should pay strict attention to the timing of the purchase. "Every business has an evolution, a natural life cycle. It must start off at an entrepreneurial level to conceive and develop the products that will be its lifeblood. Then it goes into a phase where it needs real leadership, maybe even of the Fortune 500 kind. At that point the entrepreneurs must give way."

An excellent example of Nazem's advice in action involves the case of Dresher, Inc., a brass bed maker that had rekindled an interest in brass beds in the mid-1940s and quickly became an industry leader under the guidance of founder Max Dresher. In 1979, Dresher, amid declining sales, decided to retire, sold the company to manufacturing giant Standex International Corp. Standex soon brought in Barry Merkin, former head of Xerox's publishing operation, to head up the subsidiary. One year later Dresher achieved $18 million in sales, and by 1985, that number had risen to $31 million, with projections of $40 million for 1986.

The difference? The original founder-entrepreneur had maintained such strong control of every phase of the operation that, according to some, the company suffered a sort of paralysis. Orders fell behind, accounts received the wrong parts, and Dresher's image slipped. In contrast, Merkin, who brought twenty-five years of management experience to his new assignment, created an effective tier of vice presidents to whom he wisely delegated authority. He also made sorting out the company's manufacturing problems a priority, eventually enabling Dresher once again to become the premier company in its field.

As the Dresher case illustrates, when you gracefully effect transition from the entrepreneurial phase to the mature management phase, your company can generate significantly more profits. What happens, though, when you acquire a company too soon to profit from the application of more experienced management know-how? "Then you have the potential for disaster," Nazem claims. "The parent company stifles its young, like in your scenario. The parent company might have the acquisition report to a higher level, but the only solution is to basically leave it alone. Usually the temptation is to divest itself of the acquisition. In your story, even though the parent company is a transaction company, it might ask why it acquired the company in the first place. The auto-parts distributor is no dog and certainly not a 'fluke,' as someone in the scenario said. I believe that *any* business can be salvaged if there is a basic reason for its existence. Besides, if the parent company sells it in its present state, it will get nothing for it. They've got to do something that demonstrates it is in the right phase for being sold."

Nazem sketches his own solution: "Grow the company until it sits on the threshold of the next phase. If you can't woo the founders back, find an entrepreneurial crew that can bring to the task a similar amount of spirited enthusiasm. Give them incentives and give them support. But by all means, do it without interfering with them."

## Taking Stock of In-house Talent

"We are looking at this situation from our own narrow viewpoint," says Geoffrey Rappaport, cochairman and cofounder of Supercuts, reading aloud a portion of the scenario: "We're overlooking the basics. I'd like a chance to put M&P in the black." Rappaport goes on to say, "Well, now, you've got a guy right here who understands exactly what the problem is. Get this senior vice president to document why he thinks he can turn it around. Tell him to give you a history of the disaster, going back to the beginning, describing why this acquisition made sense to Belico in the first place. If it all feels right, let him run with it for six months. Give him strict performance criteria to meet. If he can make them, fine. If he can't, then it's time to get out. Why not take a chance?"

Rappaport disagrees with most of the other panelists about the wisdom of enticing the founders back into the business. "Look," he says sternly, "this thing is past the point where you need creative entrepreneurs to run it. It's a very simple idea, and it's been executed well in the past. You really should be able to run it 'by the book' at this stage. The question isn't so much, 'What did they [the Saunders] know that we didn't?' but, 'Why can't *our* management team handle the problem? Why haven't we put together a system that's so much better than theirs?' The bottom line is that Belico should be able to make M&P better because it has the resources to do it."

Such "by-the-book" advice sounds strange coming from the man who puts his own blood and sweat behind a haircutting idea that thrust Supercuts from a single salon bankrolled with less than $2000 to an awesome national franchise operation that brings in more than $120 million a year. "Sure you've got to have passion to make the business work," he admits. "Management know-how can't substitute for employee *caring*. But you've got all the passion power you need right under your nose: the guy who wants to take M&P and run with it in a new way. Harness him and you've got all the vital energy you need to make the business fly."

Such dedication can inject life into any business in any industry. Witness the recent turnaround at the Harley-Davidson Motorcycle Company. Battered by Japanese imports and plagued by a growing reputation for poor-quality machines, the once supreme bike manufacturer began floundering in the early eighties. Before it sank deeper, however, thirteen officers bought the company and took it private, instituting a just-in-time inventory system and putting more decision-making power in the employees' hands. Costs plummeted, quality skyrocketed, and the percentage of defect-free bikes being produced by one plant went from fifty percent to ninety-nine percent. Harley expects major profits by 1987.

The Harley case clearly confirms Rappaport's point that scrappy entrepreneurs can't always provide the solution to every acquisition problem. Sometimes a blend of the entrepreneurial and "textbook" manager, the "managerial entrepreneur," can accomplish more than anyone. Take the case of Joe Wise, with his Xerox and IBM background, who bought MicroMedia Information Systems, Inc., during its entrepreneurial phase. Micromedia archives information for corporate clients, and as does M&P, it exploits a simple idea. Could a freewheeling entrepreneur have done more with it? Possibly. But Wise, with his professional management knowledge, injected needed structure and seasoned judgment into the operation, pushing sales from $500,000 to $2.5 million in five years.

Why couldn't Belico's senior VP do the same with M&P? He's got the knowledge, the energy, and the right attitude. Rappaport underscores one caveat, though: The senior VP might feel enthusiastic about giving M&P a try, but you have to make sure that the business doesn't become dependent on his personality alone. "That's a concern that my partner, Frank Emmett, and I face all the time. We don't want the world to think that they buy the 'Geoffrey and Frank' technique. It's the 'Supercuts' technique. That's why we keep a low profile when it comes to media and publicity. In order for Supercuts to grow to its full potential, it has to be able to stand on its own. We're not going to be around forever, and neither will the Belico VP. So this business about passion becomes very tricky, and you always have to make sure the company has a character of its own as it develops."

As for competition from the founders, that causes Rappaport no worry. "You've bought the original idea and supposedly have the people who can manage it. You can run the wheels off the Saunders if you want to; if you can't, then you have no business being in business. The fact that Belico is worried about the founders returning to the field indicates to me that they had no confidence about the acquisition when they made the deal. If you're afraid of competition from other people, then you're a slave to them, and you'll always be subject to their vagaries and whims. In my own business, if I spent all my time worrying about every competitor who comes on the scene—and there are plenty of knockoff companies out there—I wouldn't have time to make sure that Supercuts keeps doing what it does best, which is why it's light-years ahead of the competition."

What about the idea of getting Belico to act more entrepreneurially, as others have proposed? Again, he argues, they must
carefully examine their own actions. "They're *already* acting
entrepreneurially," he says with a laugh. "They saw a niche that
was identified by someone else and assumed that they could do
it even better. Isn't that entrepreneurial enough? We tend to
think that 'entrepreneurial' has to mean 'original idea.' You can
take *any* idea, old or new, and be entrepreneurial about what
you do with it. No, making Belico more entrepreneurial will
not solve the problem. It's getting Belico to go back and examine what it saw in M&P in the first place, to recreate the original
thinking and apply the best possible management it can."

Is this likely to happen in the real world? "Unfortunately not,"
says Rappaport ruefully. "One of the hardest things in business
is for people to admit that they make mistakes, especially in a
large company. In a small company a disaster has obvious effects. But large hierarchies are great for burying mistakes, which
makes it very easy for people to avoid accountability and owning up to their errors. So if this situation with Belico was real, I
think that the people involved would probably be inclined to
sweep it under the table rather than do anything about it. That
seems to be the mentality of corporate America today. The
ironic thing is that most mistakes aren't fatal, and you can learn
from them and get stronger. In fact, there's only one rule of
thumb that you need to remember. As my partner says, 'As long
as you don't make two bad mistakes at the time you can only
afford one bad mistake, you can stay in business.'"

## Knowing Thy Business

"The whole question for me really comes down to whether or
not they understand the business they've bought," says Charles
Levin, president of Sandler & Worth, Inc., "and in this case, the
parent company clearly isn't tuned into what makes M&P's
business tick. Furthermore, I think, given the fundamental mismatch of corporate cultures, it would probably be impossible
for anyone from the parent company to think in the way that's
necessary to run M&P."

But isn't a carburetor just a carburetor? Does it make any
difference who sells it? "A big part of M&P's success was probably its distribution and marketing," Levin answers. "The
founders worked hard, but most important, they had a unique
marketing organization and a vision for how that organization

should develop. If anyone else tries to run the company without understanding that vision, the results could be a nightmare."

Such nightmares have visited many American corporations. For an example where more familiarity would have bred more compatibility, consider the case of Ram Golf Corporation, which Colgate-Palmolive bought in 1974. Ram originally sprang into being when one of the three Hansberger brothers invented a machine for producing wooden golf clubs in 1948. Later the company swung into a wide range of golfing products, including the acquisition of a golf-ball manufacturing outfit.

What could Colgate, with demonstrated expertise in toothpaste and soap, bring to the game? A bureaucracy with proven approaches to selling consumer goods to a mass market, but little knowledge of selling premium products like Ram's to an upscale audience. As a result, Ram did not flourish under Colgate's rule, and the Hansbergers bought their company back in 1980. Today, Ram once again drives a healthy thirty percent growth rate down the fairway.

Another company that lost its fizz under a new master is C&C Cola. In 1976, C&C's founder, Charles Ferro, sold his company to ITT for $13 million and became the president of ITT's soft-drink division. But that arrangement came to an end in 1982 when ITT sold off the division to Consolidated Foods. C&C went flat, and in 1984, Ferro bought back his company for $8 million, with the added bonus of the latest bottling technology, all bought and paid for by ITT and Consolidated.

Why did C&C's bubble burst under the supervision of the two giants? Not only did the new owners tamper with C&C's original formulas, they ignored Ferro's ingenious distribution strategy, which involved selling to warehouses rather than individual retail outlets. The reduced cost of doing business had enabled "C&C Charlie," as Ferro is known in the business, to undercut the major combatants in the Cola Wars. Back in business with its original distribution program, C&C racked up more than $70 million worth of sales in 1985, a fifty percent rise over the 1984 figure.

Whether you're pumping out sports equipment, colas, or auto parts, Levin stresses that a business can't just materialize out of thin air. "All businesses evolve in response to their outside environment. Market conditions change, laws change, technology changes. And the people who are running the company have to be able to alter their planning and strategy accordingly.

Without an in-depth knowledge of those factors and how they affect the business, chances are the company will die on the vine."

Levin thinks it's hard enough for the original management of a company to stay on top of rapid change, let alone managers from a parent company who know little, if anything, about the business. And knowing the business is everything, as Avon Products learned when its demographic base dissolved right under its nose. For years "Avon calling" was synonymous with "profits rising." But in the mid-seventies, as more women left home and joined the work force, the Avon "ding dong" went unanswered. From 1978 to 1982, Avon's stock plummeted from $63 a share to the low twenties, with earnings sliding from $244 million to $164 million. And direct sales, which had pulled in nearly seventy-five percent of the company's sales revenues, declined by twelve percent each year from the late seventies though the early eighties. To combat the situation, Avon's CEO, Hicks B. Waldron, appointed in 1983, instituted an aggressive turnaround course that involved, among other tactics, sending Avon representatives into the workplace, marketing through direct mail and catalogs, and beefing up market research to determine which products its customers demanded the most.

Another famous marketer of products for the home, Tupperware, also lost customers as more and more women went to work, as homemakers grew more sophisticated, and as cheaper plastic containers became available in the local supermarket. Not only did sales and earnings fall six and twenty-seven percent, respectively, in 1984, but also Tupperware's contribution to parent Dart & Kraft's operating earnings dropped from twenty-eight to fourteen percent that same year. Fortunately for Tupperware, Dart & Kraft allowed the division's chairman, Douglas Martin, and president William Jackson to run the show without parental influence. As a result, Tupperware retained valuable aspects of its culture, including direct-sales parties, and the inspired commitment of its "dealers." The program, however, became highly flexible with shorter, less formal parties thrown during office lunch breaks and in the health clubs. To its credit, Dart & Kraft let the people who knew the business best respond to dramatic changes in the marketplace to which the parent might have responded precipitously, possibly dumping the acquisition the minute earnings began dropping.

As the Avon and Tupperware cases show, slow, insidious

changes can have a major impact on a business, and as Levin argues, it takes a keen eye to detect the situation before it becomes deleterious. With his own company, which sells high-end carpeting and Oriental rugs, a number of major factors have induced upper management to alter the way they manage Sandler & Worth. Changing interest rates, for instance, have forced them to view inventory in new ways, depending on the price of money. "We've gone though various growth plateaus where we've had years of doing more business and making less profits," he admits, "and that's forced us to put a lot of pressure on developing a profit orientation rather than a sales orientation."

Could someone, say a tire manufacturer or a bowling ball maker, step in and run Sandler & Worth? "Oh, I very much doubt it," Levin says with a chuckle. "The real expertise in our business is our ability to deal with suppliers, and that's really where the knowledge of the product is critical. We've developed relationships with suppliers over a number of years. There's a real personal element. As a result, we've learned many approaches for negotiating with them, and we've gotten to know what we can and can't do in terms of pushing for a deal that's good for us and lets them make a profit at the same time. Sure, the administrative and financial aspects of this business could be easily dealt with by any well-managed company. But the personal aspect? No way could anyone just step off the street and take over, regardless of how good at management they are. There's just no substitute for firsthand knowledge of this business or any other business."

## Healing the Parent Organization

"The real question for me," says management consultant Craig Hickman "is whether the Saunders would have been able to jump to the next level on their own. They're really in the information business. They're using information to get inventory to different places at the right time. If left alone, would the Saunders have been able to identify new business opportunities that they could use to really 'grow their business'?"

Hickman believes that if Belico decides against dropping M&P Systems, it must bring back the Saunders. He suggests, however, that Belico use more than money to entice them. "You've got to find a way to motivate the Saunders," he insists. "Sure, the potential to make the company grow faster might strongly appeal to them, along with the fact that they don't have to hassle with banks, public offerings, or other funding sources. But more importantly, perhaps, you could sit down and say, 'Yes, you're in an entrepreneurial phase, and we didn't understand how to manage a company at that stage of development, so we'll stay out of your hair for another few years. But after that we can help you plan your growth and make a transition to becoming a large corporation. You can't stay in that wild growth phase forever. We've got proven expertise in that area, and at the appropriate time we'll bring in a professional management team, along with the structure and systems that will bring some order to this rapidly growing business.' "

If the Saunders appreciate the value of such an offer, Hickman says they won't worry about adverse effects on the relationship. "A lot would really depend on the personal rapport. I think it could all be presented as a very positive situation for both parties. But you'd have to be sensitive enough to know whether the Saunders are really being truthful to themselves. Their eyes may light up with the opportunity of having the additional capital. And yet they may fight professionalizing the company's management tooth and nail. So it would really require an in-depth dialogue between the Belico executives and the Saunders to make sure that this was a *team* that could work well together and that the balancing act between an entrepreneurial company and a professionally managed company could work."

Hickman believes that large companies often make the mistake that Belico made when it comes to dealing with a small acquisition. Mismatched cultures, he says, cause some of the biggest headaches in these situations. As Jonathan Pond did, he points out that big corporations frequently underestimate the importance of passion in the start-up phase. "Passion is one of the key motivators that drives a business," Hickman asserts. "The Saunders not only had a passion for their business, but equally important, they were able to rally people's passion for building the business. That's no small thing. Research clearly indicates that satisfied employees will develop a higher level of productivity and sense of personal ownership in their jobs. In the end that will mean more to the success of a business than just about any other factor."

What kills this kind of passion in a large company? Hickman sees the shift from professional management to bureaucracy as the culprit. "You've got to watch the impulse to bureaucratize your organization," he warns. "In the entrepreneurial phase the company must be freewheeling. But as it matures and needs to stabilize, there's a tendency to go too far, systematizing everything in a way that stifles innovation and visionary possibilities for expansion."

Hickman suggests that for large companies to remain competitive in the global marketplace they must dispose of bureaucratic constraints, but not in a superficial way, such as with the current management fads of splinter R&D "skunkwork" groups or intrapreneuring. Says Hickman, "I'm not a big believer in skunkworks. I don't think they're any different from setting a new ship adrift, by saying, 'Okay, split the rebels off into a separate organization.' I think that's completely backward. We don't need to encourage large corporations to become more fragmented, to tear themselves apart into subcultures. We need to teach them how to become more *complete.* They need to learn how to integrate innovative products, services, and concepts into the way they do business every day. If you can successfully develop something in a skunkwork that couldn't be done in the normal organization, then the normal organization is sick. Besides, there's a real paradox in thinking that you have to separate your innovative resources from the rest of the company. How will you integrate the new ideas back into the rest of the organization if it can't generate them in the first place? A healthy organization should be able to innovate within its existing structure and then integrate those new ideas into its basic business."

Hickman's thinking is supported by the case of Xerox and the Star workstation, which some say is the grandfather of the modern personal computer. Xerox created this desktop marvel at its prestigious Palo Alto Research Center. Despite Xerox's track record as a master marketer in many arenas, it never did integrate this important new product that it had created outside the regular organization and, as a result, lost tens of millions of dollars on it.

As an alternative to developing a separate organization to carry out innovation, Hickman suggests what he calls a "parallel organization," which speeds up the process of *introducing* products. Hickman points to Frito Lay as an example of a company that has experimented with using parallel organizations to boost the development and testing of new processes. "The advantage," he says, "is that everyone feels they're working for the same side. That short-circuits any possibilities of people feeling like they're competing for internal recognition and resources, rather than working together in the spirit of cooperation."

To avoid tearing a company apart into subcultures and skunkworks, Hickman believes you should only make acquisitions that help the overall organization create a compatible whole. "In the seventies," he remarks, "there was a feeling that if you were a good manager and had good management structures in place, you could run anything. If you were an oil company, you could handle retail; if you were in food processing, you could manage sportswear, and so on. That, along with a foolish drive toward realizing short-term profits, led to a host of silly mergers and acquisitions."

Recommending new motivations for playing today's acquisition and merger game, Hickman holds up the GE and Kidder Peabody deal as a model. "This is a visionary move in a lot of ways. The two companies are creating a network of relationships that can lead to a self-contained economy. For Kidder Peabody, GE represents a very deep pocket. GE, in turn, will have its own investment bank right there, which will bring GE one step closer to being its own source of financial well-being and funding. If banking laws allow, I would expect in the future that GE, as a parent corporation, would in fact act as a bank for all of its subsidiaries."

He also points to GM's recent acquisition of a health maintenance organization. On the surface this seems like an odd match: a car maker and a human "body shop." Yet, on closer inspection, Hickman says the combination fits in nicely with the trend toward companies delivering health-care services to their own employees within the corporate environment. Ideally the GM merger will result in a self-sufficient, self-contained economy that could provide a model for the future.

## Lessons from the Game

1. Don't overstep your responsibility as a bank and a marketing/distribution resource when you become a parent company. Any efforts beyond that may smother the acquisition, especially one still in the entrepreneurial phase.

2. Beware the tendency of treating an acquisition like an unruly stepchild. Give it your best resources or it will wither away.

3. Think twice before tossing out an acquisition's management. People are the strongest asset of any company.

4. Think carefully before you impose any system that dramatically alters the way an acquisition does business. While the systems of a large company may bring efficiency to certain areas, they may permanently damage others.

5. Take the "ages and stages" of corporate development into account. What works for a mature organization may actually damage an entrepreneurial one, or vice versa.

6. Never underestimate the intangibles of excitement and passion for a business. When you have people who make work an organic part of their being, your company will inevitably do well.

7. When considering an acquisition, make sure it contributes to the overall wholeness of your organization. Those companies that become self-sufficient, balanced wholes will be the winners in tomorrow's global marketplace.

CHAPTER 10

# Greener Pastures:
## *Coping with a Boss Who Refuses to Retire*

### Opening Moves

At three o'clock in the morning chambermaid Maybelle Cranston pushes her cleaning cart toward the rest rooms beyond the lobby of the Thurston Central Park Hotel. Her feet hurt, her back aches, and she's in no mood to have her routine interrupted, least of all by the impeccably attired, silver-haired gentleman she finds draining the contents of the soap dispenser into a measuring cup.

"What are you doing in the women's room?" she shrieks. "Get out of here before I call the security guard and have you locked up."

The old man calmly rubs a spot from the mirror, then returns his handkerchief to the breast pocket of his tuxedo. He bows to Maybelle Cranston. "Dreadfully sorry, old girl," he says, smoothing his mustache, "but we can't overstock these rest rooms with supplies. If people always see a full soap dispenser, they'll waste it. Same goes for the paper towels!"

Stunned by the man's impertinence, Maybelle runs to find Lloyd, the night security man, but to her surprise Lloyd doubles over with laughter when he hears the story. "That 'dirty old man,' as you call him, is none other than Herbert P. Thurston III.

As in *Thurston Hotels.* You'd better go back and apologize or
he might not sign your next paycheck."

Many companies have a Herbert Thurston, a towering figure,
often the founder, who rules the company like a czar, and
whom many on the board would like to put out to pasture.
Sometimes a once effective executive refuses to step down because he can't bear relinquishing the reigns of his enterprise,
and if he has enough stock or clout with the board, he can keep
himself from being deposed.

Take the infamous case of Armand Hammer, chairman and
CEO of Occidental Petroleum. At eighty-seven years of age,
Hammer is not only one of the oldest officers of a major corporation, but has the dubious distinction of being one of the few
people to fire six presidents since 1968. In one sweep Hammer
used $194 million of Oxy's funds to buy out, at a hefty pre-
mium, investor David H. Murdock, who owned five percent of
Oxy's stock and who was allegedly plotting a takeover. When
then-president A. Robert Abboud objected, his head rolled, and
several days later the ax fell on Robert L. Peterson, chief of the
company's meat-packing division and the last member of the
board who opposed the aging chairman. The internal turmoil
could hardly escape the attention of Wall Street, and some
within the financial community lost confidence in the company.

Another CEO, Harry J. Gray, head of United Technologies,
also became noted for refusing to let go of the helm. Well
before Gray reached the retirement age of sixty-five, the company's directors urged him to pick a successor. Yet on the eve
of his retirement birthday, not only had he failed to name an
heir apparent, but four potential candidates had been driven
off. Though Gray deserves credit for shaping United Technologies into a prominent company, many question his reluctance
to turn the controls over to a new leader.

Some business experts believe that in the face of increased
takeover threats and pressure to meet financial expectations,
survival depends on managerial flexibility, and the boards of
many companies will show less tolerance of stubborn leaders.
The "sudden resignation" of James L. Dutt, chairman and CEO
of Beatrice Companies, may herald that trend. During his reign
at Beatrice, Dutt ignited heated criticism when he took the
surprising step of firing a number of key executives, including

Walter Bregman, president of Beatrice's Playtex subsidiary. Dutt also raised eyebrows in 1985 when he boosted ad budgets by twenty-five percent on such dubious projects as the $70 million sponsoring of a race-car team and $30 million on a corporate image campaign. While some inside the company lamented the loss of Dutt, outside investors clearly approved; on the day of the announcement Beatrice's stock shot up two dollars.

Just before Dutt, who had approached retirement age, received a golden shove, Apple's ex-CEO, Steve Jobs, half Dutt's age, found himself stripped of his own executive power when the very people he had imported to run his company decided on a different direction for the company. Many other executives have been caught in such crossfire, among them Edward Flannagan, former chairman of Western Union; Sanford Weill, ex-president of American Express Company; and Bill Agee, former chairman of Bendix.

In most cases, embattled executives have no choice but to vacate their offices. What would happen, though, if a board of directors wanted to remove a leader who owns more than half the company? Such a situation would call for unusually creative strategies, such as the ones our players offered in dealing with the indefatigable Herbert Thurston, emperor of the Thurston Hotels chain.

## The Game: They Shoot Horses, Don't They?

You've got a merciless migraine, your secretary has called in sick, and you're in no mood to have your misery interrupted, least of all by the general manager of eastern operations who's yelling at you over the phone. "He was in the *what* last night?" you ask in disbelief.

"The ladies room. He reprimanded a maid for filling the soap dispensers to the top and leaving an extra package of paper towels."

"That crazy old man," you mutter to yourself.

When you accepted the job as CEO of Thurston Enterprises, you had been prepared for all the headaches that come with running a sprawling chain of hotels and resorts, but you hadn't been prepared for the cantankerous chairman, Herbert P. Thurston III, whose sole mission in life seems to be making yours miserable.

For the next half hour the eastern manager details how the old man has been terrorizing hotels from Boston to Philadelphia, skulking around bathrooms to make sure they're not overstocked, poking into supply closets to count how many bars of soap have been pilfered, and monitoring the chefs to count the number of peas they place on each plate. As the eastern manager's voice grows hoarse, you think he should thank the gods of hotel management that he doesn't have to attend the board meetings at which Thurston III consistently votes against every proposal for innovation and growth. "If it was good enough for Thurston II," he proclaims, "it's good enough for me." Unfortunately half of the other directors, who have been with the company since the early days of Thurston II, always vote with Herbert, even though many would privately agree that he does more well-intentioned damage than he's worth.

Recently brought into Thurston Enterprises by top executive headhunters, you feel sabotaged, especially since Thurston III had sworn that you would receive free rein to run the organization as you saw fit. "Yep, it's time for this old horse to be put out to pasture," he had said with a chuckle. You could never imagine how much those words would come back to haunt you. Despite your growing frustration, however, you're reluctant to mount an overt campaign to depose the conservative chairman. After all, he's a likable old gent, and the Thurston family owns fifty-one percent of the stock. If anyone tries to oust Herbert P., he's likely to sell his controlling interest and see to it that *everyone* gets sent on to greener pastures.

Still, it's imperative that you do something soon, because Thurston Enterprise's chief competitor, Rumsford Hotels, has been steadily gaining ground through an ad campaign featuring the self-appointed Royal Princess of the hotel industry, Fantasia Rumsford, daughter of arch-rival hotel baron Winslow Rumsford IV. If you can't develop a way to combat Rumsford, Thurston Enterprises could be in deep trouble. Over the course of the next months you strengthen alliances with the board members who share your view that Thurston must ultimately be made chairman emeritus with no voting control. In the meantime you decide that it is crucial to get him out of headquarters, and you invite him to personally supervise one hotel (in a nice warm climate), which could then become the "standard of efficiency" for the entire organization.

To your pleasant surprise the ploy works, and Thurston III goes off to one of the company's most obscure, least profitable hotels. The following year, though, the Jacksonville Thurston nearly burns to the ground because Herbert found the expense of a new sprinkler system too frivolous. Miraculously no one was injured, but you've got Herbert back in your hair, conducting fire drills in the middle of the night and ordering the bellboys to spit-shine their shoes. Now what will you do?

## Strategies and Tactics

### Surrounding the Irritant

"You've already given us the answer to this scenario," concludes attorney and bankruptcy specialist Arnold Goldstein. "You sent Thurston down to Jacksonville, but the manager made the mistake of letting him get his hands into the operational pie. More important, you've identified the fact that this is a baby-sitting matter. What you do is call up the manager of the hotel you're going to ship Thurston to and say, 'Surprise, he's playing in your sandbox for a while. But we know this is a burden, so we're going to give you a fat bonus for the aggravation. Three months later we'll send him somewhere else.'"

According to Goldstein, you want to identify the managers whose personalities and tolerance levels will enable them to handle Thurston. "Who knows," he muses, "you might find a manager out there who likes Thurston and, for the right price, can keep him happily occupied until he's ready to retire. But the CEO in your story is clearly in no frame of mind to deal with him, so he's got to be moved on."

Goldstein goes on to suggest another alternative. "Look, the guy is in his late eighties or whatever. Chances are, all you have to do is ride it out. In a few more years he's going to have to retire, he'll pass on, or he'll just be easier to deal with. That's the trouble with this scenario—it has a built-in ending. I think it would be a hell of a lot more challenging if Thurston's grandson, a twenty-six-year-old cretin who just got an M.B.A., joined the ranks as vice president of marketing and envisioned gaining more responsibility and power each year until he worked his way up to president. That guy would be a pussycat ready to

grow into a real tiger. And if Thurston's genes are any indica-
tion, the tiger will be around for sixty or more years, devouring
chambermaids and CEOs alike. Then you've got a very challenging situation."

What to do in that case? "Well, it just so happens that I had
to deal with that situation a few years ago," answers Goldstein.
"I was a consultant for a family-owned company in the home-
health-care business. It was a healthy, great company until the
chairman and founder retired, and his son, who just got his
M.B.A., took over the management. Aside from being inexperi-
enced, he spent most of his time playing Frisbee on the front
lawn of corporate headquarters, this guy wanted to diversify
into all kinds of idiotic businesses that would have killed us. He
was also very disruptive. Good people were leaving right and
left. So we convened a secret meeting and decided that the
company's survival depended on our getting this guy [who, like
Thurston, was a majority shareholder] out of a management
role, and preferably out of the building."

Goldstein describes his strategy with a smile: "What we decided on was the 'oyster technique,' where we'd surround the
irritant. We got together with him and said, 'Hey, you're much
too creative and entrepreneurial to be running a stodgy old
company like this. Don't try to diversify this old dinosaur.
Here's $450,000—go out and start a new company, maybe
something international, based in some exciting place like Europe.' He grabbed the money and the plane tickets and was out
of our hair for three years. Then he started and ruined a high-
tech company, which probably could have been quite successful if he'd stepped aside after launching it. So he came back, and
we gave him another half million to start another company. This
one could go on some time."

Was it worth the expense? "It's saved the company," claims
Goldstein. "I'd say 150 grand a year is a small price to pay for
keeping the company alive. Wouldn't you?"

## Preserving the Sanctity of Ownership

"This is a very loaded issue," says Arthur Lipper III, publisher of
*Venture* magazine. "Number one, you have not described to me
somebody who should be fired but rather somebody who
should fire his subordinate. If Thurston counts the peas and
checks the soap in the ladies' bathroom, he's doing what an

owner of the business should be doing. Number two, a company is owned by its owners, and this man owns fifty-one percent of his, so no one has the right to fire him. If he wants to run it into the ground, that's his business. I think the issue here is sanctity of ownership and the presumptuousness of employees."

Lipper suggests that unless you can somehow persuade Thurston to step aside, you should do the only honorable thing— resign and get a job somewhere else. "I think management in this country has gone completely crazy in terms of denying the rights of its owners," says Lipper with an irritated look. "Take our antitakeover provisions as an example—they're a disgrace. Golden parachute contracts should be outlawed because they say if the ownership or control of a company changes and you're not good enough in the eyes of the new crew, you're out the door. Simple as that, with no respect for the work that you've done to build the company."

Turning back to the scenario, Lipper offers another suggestion. "What risk does the CEO who wants to fire the owner take? The owner's been at risk from day one and every day since then. It's a little ridiculous in my view for someone to be paid over $300,000 a year in today's environment for managing a company where they're not taking personal risk. If they want to buy stock in the company, fine, let them borrow the money and buy the stock, and share some of the risk."

Does management that has something on the line then win the right to make all the ultimate hiring and firing decisions? "I still believe that the sanctity of ownership prevails," insists Lipper, "but I will listen to ideas. Everybody in this company has my home phone number. I'm not interested in chain of command—you've got a problem with your area supervisor, call me and tell me about it. You've got a way that you think will enable us to do our jobs better, come and tell me. I'm willing to let people talk on for hours because it's good for them and it's good for me, but at the end of the day there has to be one person to make the decisions. And that's me. The front door works both ways."

Does everyone accept that attitude in Lipper's own shop? "There are sixty-three people out there who think they can do a better job running this company than I can," he says. "And that's fine. Let them go start their own companies."

## Rechanneling the Energy

Social psychologist Dr. Signe Dayhoff doesn't define Thurston as the culprit in this scenario, either. "One of the things I'm wondering about is why the CEO is getting so irritated by this old guy," she says. "It seems that the CEO was overly annoyed by small things that could have been taken care of with relative ease. I don't think there's been any attempt for anyone to understand anyone else—we get no sense of any communication between these guys, except at board meetings. That lack of understanding really comes through with the CEO assigning Thurston to a line position running the Jacksonville hotel—it sounds insane, given Thurston's tendencies."

How do you close this communication gap? "Sit down and talk to the old fellow," advises Dayhoff. "It's that easy. Just ask him what he wants to do with the business and what he expects of you. Even though he said, 'This old horse is ready to go out to pasture,' no one is really ready for that. The CEO was too dense to have picked up on the fact that Thurston was looking for recognition and would likely wield his power in unpleasant ways if he didn't get it."

If the CEO had tuned in on Thurston's needs, Dayhoff thinks he would have invited Thurston to function as his personal mentor and consultant. Doing so would have produced four benefits. "First, it directs his energies into something more positive, over which the CEO has control. Second, it allows the CEO to monitor Thurston's behavior. Third, if the CEO allows Thurston to become close to him, he'll understand Thurston better and will be better able to influence him. Finally, by acknowledging the experience and expertise of this person, who is undoubtedly suffering at the thought of being put out to pasture, he'll short-circuit the need for him to use his power in childish or destructive ways."

According to Dayhoff, the basic idea is to transform Thurston's destructive energies into useful ones. "If you had a classroom full of kids and you had one that was constantly being rambunctious, you'd try to rechannel his energy. For instance, if it was obvious that this child had a lot of control and could distract the class, that should indicate that he has a lot of leadership potential. Make him the class president and he'll be forced to exhibit constructive behaviors. Same with Thurston.

He's driving everyone nuts and skulking around bathrooms to call attention to himself. So if you put him in a role where he's recognized for his talents, he'll become an asset of the corporation."

Dayhoff stresses—in addition to the need to help fulfill Thurston's psychological needs—the importance of learning more about how he thinks and acts. Such knowledge will smooth once troubled board meetings, because it will enable the board members to translate innovative ideas and suggestions into terms that Thurston can eagerly accept. "If this is a horse-and-buggy person, translate them into a context that makes sense to him. A lot of Thurston's problem might come down to a real language difficulty. Oftentimes if you talk to a person in his or her own time period, it makes a world of difference."

One meaningful special project that the company should immediately embark upon is getting Thurston started on writing his memoirs, so he can share his experience and wisdom. Urges Dayhoff, "Get him a dictation machine and a special secretary or a ghost writer and make it known throughout the company that this important project is happening. Make sure board members are constantly asking him how the writing is going, so that he'll feel a need to be spending his time with the tape recorder or writer, rather than in the laundry room or kitchen."

Regardless of what specific steps are taken, Dayhoff insists that they must be approached with heartfelt sincerity. "You can't just try to slip him under the rug. Aside from his stake in the company, he's earned the dignity and right to work with the entity he created until his dying day. And as long as he isn't doing anything that jeopardizes the shareholders' best interests, it's the CEO's obligation to find suitable ways to accomplish Thurston's goals and the board's goals. But this is all sounding so complicated. Just try to treat him like a human being."

## Packaging the Global Host

Marketing consultant Pamela Alreck would also work with, rather than around, Thurston. "It sounds to me like he's too strong to be subverted, and too cagey to be tricked into weaving baskets," she observes, "so you have to concentrate on his ego needs. Put him in the spotlight and make him the Colonel Sanders of hotels. Sponsor events at every Thurston hotel around the country, giving him an opportunity to speak about the virtues of efficiency and service. I think he'd be pleased to be immortalized in history as a major figure in the hotel industry."

How do you accomplish that? "First, you hire a good PR agency, one that deals with major corporate figures. Have them assign a top person to the Thurston account, and design a campaign that turns Thurston's nit-picking behaviors into positive traits. For example, promote the fact that Thurston stands for service, right down to having the bellmen polish their shoes. Turn his eye for fine detail into a marketing theme, like Leona Helmsley did, but on a larger scale. Package him as the 'global host.' That might even be just the thing to halt the competing hotel chain—fight fire with fire."

Such a PR campaign, Alreck thinks, could work beautifully in both the print and the television media, and it would consume so much of Thurston's time with travel and photo sessions, he'd be out of the ladies' bathrooms and out of your hair. Alreck also believes that her approach solves one of the major problems posed in the scenario: Thurston's inability to accept and endorse innovative change. "I think one of the issues that comes up in the story is that the new CEO and other dissidents on the board are trying to tackle Thurston head-on. You can't revitalize his thinking, so you try to revitalize his image instead."

Although Thurston would be quite busy, he might still want to keep a hand in running the company. If so, Alreck says you can satisfy those urges by asking his advice on all kinds of matters, both large and small. "But don't talk costs with him," she cautions. "Talk profits. Get him more concerned with revenue rather than costs. That way he'll be more receptive to innovative ideas that generate money."

Alreck points out that although Thurston obviously hasn't joined the 1980s in terms of management techniques, he does bring a valuable skill to the operation. "There's nothing wrong with cost-cutting know-how. In fact, there probably isn't enough of it these days. So you have to respect him for that orientation. Besides, don't forget that he turned the company into an empire. Without him you wouldn't have a job today."

## Letting Thurston Be Thurston

Management consultant and author Ken Schatz takes a philosophical interest in what happens when people like Thurston get to the top. "Surprisingly," he says, "even with their great success, they seem to lose self-esteem and feel that they haven't been acknowledged for their achievements. As as result they often look for praise and credit and do it in ways that adversely affect other people. What this older man wants at this point in his career is acknowledgment, and the only way he knows how to get it is to keep going to work."

How can you explain the paradox of people reaching the top but losing self-esteem? "They've adopted the role of success," Schatz explains, "so they tend to generate their identity from their jobs, rather than from within. A guy like Thurston also loses the ability to separate his own identity from his role, so he *has* to keep up his business role."

If you recognize this situation, Schatz says, you can satisfy his needs while achieving your own goals. "I think a very critical point is to acknowledge Thurston's important contribution to building the business. I'm not talking about BS'ing him; I mean doing some sincere honoring. One way to do this would be to plan a phenomenal surprise 'acknowledgment party' for Thurston. Invite important people who would recognize the great job he's done and talk about the great job and contribution he's going to make to the community now that he's retired from the hotel chain. This way the event becomes an opportunity for Thurston to publicly announce his retirement."

Once Thurston has made the announcement, Schatz proposes a number of clever ways for making Thurston feel important, while at the same time keeping him out of the daily management of the corporation. "Why not provide him with resources to draw on his vast knowledge and write a textbook on hotel management? Or find a way for him to teach a course at a local college or university. You could even get him involved in some state council on excellence and ethics, or in a state or national junior-achievement program as a leader and a role model for young people. Finally, you could fly him around the country to speak in front of various business groups, stressing the importance of quality service in all kinds of businesses." Concludes Schatz, "In effect, you're asking him to take responsibility for the corporate image, acting as the king would act, leaving the CEO to function as the prime minister."

In addition to ushering Thurston into a new role outside the corporation, Schatz would launch an extensive internal-awards and acknowledgment program for performance and longevity with Thurston as the chairman. "To make this work, you have to start with a planned inspection of the chain. Before the inspection, you lay out the standards and let the various hotels conform to them. If he wants half-full soap dispensers, he gets half-full soap dispensers. Then he leads an inspection crew and gives out awards. If you can convince Thurston to don his white gloves, you could keep him so busy that he would complain about being overworked. And the more he feels overworked, the more he's out of your hair."

Should any of these ideas not appeal to Thurston, Schatz recommends an intriguing alternative: Put him in charge of on-site competitive research, poking around in your rivals' guest rooms and bathrooms. "With his passion for perfection he'd be a natural to stay in competing hotels and rate them, bringing back information about what kind of service they're providing. He might even come back with some interesting new ideas. At any rate, he could find the undercover role exciting and stimulating."

How do you pitch these ideas to Thurston? According to Schatz, the CEO should make a direct appeal to Thurston, saying, "Look, you're the king and I'm your prime minister. You've hired me to manage the place and make it more profitable, and there are some changes that have to be made. Let me make them."

Doesn't this carry some risk? "Of course it does," acknowledges Schatz, "but the CEO must put himself in a position of risk. If he just sits back and accepts the situation, then he isn't fulfilling the job he was brought in to do, and he'll probably wind up quitting in frustration. So what's the difference if he confronts Thurston and gets handed his head?

"Besides," Schatz continues, "being able to stand up to Thurston would distinguish the CEO as a leader as well as a manager." Schatz defines leadership as the total effect you have on the people and events around you, and management as the responsibility to get a job done through other people. Management, in Schatz's view, breaks into two areas: authority and influence. "On the side that goes with authority, I put in the systems and the procedures and the rights that come with the job, such as *commanding* behavior. On the side that goes with influence, that's where I look at leadership and the rights of *evoking* behaviors.

"Some managers are leaders, but most managers make their impact through what they don't do, through their passive natures, looking the other way and tolerating things they shouldn't. When I define leadership, I comment that effective leading is being consciously responsible for your influence. So when a boss says, 'I'll take responsibility for that,' I'll say, 'You already *are* responsible. Look at your behavior consciously, in a way that produces the result you are looking for.'"

According to Schatz, all of the actions he proposes would help the CEO fulfill his leadership role by evoking the desired behaviors in Thurston, without making the founder feel compromised. "In the final analysis, Thurston cares deeply about the company. Very deeply. So by asking him to change his behavior, we're also asking him to step out of character, which is a very difficult thing for him, or anyone, to do. He wants half-filled soap dispensers because that's how he was taught to run a hotel. That's what being Thurston is all about, and that's what the CEO is running up against when he tries to command Thurston to stay out of the ladies' room. A real leader will keep Thurston out of the ladies' room without even firing a shot."

## Pulling a Lateral Arabesque

PR executive Howard Geltzer, cofounder and president of Geltzer & Company, Inc., offers an interesting approach: "The management of this hotel chain should go to a local college or university and endow a program and a chair in hotel management and name it after Thurston. It would be similar to a culinary institute, with Thurston as the main chef. Let him pontificate in the university setting and preach what he believes management is all about."

Geltzer believes this maneuver would not only bestow honor on Thurston, but it would also meaningfully fill most of his time. With luck it might even create a source for competent future managers in the hotel business. "Thurston might be preoccupied with some things that seem trivial to the new guy," Geltzer says, "but he enhanced the business, and no one can deny that. So he must know what he's doing at some level and would be serving the field well if he could help impart his knowledge through the program. He's obviously a strong and intelligent man who could become a very influential spokesperson for the whole industry, not just the company."

Geltzer suggests that the hotel-management chair is a compassionate and productive measure for putting Thurston in situations where his talents can actually benefit everyone. "Why not invest in something meaningful to the person and the company? I don't like the idea of shipping him off somewhere just to get rid of him or to involve him in childish diversions. Every company owes its founder respect and the right to be heard."

At the same time Geltzer acknowledges that there comes a point where the growth might be too big for the founding entrepreneur to manage it as a sole proprietorship. "A company becomes like a child taking on a mind of its own. At some point it just won't heed you anymore. That's when difficulties arise, like the one with Thurston. In order to be an entrepreneur, there has to be a to-hell-with-you mentality: To hell with you— I'm going to do it my way! And that's essential. Otherwise the entrepreneur would be doing whatever he's doing just like everyone else, and he'd never create anything new. Unfortunately, when the company matures, you can't afford the to-hell-with-you mentality anymore, because you need too many other people. This is what happened to Thurston. He started out saying, 'To hell with you—I'm going to build a hotel chain where I'm frugal about my towels and the soap.' Now he's alienated too many people as a result."

The hotel-management program is an appropriate place for Thurston to unleash his entrepreneurial spirit, since he would be shaping young people about to enter the industry. But isn't it somewhat dangerous for Thurston to be instilling tomorrow's hotel managers with his soap-and-towels philosophy? "The people listening to him can make up their own minds about whether he's right," Geltzer says. "But there's also a strong message in his actions that goes straight to the heart of the hotel industry: cleanliness. You know why the Jets moved from Shea Stadium to the Meadowlands stadium in New Jersey? I've been told that one of the key reasons was that the owner, Leon Hess, couldn't stand the bathrooms at Shea; there weren't enough of them, and the ones they had were filthy and foul. He couldn't stand it, so he assumed his fans couldn't, either. So he packed up and left. I'd use that story as the opener for Hotel Service 101. Wouldn't that leave an impact on you?"

## Sharing the Power

This scenario strikes a responsive chord in Michael Silva, who dealt with a grand-old-patriarch chairman when he became

CEO of a private holding company, Bennett Enterprises. "In your story we have a boss who's simply clinging to what he knows. You also have a CEO who assumes that he needs to run the whole organization a different way. The fact is, they both have to let up and compromise."

Silva insists that some departments in any organization would respond better to Thurston's old style than to the CEO's new style. "A hotel is a mini-society with many segments," says Silva. "Each segment requires a different type of management, the maid service and bellhops probably being better served by Thurston's old-style spit-and-polish approach. On the other hand, you wouldn't want Thurston anywhere near sales or marketing. This is evidenced by the serious mistake the CEO made when he shipped Thurston down to Florida; Thurston could only apply the same logic of stocking bathrooms to maintaining safety. And safety is no cost-cutting thing."

Given the different talents needed to run the business, Silva suggests that Thurston and the CEO split the responsibilities according to their management talents. "If I were the CEO, I'd be thrilled at being able to get rid of managing the maid service and bathrooms by giving their responsibility to the owner."

Silva ran into a somewhat analogous situation at Bennett Enterprises when he first signed on as the company's president. "The chairman still wanted to come to the office every day, but in the end it turned out pretty well. We drew on the fact that he's an accepted symbol of the company. He loves PR and being in the limelight. I don't. He likes to go to parties. I don't. When people think of Bennett, they think of him, which is fine."

The same mechanism could work here, too, Silva says. Echoing several other players in this chapter, Silva sees numerous opportunities for Thurston to become a precious PR asset to the hotel chain. But even if Thurston stays on to manage the bathroom stocking and cleaning, the CEO must view him as a sort of marriage partner, with their relationship benefiting the corporate "family."

"In a single-parent family, one of the difficulties is that the child only has the benefit of one upbringing. So the family lacks balance. The ideal marriage consists of two unique and separate people who impart aspects of their identities to the children. If a marriage is working smoothly, the partners understand that they have different, but complementary, strengths and weaknesses. A business 'family' is no different."

## Rehiring the Boss

"What we need to do is help Thurston find another way to fulfill his need for appreciation," says Kathleen Lusk Brooke, who directs the Center for the Study of Success. "Right now he spends all his time finding faults with people and things around the hotel. Let's capitalize on his relentless vigor and put it to positive use."

How do we do that? "With 'Operation Thurston for Approval.' The basic concept is get him to give his approval vicariously. So instead of letting him run around pointing out everything that's wrong with the hotels, get him to masquerade as a bellhop, a doorman, or a janitor at various hotels, and whenever he sees someone doing something *right,* he should give them a Thurston award."

Initially the campaign would be an internal affair, aimed at keeping people on their toes. And you could launch it in one of two ways. "One is with a great deal of fanfare," suggests Brooke. "Print up buttons and circulate literature to all the hotels. But that has two drawbacks. First, some people might interpret the campaign incorrectly and just see it as a means for management to spy on them. And people don't work creatively when they feel they're being watched from above. Second, a lot of fanfare would take all the fun out of it."

As an alternative, Brooke proposes a much more dramatic launch: "Send Thurston out to some remote hotel and have him go disguised as a lowly employee and present the first award. Then write it up as a 'discovery' in the company's newsletter. (If they don't have a newsletter, use this as an excuse to start one.) The story in the newsletter might consist of an interview with the recipient, who might say. 'Well, gee, I was just helping this customer with her bags and I saw this new bellhop standing around looking at me. I sure didn't know it was the chairman of the board. What a great surprise to get an award from him!' After that you can have a regular column listing the award recipients of the month, listing the place and circumstances and various human-interest facts."

But wouldn't the idea of a "secret agent" stalking the hotel chain still offend employees? Not if you tie it into cash incentives. "You couldn't just come out and give people cash with the award," Brooke cautions. "Thurston would never stand for people getting bonuses to do what they're supposed to do. But there could be an unwritten understanding that when people come up for review, they're more likely to get a salary increase if they've been given a "Thurston for Approval Award.' People would then see it more like a reverse of the Burger King contest where you could win a cash prize if you were the first to spot this nerd named Herb. The only problem was that Herb was so unappealing that you wouldn't want to identify with him. By contrast, Thurston should be promoted as a royal knight on a sacred mission."

This last point leads into what Brooke sees as phase two of the campaign: turning Thurston into a media symbol. "This serves a very important purpose. It enables him to give positive strokes, rather than negative ones, because he'll be the center of all the attention. Remember, his negative strokes had come out because he felt thwarted. Now that he's at the pinnacle of recognition, perhaps even the quintessential symbol for the hotel industry, he has less reason to be looking at the world in terms of what's wrong with it."

The entire "Thurston for Approval" concept is based on a general principle that Brooke has developed in her years of studying success—"A Hire Authority." "Your car is bigger than you," she says, "but you drive it. It's really the same here. You're actually hiring Thurston's talents to accomplish *your* goals. But you'll never see it that way if you go into it with an adversarial frame of mind."

According to Brooke, you want to "hire" Thurston in a way that matches his goals with your own. "For instance, perhaps you want to get a new computer system that will cost a lot of money. Judging from the fact that Thurston wouldn't spring for a new sprinkler system, I doubt that he'd go for an upgraded computer. So you have to put in terms like, 'A new system will help us better track the awards system and monitor the progress in shaping up the various hotels . . . it will go a long way toward insuring that our customer service is the best in the world.' You could probably argue that case with almost any management plan you want, putting it in terms that make it seem like it's achieving his goals rather than yours."

But aren't we just playing with the Thurstons of the world when we "hire" them as bosses? "Perhaps," says Brooke, "but our institutions are always about twenty or thirty years behind what's really happening in terms of actual demographics in this country. Right now, for example, many support-staff jobs are planned for people who stay in the work force for three years; that is, they're based on women's traditional working patterns of the last two decades. Today women want to be in the work force for thirty years, just like their male counterparts. So they don't want to be wasting three years in dead-end support jobs. They want to grow. The changes will be slow in coming but will happen from within the organizations."

According to Brooke, a similar situation exists with older executives, despite such gestures as the Small Business Administration's SCORE (Service Corps of Retired Executives). "We have our Young Presidents Organization, so why not have an Old Presidents Organization? Unfortunately our institutions aren't set up to give older people the kind of stimulation and recognition they need. If they aren't kicked out, they get kicked sideways. Given our population trends, organizations of the future will somehow have to do a better job of accommodating them, or there will be a lot of unhappy people out there with little to look forward to."

How will organizations of the future accommodate their Thurstons? "Well, that depends on what kind of approach we take," Brooke says. "I think today there's too much emphasis on a problem-solving approach. Problems are easy to identify— they stick out, and anyone with a critical capacity can see them. Problems are certainly important, but looking at solutions yields more useful information. I believe that if you study an issue from the point of view of success, rather than a point of view of failure, you'll come up with better solutions."

Brooke hopes that tomorrow's organizations might install a variety of positions beyond chairmanship, based on the kinds of successful roles that resourceful executives create on their own after retiring. For instance, the recipients of the "consultant emeritus" title would be "hired" out to various departments within the company to solve pesky problems. A "senior trainer emeritus" might supervise the education of middle managers and even line workers. And a "corporate historian emeritus" might serve as a resource for explaining to younger managers how the company solved problems in the past, passing on wisdom, lore, and tales that would strengthen the corporate culture.

Another exciting possibility would be a program that uses executives to rejuvenate the company. "With this plan you wouldn't send your young hotshots out to creativity seminars and creative-management training courses. You'd send your older executives and then strategically redeploy them around the company. The idea is that their asset—knowing everything about the company—has become a liability. They get encrusted, thinking in the same patterns. If you can shake them up and radicalize them a bit, you have a very powerful combination of a freethinking person who also knows the history of the company, its problems, its mission, and its goals. So that person will be in a great position to bring about change where it's needed."

Finally Brooke returns to her notion of emeritus executives masquerading as clerks, data-input people, tellers, janitors, line workers, and other nonglamorous positions. "These workers are really the ones who contribute to a company's productivity, and yet they are motivated and recognized the least. Showing them that the chairman of the board can find something important in their jobs says there is a path, a hidden ladder from the bottom to the top. Besides, who can understand the need for recognition better than an executive who is about to enter the 'twilight zone' of retirement? Both the outgoing executive and the lower echelons share the same frustration—they both know that they have so much valuable knowledge to give, but they are denied corporate currency. This is a way to pass out the chips."

## Lessons from the Game

1. Open communication channels. Adversarial relationships at the top usually stem from a lack of understanding that you can easily overcome with frequent and honest talking.

2. Keep an eye open for symptoms of "recognition syndrome." Many successful bosses paradoxically lose their self-esteem and compensate for it by asserting their wills in nonproductive ways. Solving the recognition problem often solves the behavior problem.

3. Create meaningful projects for a retiring boss. Anyone who's been building a company for forty of fifty years will see

through hollow attempts to keep him preoccupied. Besides, it's a waste of talent. An aging boss can be become an invaluable mentor, an in-house consultant, and a culture builder.

4. Search for ways to transform undesirable behaviors into useful work. A soap dispenser can be half empty or half full, depending on how you want to see it.

5. Translate contemporary concepts into terms that the boss can appreciate. Sometimes language forms a major barrier to someone who still thinks in another era.

6. Don't put your goals against those of the boss. You can get what you want by making it appear that your goals and his coincide.

7. Consider harnessing an aging boss as a powerful comanager. If he built an empire and wants to continue, use his or her strengths to complement your weaknesses.

8. Pay attention to individuals who have successfully become "emeritus." The answer to managing a boss who won't retire will differ at each company. But if you focus on models of success rather than solutions to failure, you've got the best chances of creating a win-win situation.

9. Treat outgoing bosses (and all other retiring employees) with the compassion and respect they deserve. Remember, you'll be retiring yourself someday.

CORPORATE NIGHT

EPILOGUE

# Post-Game Highlights

At the end of every great chess match, the experts convene to analyze the moves that led to victory. While we don't pretend to be the world's foremost specialists on business problem-solving, we have picked up a few valuable lessons as we talked for hundreds of hours with the forty-five executive chess players featured in this book. Their solutions ranged from classic moves to outlandish maneuvers, but as we wove them together, two clear patterns emerged.

First and foremost, we found that our players' advice invariably depended on their own definitions of the severity of the problems we posed. In essence, before suggesting a solution, each player asked, "How serious is the problem here?" Each answer to that question, it turned out, tended to place a problem in one of five basic categories:

- a true emergency;

- an ongoing and foreseeable consequence of doing business;

- a domino in a series of preceding and succeeding crises;

- a recurring nightmare;

- no real problem at all.

For example, in Chapter 2, Attorney Bruce Sunstein focused on the grave legal consequences of Flagship Food's espionage caper (a true emergency); Reebok International president Paul Fireman sadly pointed to the fact that "ethics by convenience" has become too common in business today (ongoing problem); competitor intelligence expert Leonard Fuld described how unethical behavior can snowball into a series of problems (domino effect); psychologist Signe Dayhoff and corporate ethicist Richard Sanner pointed to the fact that a corporate culture may signal people that it's okay to carry out illegal behaviors (recurring nightmare); and marketing experts Rob Settle and Pamela Alreck both condemned the illegal action, but pointed out that if you took the course of lying low and not introducing the stolen product, the crisis would dissolve and might even turn into a marketing opportunity (no problem).

One player's emergency can be another player's good fortune. For example, in Chapter 8, some players saw the bizarre eye discoloration caused by MaxLite's contact lenses as a threat to the company; others saw it as an opportunity to start a fashion trend. In Chapter 6, some worried that the everlasting running shoe would cannibalize Trident Running Shoe's existing lines, while others saw it as an opportunity to set a new standard for the industry; and in Chapter 10, some pictured the aging hotel mogul Herbert Thurston III as a barrier to progress, while others understood him to be a fabulous source of experience and knowledge.

Regardless of a player's definition of the problem, he or she then tended to approach that problem with one of five styles:

• attacking the problem with brute force;

• employing the element of surprise;

• acting as a catalyst for a team effort;

• retreating today, winning tomorrow;

• ignoring the problem and seeing if it goes away.

Consider the problem in Chapter 1, in which *FeelGood!* encroaches on the turf of mighty Mocha and DaisyCo by offering a new drink that tastes great and fights plaque. Our players' suggestions included:

- buy *FeelGood!*'s manufacturer;

- turn *FeelGood!*'s assets into liabilities by suggesting that your rival's active ingredients may be dangerous;

- fight fire with fire by bringing in an entrepreneur to battle *FeelGood!*;

- let *FeelGood!* prove there's a market for plaque-fighting colas, then steal the show;

- react by not reacting. If you're top dog, why worry about underdogs?

We believe that the five problem-solving styles can effectively be used to tackle any basic business dilemma, whether it's a problem with R&D, marketing, personnel, finance, or public relations. Whenever you encounter a frustrating business problem, try this: define it within each of the five basic categories and then apply one of the problem-solving styles to each of your definitions. Create hypothetical scenarios, always remaining alert for the best and worst possible outcomes. Before long, you may find yourself thinking in new ways and developing a more creative problem-solving style. Perhaps you'll win distinction as a new corporate knight.

CORPORATE
KNIGHT

# Biographies of the Players

PAMELA ALRECK directs Associated Business Consultants (San Diego, CA). She holds a doctorate in business administration from United States International University, and an M.S. and a B.S. in business administration from San Diego State University. Formerly the Director of Psychometric Systems and the Market Research Director for San Diego Surveys, Alreck has consulted to numerous corporations and government agencies, including Prentice-Hall, Inc. and Wickes Corp., and has coauthored more than twenty-five papers on marketing. She is the coauthor of *Why They Buy: American Consumers Inside and Out* (John Wiley & Sons), *Marketing Research Computer Analysis Software* (Random House), and *The Survey Research Handbook* (Dow-Jones Irwin).

(CHAPTERS 2, 7, 10)

NICOLAOS V. ARVANITIDIS cofounded Liposome Technology, Inc. (Menlo Park, CA) in 1981, to develop and commercialize liposome/lipid-based drug-delivery systems. He serves as the company's chairman and CEO. Arvanitidis holds a Ph.D. in engineering and economic systems from Stanford University, an M.Sc. in electrical engineering from Stanford, and a B.S. in elec-

■□ 233

trical engineering from Seattle University. Prior to forming Liposome Technology, Arvanitidis served as an adjunct professor at Stanford University, and as the President of INTASA, Inc., which consulted on natural-resource management and economic issues to state and federal agencies.

(CHAPTER 5)

---

KATHERINE AUGUST serves as Executive Vice President of First Republic Bancorp, Inc. (San Francisco, CA). She received her bachelor's degree from Goucher College and an M.B.A. from Stanford University. After serving as a McKinsey consultant for three years in San Francisco and London, August joined Itel Corporation as Director of Finance, and then PMI Mortgage Insurance, where she served consecutively as Treasurer, Vice President, and Senior Vice President—Chief Financial Officer.

(CHAPTERS 4, 7)

---

HERBERT M. BAUM joined Campbell Soup Company (Camden, NJ) in 1978 as Associate Director of New Products in the Canned Foods Division and during the next seven years was promoted to Director of Marketing Services, Corporate Vice President of Marketing, and in 1985, President of Campbell U.S.A. Division. Baum, who received a B.S. from Drake University, served as an account executive with Doyle Dane Bernbach and as Vice President at Needham, Harper, & Steers prior to his employment with Campbell.

(CHAPTER 1)

---

MARC L. BENDER (Newton, MA) serves as an independent communications consultant and advertising producer for corporations, law firms, and political candidates; and as a professor of advertising, public relations, and business communications in the Massachusetts state college system. He received a B.A. from Harvard College in history and an M.A. from Harvard University in East Asian Regional Studies. In addition to creating marketing materials for the Peace Corps and the Department of Energy, he served as National Media Director for the Democratic National Committee and has consulted to numerous federal, state, and municipal agencies on public relations. Bender's international work has taken him as far as the mountains of Chinese Turkistan, where he was the first American to research consumer attitudes among Uighur tribesman.

(CHAPTER 8)

MYRON I. BLUMENFELD has served as vice president of three retail chains and as a consultant to numerous others throughout the U.S. and Mexico. He was Manager of International Retail Consulting Services for Ernst & Whinny and since 1981 has been president of his own consulting firm, Myron I. Blumenfeld & Associates (New York, NY). Blumenfeld holds a B.S. in economics from the Wharton School, University of Pennsylvania, and an M.B.A. from New York University, where he now teaches part-time.

(CHAPTER 7, 8)

KATHLEEN LUSK BROOKE holds a Ph.D. from Harvard University and is the author of *Hidden Ladders* (Doubleday). She taught courses on success at Harvard and failure at M.I.T., and is now Director of the Center for the Study of Success (Boston, MA), and its adjunct search service, Executive Assistance, which is retained by major corporations and organizations in the U.S. and abroad. A former fashion model, Brooke is a frequent public speaker and talk-show guest, and her research on success has been published in numerous national newspapers and periodicals.

(CHAPTER 10)

CHRISTINA DARWALL is founder and President of New Ventures Services, Inc. (San Mateo, CA), a "hands-on" consulting firm that helps start-ups locate funding sources and develop marketing plans. Darwall holds a B.S. from the University of Michigan and an M.B.A. from the Harvard Business School. Prior to starting her company, Darwall served as Senior Vice President in charge of finance, human resources, computer systems, and planning/business development at Impell Corporation, an engineering and software company. She was also a principal in the strategy consulting firm, McKinsey & Company, Inc. Darwall sits on the boards of three companies: ViewStar Corporation, MBA magazine, and Bell Bicycle, Inc.

(CHAPTERS 3, 4, 6)

SIGNE A. DAYHOFF received her Ph.D. in social psychology from Boston University, where she was a National Institute of Mental Health Research Fellow. She is President of The Mentoring Network (Wellesley, MA), an organizational-behavior consulting firm. Dayhoff has taught at Boston University, the University of Massachusetts, and Framingham State College. She is the author of *Create Your Own Career Opportunities* (Brick House Publishing) and coauthor of *Decision Making for Managers* (American Management Association), as well as numerous articles in business periodicals. She is also producer and host of *The Inside Track,* a career-development interview program for cable television.

(CHAPTERS 2, 10)

PIERRE DERSIN studied electrical engineering at M.I.T., where he earned his Ph.D., with a minor in management from M.I.T.'s Sloan School. He is President of Transimatics, Inc. (Burlington, MA), which produces diagnostic devices for automated manufacturing and processes. He also serves as Vice President of Fabricom Corp. of America and has been a director of both companies since 1985. Dersin was the Technology Attaché for the Belgian Embassy in the United States from 1981 to 1983.

(CHAPTER 5)

SALLY EDWARDS has participated in six Ironman Triathlons, placing in the top five in each. She also won the Ultra-Marathon and placed first in the Western States 100-Mile Endurance Run. Edwards holds an M.A. in exercise physiology from the University of California, Berkeley, and an M.B.A. from National University. She is the founder and President of Fleet Feet, Inc. (Sacramento, CA), a sporting-goods franchiser with thirty stores. Edwards is the author of several books, including *Triathletes: How They Train and Race* (Contemporary), *Triathlon: A*

*Triple Fitness Sport* (Contemporary), and *The Equilibrium Plan: The Diet and Exercise Approach to Lifetime Fitness* (Arbor House).

(CHAPTER 6)

---

PAUL FIREMAN is President and CEO of Reebok International Ltd. (Canton, MA), a major manufacturer of athletic footwear and performance sportswear. With U.S. sales at $66 million in 1984, Fireman organized a buyout from the British founder and reorganized the company as Reebok International Ltd., which sported sales of $390 million in the first six months of 1986. Prior to joining Reebok, Fireman, who was educated at Boston University, was Vice President of Sales and then Treasurer for BC Recreational, a distributor of outdoor sports equipment.

(CHAPTERS 2, 6)

---

LEONARD FULD has been performing corporate research for almost a decade and is the founder and President of Information Data Search, Inc. (Cambridge, MA), which specializes in the field of competitor information and sponsors seminars on corporate research techniques and ethics. Fuld has been a featured speaker of the American Marketing Association and the Conference Boards of New York and Canada, a talk-show guest on national newsmagazines, and is the author of *Competitor Intelligence: How to Get it—How to Use it* (John Wiley & Sons). He is currently completing a second book on corporate intelligence systems to appear in 1987. He obtained his undergraduate degree from Yeshiva University and his M.S. in communications from Boston University.

(CHAPTER 2)

---

HOWARD GELTZER is the cofounder and President of Geltzer & Company, Inc. (New York, NY), a public-relations firm. Geltzer trained in General Electric's advertising and public-relations training program and later served as a promotion manager at McGraw-Hill. Geltzer & Company has offices in New York and Los Angeles, and a client list that includes Sony Corporation of America, Dow Chemical, Prince Tennis, Commodore Computers, and others in technical, as well as non-technical industries.

(CHAPTER 10)

ARNOLD S. GOLDSTEIN specializes in small business matters. An author and attorney, he is a senior partner in the law firm of Meyers, Goldstein, Chyten & Kosberg (Chestnut Hill, MA). Goldstein has written twenty-one books on small business, including *The Basic Book of Business Agreements* (Enterprise Publishing), *The Complete Guide to Buying and Selling a Business* (John Wiley & Sons), and *Starting on a Shoestring* (John Wiley & Sons). Goldstein received a B.S. from Northeastern University, a J.D. from New England Law School, and an M.B.A. and an L.M. from Suffolk University. He is a professor at Northeastern University, where he teaches management and law.

(CHAPTERS 3, 9, 10)

JAMES H. GREGG is President and CEO of Applied Immune-Sciences, Inc. (Menlo Park, CA), and has twenty-five years of sales, marketing, and general-management experience in the health-care field. Before joining AIS, he was President of Telectronics, Inc., a $40-million manufacturer and marketer of pacemakers and, before that, served as Vice President of Operations for Squibb Medical Systems. His other previous experience in the health-care field includes executive and management positions with Spacelabs, Inc., NDM Corporation, IVAC Corporation, and American Hospital Supply Corporation. Gregg holds a degree in business administration from the University of Southern California.

(CHAPTERS 4, 5)

CRAIG R. HICKMAN (Salt Lake City, UT) provides management-consulting and training services to Fortune 1000 companies. He coauthored the best-selling *Creating Excellence* as well as *The Future 500,* and previously served as President of the Bennett Information Group, a research and consulting arm of Bennett Enterprises. He also served as the director of Arthur Young's strategic-management practice throughout the western

United States. Hickman holds a B.S. from Brigham Young University and an M.B.A. from the Harvard Business School.

(CHAPTERS 7, 9)

PHILIP KEMP joined Dawson International, a knitting and spinning company based in Scotland, in 1983 to help locate a U.S. acquisition. Dawson not only accepted Kemp's recommendation and acquired J. E. Morgan Knitting Mills (Hometown, PA and New York, NY), the largest manufacturer of thermal underwear in the U.S., but also named him Morgan's president. Under Kemp's direction Morgan saw a twenty-five-percent increase in sales within the first two years of his appointment. Born in Manchester, England, Kemp has held marketing positions with numerous British companies and has done business as far away as Sri Lanka and Australia. Today he divides his time between Pennsylvania and New York City.

(CHAPTERS 1, 8)

MICHAEL KILLEN spent six years working with Dr. An Wang as a business strategist and is now a telecommunications industry expert. Killen is founder of Killen & Associates, Inc. (Palo Alto, CA), a management-consulting firm and publishing company that specializes in tracking and predicting the strategic behavior of IBM and AT&T. Killen publishes more than thirty major reports a year and writes five regular columns for telecommunication publications in the U.S. and Japan. He lectures on business at the University of San Francisco and speaks at executive-strategy sessions sponsored by federal and state agencies and major high-tech corporations.

(CHAPTER 4)

JAMES F. KOEHLINGER brings twenty-seven years of financial experience to *Executive Chess*. A C.P.A. and partner in Boston Financial Resources (Boston, MA), he functions as temporary chief financial officer for client companies. Prior to joining BFR, he spent seven years as Group Controller for Digital Equipment Corporation and three years as Controller for Rust Craft Greeting Cards. He also served as General Manager for a division of

ITT. Koehlinger started his career in public accounting by spending six years at Price Waterhouse & Co., and Main, Hurdman & Co. He received his B.S. from Indiana University and an M.B.A. from Clark University.

(CHAPTER 7)

---

GARY S. KREISSMAN holds a B.A. from the University of Michigan and an M.B.A. from the Harvard Business School. He joined VAL-PAK, (New York, NY), the largest network of cooperative direct-mail distributors in the country, as Corporate Vice President of Marketing and Product Development. Before coming to VAL-PAK, Kreissman served as Marketing Manager and then Director of Marketing for Rémy Martin Amérique, where he is credited with a forty-one percent growth increase in U.S. sales and with the development and introduction of RMS, the first world-class California alambic brandy. Kreissman's experience also includes a five-year stint as an account supervisor and account executive at Ogilvy & Mather for Maxwell House, Post cereals, and the Main Meal Division.

(CHAPTERS 1, 6)

---

CHARLES LEVIN is President of Sandler & Worth, Inc. (Springfield, NJ), a high-end broadloom carpeting and Oriental rug chain with seventeen outlets on the East Coast. He received his B.A. from the University of Rochester and studied law at Boston College. In addition to his responsibilities as the President of Sandler & Worth, Levin has served as the Executive Vice President of Syntonic Systems Inc., a software development firm specializing in time-management programs.

(CHAPTERS 3, 9)

---

ARTHUR LIPPER III wears many hats in the business world: international financier, consultant, and author. He is chairman, publisher, and editor-in-chief of *Venture* magazine and is also cofounder and Chairman of the New York Securities Corporation (New York, NY), a securities brokerage and investment banking firm. Lipper is the author of *Venture's Guide to Investing in Private Companies* (Dow Jones-Irwin). In addition to his activities as a publisher and venturist, Lipper serves as an adjunct associate professor at New York University Graduate School of Business and as a Trustee and Founder of The Lipper Foundation, which is dedicated to the recognition and development of gifted children. He is also a Trustee of the Institute of Private Enterprise of the University of North Carolina at Chapel Hill and Director of the International Council for Small Business.

(CHAPTERS 3, 10)

ALAN M. LUSTIG is President of Fabrics International Corporation (Andover, MA). Prior to founding the company, he served as Marketing Manager for Malden Mills and before that as Chief Industrial Engineer and Director of Production Control and Inventory Control for the industrial products division of Honeywell. Lustig was also a supervisor at Curtiss Wright Aircraft Corp., where he participated in the start-up team for converting turboprop engines to jet-engine production. He received a B.S. in business administration from the University of Massachusetts and an M.S. in industrial engineering at Columbia University.

(CHAPTER 9)

FRED NAZEM is a scientist, entrepreneur, and venturist. He is the founder and Managing General Partner of Nazem & Company (New York, NY) and the Managing General Partner of Nazem & Lieber, private venture-capital partnerships. Prior to forming the partnerships, he founded and was the Managing Director of Collier Enterprises, a technology-based venture-capital organization and was the founder and CEO of Geo-Capital, an investment advisory firm. In addition, he held key positions at Charter New York and Irving Trust Company. Nazem holds a B.Sc. in biochemistry, an M.Sc. in physical chemistry, and has done research and doctoral work in nuclear physics. He also holds an M.B.A. in finance from Columbia University.

(CHAPTERS 3, 4, 9)

THOMAS B. OKARMA is Senior Vice President for Research and Development at Applied ImmuneSciences, Inc. (Menlo Park, CA). He received a B.A. from Dartmouth College, a Ph.D. in pharmacology, and an M.D. from Stanford University. He has taught pharmacology at the University of Vermont School of Medicine and Immunology at the Stanford University School of Medicine. In addition, Okarma is a member of the clinical faculty at Stanford Hospital and has written more than thirty publications in fields related to immunology.

(CHAPTER 5)

JONATHAN POND founded and serves as President of Investment Management Information, Inc. (Cambridge, MA), a firm that offers publications, lectures, and consulting in the area of personal financial planning. Pond studied accounting and finance at the University of North Carolina, Chapel Hill, Emory University, and the Harvard Business School. He is also a C.P.A. and a certified management accountant. Mr. Pond has authored numerous publications and videotape training programs, including: *The Personal Financial Planning Handbook* (Warren, Gorham & Lamont), *An Integrated Approach to Personal Financial Planning* (American Institute of C.P.A.'s Videotape Master Series), and the *Wiesenberger Mutual Funds Investment Report.* In addition, Pond markets a software package called the Personal Financial Planning Program.

(CHAPTERS 7, 9)

JAMES H. QUEST has spent his entire business career in marketing and advertising, beginning in brand management with Procter & Gamble. Through his experience as Senior Vice President and a member of the Board of Directors of The Marschalk Company, Quest gained experience marketing products in fields ranging from beverages and consumer electronics to proprietary drugs and frozen foods. He holds a B.S. from Cornell University School for Hotel Management and currently serves as President and CEO of Posey Quest Geneva, Inc. (Greenwich, CT), an ad agency.

(CHAPTER 1)

JOSEPH A. RAELIN (Needham, MA) is Associate Professor of Administrative Sciences at the Boston College School of Management, a management consultant, and an expert on salaried professionals. He received his B.A. and an Ed.M. from Tufts University and his Ph.D. in policy studies from the State University of New York at Buffalo. He has written more than forty articles on human-resource concerns and is also the author of *The Salaried Professional: How to Make the Most of Your Career* (Praeger) and *The Clash of the Cultures: Managers and Professionals* (Harvard Business School Press). He has been widely quoted in the popular press about career-development issues.

(CHAPTERS 4, 5)

ALEXANDER RANDALL 5 holds a B.A. in psychology from Princeton University, an M.A. in communication technology, an M.A. in international development, and a Ph.D. in general systems research from Columbia University. After receiving his doctorate, Randall joined the University of Maryland's overseas division and taught social technology in more than forty countries. In 1981, he and his wife founded The Boston Computer Exchange (Boston, MA), the nation's largest broker of used computer equipment. Randall has an active consulting practice in the fields of computer networking and creative problem solving, and has been retained by state and federal agencies, as well as IBM, GTE, Standard Oil, and other major corporations.

(CHAPTERS 1, 4, 6, 7)

GEOFFREY RAPPAPORT cofounded Supercuts (San Rafael, CA) and serves with Frank Emmett as the cochairman of the nation's most successful haircutting franchise operation. Rappaport received a B.A. from Montieth College and later entered the Ph.D. program at the University of California, Berkeley, where he received an M.A. in the philosophy of education. Supercuts recently celebrated its tenth anniversary; a single store started with $2000 has grown to a thriving chain of more than 500 stores with combined gross sales of more than $120 million a year.

(CHAPTERS 3, 9)

RICHARD E. SANNER (Wellesley, MA) holds a B.S. and an M.S. in industrial management from Georgia Institute of Technology, a B.D. and a Th.M. from Columbia Theological Seminary, and a Th.D. from Boston University School of Theology. He has taught extensively in the fields of organizational behavior, labor relations, personnel management, and corporate ethics. Sanner is currently a Senior Associate at Organizational Dynamics, a consulting firm specializing in personnel and management training and has served clients such as Federal Express, A. C. Nielsen Co., the Federal Aviation Administration, and other private and public concerns.

(CHAPTER 2)

---

ROBERT SAVAGE (New York, NY) is an independent marketing consultant with thirty years experience in the marketing of consumer products and services and the management of creative organizations. He has served as the Managing Director and Chief Operating Officer of Henson Associates, Inc., creators and producers of the Muppets. Prior to joining Henson, he was President of Saatchi, Saatchi, and Compton Advertising, Inc. Savage has also served as Chairman and CEO of Ketchum Communications/San Francisco and as a member of the Board of Directors and a Management Supervisor at Ogilvy & Mather, where he was responsible for accounts such as General Foods, Campbell Soup, Merrill Lynch, IBM, and American Express. Savage received a B.A. from Principia College and an M.B.A. from the Harvard Business School.

(CHAPTER 1)

---

KEN SCHATZ offers leadership concepts to hundreds of top managers and executives through Schatz & Company (Alexandria, VA), of which he is founder and President. He holds a B.A. in mechanical engineering from Rensselaer Polytechnic Institute and an M.B.A. from The Wharton Graduate School. Schatz is the author of *Managing by Influence* (Prentice-Hall) and sponsors programs based on the book in areas such as direct communication, dynamic teamwork, innovation, self-confidence, and increased productivity.

(CHAPTER 10)

MICHAEL P. SCHULHOF is Chairman of the Strategic Planning Committe and a Director of Sony Corporation of America (New York, NY). Previously he was President of the division of Sony responsible for all nonvideo activities, including office equipment, professional audio, and tape products. Schulhof earned a B.A. from Grinnel College, an M.Sc. at Cornell University, and a Ph.D. in physics at Brandeis University. As a solid-state physicist, he published twenty-seven papers and was associated with Brookhaven National Laboratory. Mr. Schulhof also serves as an officer and director of Reproducta Company, Inc., and is a member of the board of directors of the Computer and Business Equipment Manufacturing Associations.

(CHAPTERS 5, 6)

SANFORD SCHWARTZMAN is President of American Carbonyl, Inc. (Garfield, NJ), which he founded in 1979 to create process technology for patented specialty chemicals used in the graphic-arts industry. During the past thrity-five years he has started and/or held executive management positions with eight companies in the specialty chemistry field. Schwartzman holds a B.A. from New York University.

(CHAPTERS 6, 8)

ROBERT SETTLE (San Diego, CA) received a B.A. from Dominican College, an M.B.A. from the University of Wisconsin, and a Ph.D. in business administration from the University of California, Los Angeles. Currently a Professor of Marketing at San Diego State University, he is the author of more than fifty articles on marketing issues and has coauthored several books, including *Why They Buy: American Consumers Inside Out* (John L. Wiley & Sons), *Marketing Research in Action* (Random House), and *The Survey Research Handbook* (Dow Jones-Irwin). Settle's client list includes Rohr Industries, Wickes Corp., Ziff Davis Publishing Corp., the U.S. Navy, and numerous other organizations in the private and public sectors.

(CHAPTERS 1, 2, 6)

MICHAEL A. SILVA coauthored *Creating Excellence* and *The Future 500*. He is President of Bennett Enterprises (Salt Lake City, UT), a privately held conglomerate that includes manufacturing, computer retailing, banking, and consulting operations. Formerly a management consultant with Arthur Young and Company, Silva received his B.A. and M.B.A. degrees from Brigham Young University, where he specialized in organizational development.

(CHAPTERS 7, 8, 10)

DAVID H. SIMON founded and serves as President of Simon/ McGarry Public Relations, Inc. (Los Angeles, CA), which has offices in Los Angeles, Sunnyvale, CA, and Dallas. Simon/McGarry is the nation's first PR firm to deal exclusively with high-tech clients. Simon has more than twenty years of experience in public relations and advertising, including financial relations, corporate counseling, promotions, and marketing communications. Prior to forming his agency, Simon served as Corporate Director of Advertising and Public Relations for Teledyne, Inc. He is also the founding president of the Los Angeles Chapter of the National Association of Corporate Directors. Simon holds a B.A. in electrical engineering from Cornell University.

(CHAPTER 8)

JAMES E. STANCHFIELD holds a B.S. from the University of Massachusetts and a Ph.D. from Dartmouth College in cell biology. He is currently the founder and CEO of Betagen Corp. (Cambridge, MA), which develops and markets computerized instruments for genetic research. Prior to forming Betagen, Stanchfield served as COO of American Bionetics, Inc., a supplier of products for genetic engineering research. He was also National Sales Manager for Bethesda Research Laboratories and served as a staff scientist at the National Cancer Institute.

(CHAPTERS 4, 5)

BRUCE D. SUNSTEIN is a partner in the law firm of Bromberg, Sunstein, & McGregor (Boston, MA), where he concentrates on business and patent law, trademark, and copyright matters. He holds a B.S. in applied mathematics and literature from M.I.T., an M.A. in English from Indiana University, and a J.D. from the University of California, Berkeley. He is a member of the Institute of Electrical Engineers and the American Intellectual Property Association.

(CHAPTER 2)

ARTHUR TAUDER (New York, NY) has spent the past twenty-five years in the advertising field. He has consulted to the Campbell-Edwald Company, Coca-Cola, Gillette, McCann-Erickson, and Revlon. He also served as the Chairman of the Media Advisory Group of Interpublic, where he was appointed to the Operations Committee. Prior to his work at Interpublic, Tauder was Executive Vice President and General Manager of The Marschalk Company, and an account supervisor at Ogilvy & Mather and BBDO. He received a B.S.J. from Northwestern University's Medill School of Journalism and currently lectures in its Graduate Advertising Program.

(CHAPTER 6)

HERBERT TEMPLE III is Chairman of the Board of Temple, Barker, & Sloane, Inc. (Lexington, MA) and one of its founders. As a business economist and specialist in corporate strategy and organizational planning, he is consulted primarily on issues relating to telecommunications, aerospace, broadcasting, transportation, industrial and agricultural equipment consumer durables, real estate, financial institutions, and conglomerates. Temple has been an adviser on policy and administrative issues to the White House as well as to numerous federal agencies. Prior to funding TBS, Temple was an Executive Vice President of Harbridge House, Inc., where he directed the firm's consulting services to the private sector and in weapons and space systems development. He holds a B.A. from Harvard College and an M.B.A. from The Harvard School of Business Administration.

(CHAPTER 4)

MAX A. TESLER holds an M.D. from New York University and carried out specialty training in gastroenterology at Cornell and Yale Universities. Formerly the director of medicine and medi-

cal education at French Hospital. In 1979, he founded
PharmaControl Corp. (Englewood Cliffs, NJ), a research and
development company for the pharmaceutical industry that
holds exclusive patents on water-soluble aspirin and a nonin-
vasive glucose monitor. Dr. Tesler serves as PharmaControl's
Chairman, President, and CEO and sits on the board of two
biomedical companies, Ifex and Enzymes of America.

(CHAPTERS 3, 5, 9)

DOUGLAS WISE holds a B.A. from Dartmouth College and an
M.B.A. from Columbia University. He came to the Interpublic
Group in 1965, first working for The Marschalk Company,
where he served on accounts such as Coca-Cola Foods, Coca-
Cola USA, Goodyear International, and Bristol Meyers. He later
earned the title of Senior Vice President and became a member
of the Board of Directors. Wise currently serves as Senior Vice
President of McCann-Erickson (New York, NY) and manages
the Goodyear and Gillette International accounts. His previous
assignments at McCann have included management of the Coca-
Cola account in Japan, as well as working with the Pabst Brew-
ing Company and Ponderosa Steakhouse chain.

(CHAPTER 1)

# Index

Accountability, forcing, 51–54
Acquisition, turning around a
    troubled, 184–208
  the game, 185–86
  lessons from the game, 207–208
  opening moves, 184
  strategies and tactics, 187–208
  *see also* Buying out a
    competitor
Adidas, 137
Advent company, 98
Advertising, 20
  challenging claims of
    competitor, 3–5, 14–16, 17–
    18, 21–22
  competitive, 12, 20
  to introduce the perfect
    product, 121–22, 124, 130,
    136
  to restore public's trust, 175–78
A. H. Robins, 167
Alka-Seltzer, 9
Alreck, Pam, 31–33, 143–46, 217–
    18, 230, 233
Amdahl, Gene, 72, 82

American Airlines, 84
American Can Company, 40
American Carbonyl, Inc., 129
American Express Company, 211
Apple Computer, 51, 83–84, 145,
    159
Applied Immune Sciences, Inc., 52,
    64, 146
Aries, Robert K., 35
Arity Corporation, 75
Arvanitidis, Dr. Nicolaos, 112–14,
    233–34
Ash, Mary K., 61
Associated Business Consultants,
    31, 143, 233
AST Research, 66
August, Katherine, 79–81, 151–
    54, 234
Avis, 90.
Avon Products, 203

Balanced team approach, 59, 67
Bank of America, 193
Banquet microwave dinners, 18
Baum, Herbert, 17–18, 234

Beatrice Companies, 210–11
Bell Labs, 114, 128
Bender, Marc, 175–79, 234–35
Bennett Enterprises, 157, 160, 172, 223
Betagen, Inc., 81, 105
*Beverage Digest,* 20
Big Bite chain, 7
Biogen Inc., 106
Biographies, 233–48
Blumenfeld, Myron, 148–51, 166–69, 235
Boeing Corporation, 111
Bon Vivant, 163
Boston Computer Exchange, 6, 71, 124, 142, 243
Boston Consulting Group, 87
Boston Financial Resources, 239
Brain drain, 68–92
    the game, 69–71
    lessons from the game, 91–92
    opening moves, 68–69
    strategies and tactics, 71–91
Brooke, Kathleen Lusk, 224, 235
Burger King, 7
Buying out a competitor, 13, 17, 156
    *see also* Acquisition, turning around a troubled
"Buy-now" technique, 21

Cadillac, 9
Campbell Soup Company, 17, 18
C & C Cola, 202
Canon, 30
Capri Beachwear, Inc., 148
Capsco Sales, Inc., 84
Career ladders, dual, 107, 108, 115
Caterpillar Tractor Company, 42
Center for the Study of Success, 224, 235
Chemical Bank, 40
Chevrolet, 187
Chrysler Corporation, 152
Cinch spray cleaner, 21
Clark forklifts, 30
Coca Cola, 13–14, 15–16

Colgate-Palmolive, 202
Compaq Computer, 59, 90, 153
Compensation, *see* Incentives
Competition, *see* New competitor
Competitive advertising, 12, 20
Conant Associates, 114
Confidentiality agreement, rights and, 88
Consolidated Foods, 202
Control Data Corporation, 111
Corning Glass Works, 165
Cost-cutting, 148, 155, 161
*Creating Excellence* (Hickman and Silva), 156
Creative talent, caging the, 59–62
    *see also* Scientists and researchers, getting the most from
Creative thinking, 8, 22, 138, 142
    nonlinear, 172–74, 182
Culture, corporate, 41–44, 192–93, 201, 205–206
Cybernex, 90

Dalkon Shield, 167
Dart & Kraft, 203
Darwall, Christina, 62–65, 76–79, 132–34, 235
Data General, 77
Dayhoff, Signe, 41–44, 216–17, 230, 236
Dayton Hudson, 61
Defining the severity of the problem, 229
DelMonte microwave dinners, 18
DeLorean, John, 82
Delta Airlines, 172
Departing employees, *see* Brain drain
Dersin, Pierre, 110–12, 236
Diolight Technology, Inc., 132–33
Direct Mail Marketing Association, 147
Disincentives to prevent brain drain, 90
Distribution, 13, 202

Dolby, 123
Don't-stand-where-they-can-hit-
you strategy, 7
Dow Chemical, 101
Dresher, Inc., 197–98
DuPont, 35, 126
Dutt, James L., 210–11

Eastman Kodak, 111
Edison, Thomas, 4
Edwards, Sally, 136–38, 236–
37
E. F. Hutton, 90
Emmett, Frank, 66, 200
Energy Conversion Devices, 98
Entrepreneurial spirit within a
company, see Acquisition,
turning around a troubled;
Brain drain
Ericksen-Desaigoudar, Billye, 84
Espionage, see Spying, corporate
Ethical guidelines, 28, 32, 34, 37,
39–40, 45
curing a sick corporate culture,
25–27, 41–44
rebuilding corporate trust, 38–
41
Ethyl Corporation, 82

Fabrics International Corporation,
193
Family and friends, doing business
with, 46–47
the game, 47–49
lessons from the game, 67
opening moves, 46–47
strategies and tactics, 49–67
Fast-food restaurants, 11
see also individual companies
Federal Bureau of Investigation
(FBI), 27
Federal Trade Commission (FTC),
5, 15–16, 18, 30, 31
Ferro, Charles, 202
Fireman, Paul, 33–36, 119–22,
230, 237
Firestone Tire and Rubber, 167

Firing:
to cut costs, 149
of key employee, 51, 56, 61, 67
First Republic Bancorp, Inc., 79,
151, 234
Fleet Feet, Inc., 136
Food and Drug Administration, 4,
16, 178
Forbes, 98
Ford Motor Company, 11, 51, 60,
127
Formula 409 spray cleaner, 21
Friends, doing business with,
see Family and friends, doing
business with
Frito-Lay, 24, 206
Fry, Art, 82
Fujitsu, 72
Fuld, Leonard, 26–29, 230, 237

Gallo Winery, E. & J., 61
Gelltzer & Co., Inc., 221, 237
Geltzer, Howard, 221–22, 237
Genentech, 107
General Dynamics, 39, 40
General Electric, 207
General Mills, 33
General Motors, 9, 60, 82
Genesco, 55
Gerber, 170
Gilbert, Walter, 106
Golden parachute contracts, 215
Goldstein, Arnold, 49–51, 187–
88, 213–14, 238
Goodrich, Charles, 99
Goodwill:
of departing employee, 73
restoring the public's, 175–76
Gore, W. L., 77, 122–23
Gore-Tex, 122–23
Grace Corporation, W. R., 188
Gray, Harry J., 210
Gregg, Jim, 84–85, 238

Häagen-Dazs, 191
Hammer, Armand, 210
Hansen Juice, Inc., 53

Harley-Davidson Motorcycle
Company, 199
Harper & Row, 61
Harrell, Wilson, 21
Hertz, 90
Hewlett, Robert, 50
Hewlett-Packard, 11, 50, 83, 145,
196
Hickman, Craig, 156–58, 204–
207, 238–39
Hitachi, 27
Honda, 77
Honeywell Corporation, 111, 196
Hrudka, Joseph, 188
Hygrade Food Products, 168
Hypergrowth, surviving, 143–60
the game, 140–42
lessons from the game, 160–
61
opening moves, 139–40
strategies and tactics, 142–61

Iacocca, Lee, 51, 152
IBM, 28, 60, 90, 173, 187, 196,
200
Identity of your product,
maintaining the, 6, 9–10, 21,
157, 160
Imitations and line extenders, 7,
13, 18, 20, 30, 134, 143, 144
Inc., 81
Incentives:
deferred compensation, 79
for performance, 58, 60, 67, 86,
99–100, 224–25
to prevent brain drain, 79, 85,
87–88, 92
Information Data Search, Inc., 26,
237
In Search of Excellence (Peters),
83, 187
International Harvester, 30
Intelligence gathering, ethical, 26–
27, 32, 35–36, 37, 44–45
International marketing, 14
Intrapreneuring program, 71–72,
83, 85–86, 91, 206

Investment Management
Information, Inc., 192
Investor confidence, restoring, 177–
78
Isolation of feuding partners, 51,
59–60
ITT, 202

Japan, 13–14, 30
Jarman family, 54
J. C. Penny, 156–57
J. E. Morgan Knitting Mills, 4, 169,
239
Jobs, Steven, 51, 90, 159, 211
Johns Manville, 163
Johnson & Johnson, 167, 171, 173,
177, 178
Joint ventures, 78, 82, 111–12

Kapor, Mitch, 75
Keating, Kevin, 132
Keebler, 24
Kellogg family, 55
Kemmler, George, 5
Kemp, Philip, 4–6, 169–71, 239
Kentucky Fried Chicken, 7
Kettering, Charles, 82
Key employees:
keeping, see Brain drain
firing, see Firing
Kidder Peabody, 207
Killen, Michael, 88–91, 239
King Arthur Flour, 54
Kleber company, 167–68
Knee-jerk reactions, avoiding, 6,
10–12, 14, 21
Koehlinger, Jim, 154–56, 239–
40
Komatsu, 30
Kreissman, Gary, 18–21, 134–36,
240

Land, Edwin, 98
Lattice structure, 77
Lawsuits:
against departing employees, 90
product liability, 162, 170, 177

Levin, Charles, 51–54, 201–204, 240
Liability, *see* Product liability crisis, recovering from a
Licensing, 123
Life cycle:
  of a business, 197, 208
  of a product, 12, 146
Lillian Vernon, 150
Line extenders, *see* Imitations and line extenders
Liposome Technology, Inc., 112
Lipper, Arthur, III, 59–62, 214–15, 240–41
Listerine, 9, 18
L. L. Bean, 150
Loews Corporation, 61
Long-term vs. short-term research, *see* Scientists and researchers, getting the most from
Lotus Development Corporation, 75, 154
Loyalty of customers, 14, 19, 163
Lustig, Alan, 193–96, 241

McArthur, Douglas, 174
McCann-Erickson, 12
McDonald's, 7
McDonnel Douglas Corporation, 40
McKinsey & Company, 73–74, 79, 151
Managers, 220–21
  of acquired companies, 189–90, 191–92, 194, 198–207, 208
  for company suffering from hypergrowth, 148, 150, 151, 153–54
  relationship between scientists/ researchers and, 93–115
  -scientists, 101–103, 105, 108–109, 111, 115
  separating professionals from, 74–76, 81
Market research, *see* Product research

Market saturation, 142–45, 152, 155, 160
Market segments, introducing the perfect product in selected, 132–34, 138
"Marriage counselor," venture capitalist as, 62–65
Mary Kay Cosmetics, 61
Matrix organization, 76–77
Mattus, Ruben, 190
MCI, 174
Mentoring Network, The, 236
Mercedes Benz, 9
Mercke & Company, 35
Merrill Lynch, 90
Michelin, 120
Microelectronics & Computer Technology Corporation, 111–12
Minolta, 30
Mr. Gasket Company, 188
Mitsubishi, 30
"Mixed-messages trap," 9, 157
Mondavi family, 50
Monsanto Corporation, 150
Murdock, David H., 210
Mustang, 11, 51

Nabisco, 24
National Advertising Review Board, 17
Nazem, Fred, 57–59, 73–74, 196–98, 241
NCR, 111, 173
New competitor, 1–22
  the game, 2–3
  lessons from the game, 21–22
  opening moves, 1–2
  strategies and tactics, 4–21
New technology, introducing, *see* Perfect product, introducing the
"Newness threshold," 120
New Venture Services, Inc., 62, 132, 236
Next Computers, 90
Nike, 137

Nissan, 30
Nonlinear thinking, 172–74, 182
NutraSweet, 5

Objectivity with family or friends
    in business, 55–56, 61, 67
Occidental Petroleum, 210
Okarma, Dr. Thomas, 100–104,
    241–42
Orvis, 123
Osborne, Adam, 82
Osborne Computer Company,
    145, 153, 154
Ovshinsky, Stanford, 98
Owner of the company:
    refusing to retire, 209–27
    succession planning, 53, 55, 61–
    62, 67, 84

Packard, Donald, 50
Parent company, see Acquisition,
    turning around a troubled
Patriotic associations with your
    product, 16
Pepsi, 14, 16
Perfect product, introducing the,
    117–38
    the game, 118–19
    lessons from the game, 138
    opening moves, 117–18
    strategies and tactics, 119–38
Perrier, 19
Peters, Tom, 83, 84
Peterson, Robert L., 210
PharmaControl Corporation, 54,
    96, 189
Philips, 109
Pillsbury Company, 190
Planning, long-range, 52–53, 62
Polaroid, 98
Pond, Jonathan, 146–48, 191–93,
    242
Posey Quest Genova, Inc., 14
Post-It notes, 83
Price strategy, 15, 20–21, 127,
    129, 130, 134–37
Problem-solving styles, 230–31

Procter & Gamble, 21, 24
Product liability crisis,
    recovering from a, 162–82
    the game, 163–64
    lessons from the game, 182–83
    opening moves, 162–63
    strategies and tactics, 165–66
Product life cycle, 12, 146
Product research, 10–11, 14, 18–
    19
Professionals:
    getting the most from, 93–115
    separating managers from, 74–
    76, 81
Public relations, 16, 134, 218, 223,
    225
    product-liability problem and,
    179–82
Puma, 50

Qureshey, Safi, 66
Quest, Jim, 14–17, 242

Raelin, Joe, 75–76, 106–108, 242–
    43
Ram Golf Corporation, 202
Randall, Dr. Alexander, 6–8, 71–
    73, 124–27, 243
Rappaport, Geoffrey, 65–67, 198–
    201, 243
RCA, 128
Reebok International Ltd., 33, 36,
    120, 237
Rémy Martin Amerique, 18, 20–21
Researchers, see Scientists and
    researchers, getting the most
    from
Reston, Brady, and Winthrop, 71
Retail business to support catalog
    business, 147, 149
Retirement, coping with a boss
    refusing, 209–27
    the game, 211–13
    lessons from the game, 227–28
    opening moves, 209–11
    strategies and tactics, 213–28
"Reverse engineering," 37

Revson family, 50
Ricoh, 30
Rolm, 174, 187
Rosen, Benjamin, 154

Safety of a product:
　challenging, 4–6, 14
　restoring public's faith in, 175–77
Sandler & Worth, Inc., 51, 53, 201, 204
Sanner, Richard, 38–41, 230, 244
Savage, Robert, 8–10, 244
Scarcity of a product, creating, 137
Schatz, Ken, 218–21, 244
Schulhof, Michael P., 108–10, 131–32, 245
Schwab, Charles, 193
Schwartzman, Sanford, 129–31, 165–66, 245
Scientists and researchers, getting the most from, 93–115
　the game, 94–96
　lessons from the game, 115–16
　opening moves, 93–94
　strategies and tactics, 96–115
　see also Creative talent, caging the
Scope, 9
SCORE (Service Corps of Retired Executives), 226
Scully, John, 51, 159
Searle, G. D., 5
Sears, Roebuck, 130, 157
Sebastiani family, 49
Segmenting the organization, 158–60
Selling your company, 72
Settle, Rob, 10–12, 29–31, 127–29, 230, 245
Seven-up, 13
Sharper Image, 147
Shelf-space, dominating, 15
Shoen, Samuel, 120
Short-term vs. long-term research, see Scientists and researchers, getting the most from

Silva, Michael, 157, 158–60, 172–74, 222–23, 246
Simon, David, 179–82, 246
Simon/McGarry Public Relations, Inc., 179, 246
Smart teams, 58
Smucker Company, 5
Sony Corporation of America, 108, 131, 245
Sorrell Ridge, 5
Soul of a New Machine, The (Pulitzer), 77
Spencer Gifts, 150
Sperry Corporation, 111
Spin-offs for new technology, 126, 129, 138, 155
Spoor, William H., 190
Spying, corporate, 23–44
　the game, 25–26
　lessons from the game, 44–45
　opening moves, 23–25
　strategies and tactics, 26–44
Stanchfield, Jim, 81–84, 105–106, 246
Standard Oil Company, 98
Standard Oil of Indiana, 101
Standard Oil of New Jersey, 82
Standex International Corporation, 197
"Step-aside" strategy, 7
Stock ownership, see Incentives
Succession planning, 53, 55, 62, 67, 84
Sugar Association, 5
Sunstein, Bruce, 36–38, 230, 246–47
Supercuts, 66, 198, 199
Swanson, Robert, 107
Swanson microwave dinners, 18

Tauder, Art, 121–24, 247
Technology, product incorporating new, see Perfect product, introducing the
Temple, Herbert M., III, 85–88, 247

Temple, Barker & Sloane, 85, 247
Tesler, Dr. Max, 54–56, 96–100,
    189–91, 247–48
Texas Instruments, 11, 90
Thalheimer, Richard, 147
3M, 82, 111
Thunderbird, 11
Toyota, 30
Trade secrets, 36, 38, 90
Trading down, 127
Trade-off strategy, 31–33
Transimatics, 110
Trilogy company, 72, 82
Tupperware, 203
Tylenol, 167–68, 171

U-Haul, 120
Underdog, playing the, 7
United Technologies, 210
University(ies):
    business research at, 110–11
    endowing a chair at a, 221–22

Val-Pak, 18, 134, 240
Value structure of partners, 63–
    64
*Venture* Magazine, Inc., 59, 214,
    240
VisiCorp, 75
Vision or corporate purpose, 54,
    66, 67

Wadsworth, 71
Waldron, Hicks B., 203
*Wall Street Journal,* 111, 190
Wendy's International, 7
Westinghouse, 128
Westinghouse, George, 5
Wilkinson Sword Ltd., 123
Wise, Doug, 12–14, 248
Wong, Albert, 66

Xerox, 30, 37, 83, 197, 200, 206

Yuen, Tom, 66